For old times sake ———
Brad + Edna
from
Mother Manker.
Christmas 1942

Montreal

A View of Montreal from St. Helen's Island. Published by A. Bourne, Montreal, 1830.

Montreal

SEAPORT AND CITY

By
STEPHEN LEACOCK

Doubleday, Doran & Company, Inc.

GARDEN CITY 1942 NEW YORK

PRINTED AT THE *Country Life Press,* GARDEN CITY, N. Y., U. S. A.

Preface

THE GREAT AUTHORITIES at first hand for the earlier
history of French Canada and of Montreal are the narratives
written by Jacques Cartier and by Samuel de Champlain. With
these are the collection of reports, letters, and documents gathered by the Society of Jesus and known as the *Jesuit Relations;*
and the *History of Montreal,* written by Dollier de Casson in
1672. Notable firsthand material about Montreal of the Old
Regime (1721) is found in the *La Nouvelle France* of Father
Charlevoix, published in 1744, and in the celebrated *Travels
(1749) in North America* of Peter Kalm, the Swedish naturalist.
By the time the Conquest is reached and the age of newspapers,
journals, and government reports, firsthand documents became
as numerous as Maisonneuve's Iroquois.

But all writers are indebted, and none more than the present,
to certain great sources of information, secondhand in the historic sense, but representing the labors of a lifetime and the
search of libraries and repositories inaccessible to the public at
large. Here the volumes of Francis Parkman, a marvelous blending of genius and accuracy, of picturesque charm and reliable
fact, have never been excelled. Nor are they likely to be. Too
many newer historians are afraid to be interesting for fear of
being thought shallow, afraid of any attempt at humor and in any
case unable to call it into their service, omit all mention of

scenery and wind and weather as immaterial to history, and thus substitute for the moving, animated narrative of a Macaulay or a Parkman a dull, indigestible record of facts that defeats its own end and buries the past in oblivion. Conspicuous exceptions break the rule, but the trend is all too obvious.

Nor can anyone write of Montreal without paying tribute to the monumental work of Dr. W. P. Atherton, whose three volumes on Montreal, its history and its institutions, are beyond competition. Talleyrand once said of Jeremy Bentham's works, "Pillaged by everybody, he is still rich." So let it be with Dr. Atherton. We all acknowledge our debt only to leave it unpaid and borrow more. I have not attempted to include in this book any general bibliography of Montreal. I have only indicated in the notes certain firsthand authorities for corroboration of the text where the matter is curious or contentious.

But I have to acknowledge here in the composition of this book debts of a more intimate and personal kind. I have the honor to be a member, since its foundation, of the University Club of Montreal, whose club building occupies, as said in this book, the center of the site of Hochelaga. Several of my fellow members belong to old Montreal families, French and English, who have transmitted and treasured information, maps, papers, pictures, relics. These they have kindly placed at my disposal. I should wish to make honorable mention here of my friends Mr. Stanley Coristine, Mr. Arthur Terroux, and Col. Fred Gaudet, not if this meets their eye, but taking care that it shall meet their eye. I am also greatly indebted to my old friends Dr. John L. Todd and Mrs. Todd, the owners and occupants of Boisbriant, the beautiful estate at Senneville that was the fief and Seigneurie le Ber, as mentioned in the text.

I am greatly indebted, as I have been on many previous occasions, to my old friend Mr. Murray Gibbon of the Canadian Pacific Railway Company. Not only has he supplied me with material from his ample resources but also with advice and suggestion from his ample brain.

I am under a very special obligation for my chapter on McGill University to my friend and colleague of many years, Professor

Thomas Matthews, registrar of the university, without whose help and guidance I should hardly have ventured on ground, fertile and familiar, but in its very fertility favoring the weeds of hidden error. It is only fair to say that if any of these errors still remain uneradicated the full credit must be given to Mr. Matthews. I am under a similar obligation to another old friend and former colleague of my own department, Professor John Culliton, who has very kindly checked over the economic material of this book, with a view to eliminating errors. Any left are his.

I have also received most valuable help in regard to the present medical curriculum of the college from my friend Dr. E. Kenneth Smith, one of the latest of its graduates on the roll of the faculty and certain, I am sure, to prove worthy of it. It is proper to add that in the preparation of this book I have from first to last been greatly aided by the continuous and courteous assistance of the highly trained staff of the Library of McGill University. In this connection it is proper also to express my appreciation of the research work in the library done for me by Mrs. H. T. Shaw.

Acknowledging all these debts, I feel also that I owe a good deal of this book to my own industry and effort.

McGill University   STEPHEN LEACOCK
1942

Contents

x   Contents

Illustrations

CHAPTER I

Hochelaga

*Jacques Cartier's Discovery of the St. Lawrence.
The Empty Continent. The Norsemen. John Cabot's
Voyages. The Newfoundland Fisheries. Cartier's
Voyage of Reconnaissance (1534). Discovery of the
St. Lawrence (1535). Cartier at Hochelaga. The
Winter at Stadacona.*

MORE THAN A HUNDRED YEARS went by between the discoveries of Columbus and Cabot and the first permanent settlements of North America in Quebec, Virginia, and New England. Tropical America fell an easy prey to the arms, the enterprise, and the rapacity of Europe. The feeble natives of the Caribbean had no answer even to the clumsy fire-arms and the awkward ships of the sixteenth century; the half-civilized Aztecs and Peruvians little better. Force opened the way; gain and the lure of adventure furnished the motive, religious zeal the cloak of justification. None who went to America meant to stay there.

With North America it was different. For centuries after the discovery of the North American coast nature jealously guarded the access to the vast resources of the interior. On the north a great barrier of ice blocked all approach. The Elizabethan explorers, interested not in America but in what might lie behind it, strove against this barrier in vain. On the south, along the Gulf of Mexico, the tropical heat, the fevers of coastal swamps, the tangled delta, and the shifting channels of the Mississippi long held all intruders at bay. The western side of North America remained thus utterly unknown and beyond reach. The passage around the bottom of South America, achieved by Magellan and by Drake, was impossibly far and impossibly dangerous. Even after Núñez Balboa had seen the unlimited Pacific, during his famous silence on his peak of Darien,[1] the route over the jungles and mountains of Panama was barely more than a war trail for buccaneers and plunderers, too arduous for the path of peace.

Only on one side was the coast of the continent of easy access. The incomparable series of inlets, bays, and river mouths which indent the Atlantic coast from the Bay of Fundy to the sands of Carolina offer everywhere easy landings and ample shelter. But it was only the coastal margin which was thus accessible. The mountain rock and forest of the Adirondacks and the Appalachians still blocked the interior. In a few places access might be effected by the valleys of the rivers. But only in one place was there a wide-open break in this barred coast. Right in its center the sheltered waters round what is now New York led into the broad placid stream of the Hudson that carried ships under sail 150 miles inland and showed them, when ship navigation ended, the open valley of the Mohawk, an easy pathway into inland America. For over a century the coastal voyages of explorers (Corte-Real, Verrazano, Gómez) passed this opening by. They too were looking for something else. The "stern and rockbound coast," the forest torn by the wind, the lurking savages meant nothing to men whose eyes expected at each new cape and corner to see the crowded seaports and the sunlit cities of the Orient, and whose ears ever listened for the bells in the pagodas of Cathay.[2]

[1] Keats of Cortez in error.
[2] S. E. Dawson, *The St. Lawrence*, 1905.

It is a humiliating thought for us to realize that these early discoverers saw North America and didn't want it. A few attempts on it were made. Ponce de León, searching, as old men ever do, for the Fountain of Youth, looked for it, as old men still do, in Florida. De Soto and others, looking for gold and the "Seven Cities of Cibola," struggled as far as the Mississippi. Raleigh even attempted a real settlement. Henry Hudson, after sailing his ship against the ice of Spitzbergen and Novaya Zemlya, with the same pagoda bells in his ears, turned right about westward and left his name forever on the great fresh-water river and the great salt sea which he discovered. Of the two the great sea seemed at the time vastly the more important. Then came the Pilgrims looking for the wilderness and finding it.

Thus slept North America. It was indeed an empty continent; empty and silent. Except perhaps on the British Columbian coast its aborigines were so few that all was solitude. Here and there a few thousand Indians might cluster, as in the wigwam lodges of the Hurons below the Georgian Bay, or the Onondagas beside Oneida Lake, or the group which Jacques Cartier was to find at Hochelaga. But such open spots were rare in the unbroken forest which then covered all eastern Canada, New England, and the shores of the Great Lakes. A voyager making his way along the rivers that pierced the forest or along the streams where the forest trees met over his head, might pass days and days—indeed expected to do so—without sight or sound or evidence of human life. Our Canadian west was one vast solitude over which passed at intervals great droves of buffalo, attacked by nomad savages, without as yet the European horses that later gave them mastery. Nearly four hundred years after Columbus the famous English soldier and writer, Captain Butler,[3] could still speak of the inconceivable solitude of the West. "You may travel," he wrote, "five hundred miles in a straight line without meeting a human being." Thus slept America; thus waited the best of it for man's use— the riches of the Ohio valley, the alluvial soil of the prairies, the garden valleys of British Columbia; its very uses slept with it, still unusable. What were rock oil and hard coal to people who

[3](Sir) William Butler, *The Great Lone Land*, 1872.

traded in little shipfuls of spices, sandalwood, and nutmeg, thinking pepper priceless? Today the kitchen holds unheeded all their little treasures. Even gold: all the gold and silver of Mexico and South America was as nothing beside what was hidden in the fastnesses of the silent continent. All that came to Europe in a hundred years of the days of Cortez and Pizarro was nowhere beside what later came from California in twenty years and out of Canada in the last ten.

It is necessary to lay stress on this unused aspect of our continent, and especially of Canada. It has served to turn the course of our history aside, false values blocking the true direction. We cannot understand the history of Montreal without it. This failure to appreciate the latent wealth of the North is not a mere curious relation of the romance of the past, of the irony of history. It counts now. It explains the common failure to understand that Canada is today still relatively empty—12,000,000 people instead of ten times as many. The material changes of machine civilization (we dare no longer call it progress) have shifted all physical values. What now is a little pot of pepper, or even a rajah's emerald, as beside water power, minerals, coal, rock oil? Man now can live sheltered from the cold, serving iced drinks where Indians froze. Civilization moves north, steadily as a star drifts across the sky. Unless we take full account of these broad features, this shifting frame of human history, we cannot estimate the oncoming future of North America.

All this we have said of the Hudson River access to the continent. But above the Bay of Fundy a greater and easier one, the entry of the St. Lawrence, lay concealed, to be revealed for one brief moment by Jacques Cartier in 1535, lost then for sixty-eight years till Samuel de Champlain rediscovered it forever. If it were not for the northern ice, this entry indeed to the very heart of the continent would surpass all others to an incomparable degree. It leads by water, so to speak, to everywhere. But the "if" is large enough to blot out all the rest of the clause. Indeed in past history, in sailing-ship days, this factor governed all. We do not realize how few people ever came that way before the steamship revolutionized it after 1809. A hundred years after

Cartier there were only sixty-five French people in Quebec and none (over the winter) in Montreal. At the close of the seventeenth century New France had only about 12,000 French inhabitants. The population of the British Atlantic seaboard was nearly a quarter of a million. The chief glory of the St. Lawrence was as yet in what it was going to be rather than what it was. It still is.

Cartier's discovery came about thus. The northeastern coast of North America had long been dimly known to Europe—known and disregarded. The Norsemen had been established in Greenland for over four hundred years. As a result their ships were at times driven by bad weather, or tempted by good weather, along the shores of the mainland of America. Here they found a coast of rock and slate that they called Hulluland and a seaside forest land that they named Markland. They even went south to the warm temperature of a fertile district called Vinland, all of which places are now a puzzle to the historian. But the Norsemen had enough of them. As soon as random voyages led to an attempt at real settlement in Vinland (Thorfinn Karlsefni, A.D. 1007), the Norsemen came in contact with the American savages, the treacherous ambush, the war by night and cruelty by day that were to be the curse of North America.[4] These tangled woods, these stealthy, whispering waters became, in old classical sense, a "horror" to the Norsemen. They drove their ships back again, back to the bright emptiness of Greenland, its green meadows and its glistening ice, all adrip in the sunshine—God's country, brave and open, where men were men. They never came to Vinland again, except in short voyages to snatch away timber. They knew quite enough about North America. They too didn't want it.

Neither did John Cabot, who did not live to know that he had been there. He came back to his parsimonious patron, Henry VII, with brave talk of the "new Isle" that he had discovered. He reported that he had reached the country of the Great Khan; that it was seven hundred leagues beyond Ireland. He offered to go again and sail farther south to reach Cipango, which was

[4]F. Nansen, *In Northern Mists*, 1911.

nearer the equator, and to bring back spices. This first voyage of Cabot and his sons had been, like the later journeys of the Pickwick Club, conducted "upon their own proper costs and charges." But the King now, evidently deeply moved, gave Cabot £10 for having "found the new Isle." He commissioned him at once to make a new voyage by this happy route to Cipango for spices, with a promise of £20 a year for life and of a fleet of ten ships and three hundred sailors for 1498.

There was great excitement in Cabot's home town of Bristol from which he had sailed over this new route. We read how the sailors followed him around. Sailors and merchants foresaw a great trade in spices between Bristol and Cipango. But we know now, thanks to painstaking scholarship, where Cabot had been on his famous first voyage. Sailing from Bristol May 2, 1497, he had landed, fifty-two days out, on Cape Breton Island, claimed it and named it Cape Discovery, sailed north, saw and named Cape Ray on Newfoundland, the near-by islands of St. Pierre and Miquelon (rediscovered by the world in 1942), passed the bold headland of Cape Race (he called it England's Cape), and thence home to drop anchor in Bristol on August 6, 1497, with Asia in his pocket.

Such was Cabot's first voyage. Like so many American voyages of discovery, from Columbus' first error onward, it was utterly futile in its intended purpose, immeasurable in its unplanned results. For Cipango take the Grand Banks; from their codfish trace Cartier, and from Cartier the St. Lawrence, Montreal, and the vision of the future. Meantime preparations went forward for the second Cipango voyage. The King was as good as his word, or as nearly good as kings then were. Cabot got two ships and three hundred men with letters patent (February 3, 1498) wide enough to reach Asia. A few small trading vessels joined fortunes with him. He set out in May 1498 on a voyage in defiance of geography, dreary with cold and hardship, broken with mutiny, and utterly fruitless. Cabot pushed up the east coast of Greenland till the sheer futility of it led him to the west coast, thence across the Straits to Baffin land (latitude 66° north), then south past Newfoundland, and then along the everlasting coast of forest and rock and empty sand, looking for what was not there. Somewhere off the coast of Maryland (latitude 38°), with stores low and hope dead, Cabot turned for England. He reached Bristol late that autumn to die—why not?—soon afterward. His son Sebastian had a later career, but as far as North America was concerned, the Cabots ended with 1498.

Not so the "new Isle." Cabot's sailors brought home to Bristol and from there to all western Europe the news of the marvelous codfisheries off the "new Isle." Till then the English codfishing fleets went out, mostly from London and the east ports, but also from Bristol, to fish off the coast of Iceland. But the fishing was limited and restricted by the regulations of Danish sovereignty. These new fisheries, free and open, literally "beat all." There is a famous letter in which an Italian diplomat wrote home: "Cabot's sailors, practically all English and from Bristol . . . affirm that the sea is swarming with fish which can be taken with baskets let down with a stone."[5]

For once sailors' tales of wonder held true. The North Atlantic Ocean, at the full depth of its sunken bed between America and Europe, is five miles deep. But all around the northeastern coast of North America from Cape Cod to Labrador there projects an outlying "continental shelf," only "recently" submerged. Here are great "banks," like Georges Bank east of Nantucket and the Grand Bank southeast of Newfoundland. The line that marks a depth of only six hundred feet runs all round this continental shelf. The area of the whole submarine plateau is computed at 500,000 square miles. There are great stretches on the Banks where the depth is only from 180 to 420 feet. Here, as a French writer has said, "the land is infinitely silent, but the sea harbors every form of life." The temperature, the ocean bed with an infinity of small fish, and salt cold water combine to make an ideal environment (for a codfish). Here close to the surface, upheld by the salt of the icy water, float the infinite quantities of "plankton," the microscopic life of ponds and seas. On this feed the larvae of the codfish. Later the fry descend to live on shell stuff, then come again up to live, voraciously, on everything

[5]H. A. Innis, *The Cod Fisheries*, 1940.

afloat. A codfish is mature at three years, lives easily beyond five, weighs from three to four pounds inshore and about twenty-five to thirty-five on the Banks. They vary greatly. The record reaches over two hundred pounds, a six-foot length. Small varieties are mature at three years, large ones at five. A sizable cod when it spawns leaves 3,000,000 eggs a year floating among the plankton. Each egg only asks a chance to leave 3,000,000 more. Malthusian despondency is staggered at the prospect. But at least it makes our history easier to understand, our future easier to secure.

That is what Cabot's sailors saw when they lifted in the cod in basketfuls. That was the news that sent all Brittany and Normandy to the Banks. Bretons, Normans, and Basques, even the Portuguese, came before the English themselves; the latter still clung with insular conservatism to their Iceland fishing. Later, after Cartier's time, they came in a flock.

All through the fifteen hundreds the fishermen came in increasing numbers to the Newfoundland Banks. But they came and went like a flock of sea birds in unrecorded voyages in the summer season of the spawning of the codfish. They drove home with the strong west winds of the equinox in a voyage of about a month. Later sailing ships have run across in two weeks. History took but little count of the fishing fleet, though we read that Henry VIII once sent out ships of the new Royal Navy to shepherd them safely into the Channel. History was too busy with the new splendors of the monarchies of the Renaissance and with the Italian wars. Only today patient scholarship traces out the record from seaport entries.

The cartographers of the day gathered up the rough charts of the fishing pilots and made out of them the maps and globes that have been preserved. These show the coast and islands recognizable from the Bay of Fundy to Labrador. But the Gulf of St. Lawrence is marked as a huge inlet closed in on the west, beyond the Strait of Belle Isle, and marked the Great Bay. The fishing boats did not push far into the gulf since the fishing is less good as the water gets less salty.

There must have been much information handed round in the

seaports about the strong currents that came down and much suspicion that the Great Bay led somewhere. After all, the ground was as familiar to them as Saint-Malo itself. Lescarbot, the later companion of Champlain, tells of knowing one old man who had made forty-two round trips (eighty-four voyages). We still retain some of the place names given by the fishermen before history began—the Cape of the Bretons, the Harbour of St. John.

This was the situation that led Francis I of France into North American exploration. Francis was one of the glittering kings of the new monarchy, as who should say, the "opposite number" of our Henry VIII and the Spanish Charles V. He threw himself eagerly into the glory of war and the invasion of Italy till his defeat at Pavia left him a prisoner with "all lost but honor." Set free with his honor—by trading off Burgundy—he threw himself into the current of the Renaissance, a patron of the glory of Paris in art and letters. Then for a brief moment—a break in the clouds—into North American adventure, and then finally into the crowning glory of the persecution of the peasant heretics of Vaudois (the Waldenses). The brief American episodes of his reign were found in the voyage of Giovanni Verrazano, commissioned by King Francis before his Italian disaster, and by Jacques Cartier's discovery of Canada.

Verrazano's voyage and his later fate have left only a twilight record. He sailed across the Atlantic until he struck land, skirted northward, looking always for something better, landed here and there but nowhere north of the present New Hampshire, then up along the fishing coast to the frozen seas, then out and home. The voyage was fruitless, leaving nothing but the name New France, lost and found again, and needless as a French claim when Cartier's voyages superseded it.

These voyages were another matter. Cartier was a pilot of Saint-Malo, a man in middle life, courageous and devout and of a vision that looked beyond sea fishery to the apostles' higher calling. He had already made a voyage to South America, perhaps had been to the Banks. We do not know whether the King's admiral, Chabot, heard of Cartier and summoned him or whether

Cartier made proposals to the admiral. At all events he was given a royal commission for a voyage of discovery.

Cartier seemed to know well enough where he was going—straight through the Belle Isle Strait and on. The fact that after he passed the Strait he met, without surprise, "a tall ship out of Rochelle" shows how familiar already was the outer coast.[6] He passed along the stern and forbidding north shore of the Gulf. He decided that this must be the land that God gave Cain. This was not a joke. It was, after the fashion of the day, a pious confirmation of the truth of Scripture. But Cartier's attempt to get past Anticosti Island by the north channel, against wind and current, proved hopeless.

The art of "tacking," sailing in zigzags against the wind, was unknown, or perhaps previously known and lost, in the Middle Ages. One recalls the contrary winds which held Richard II in Ireland and lost a throne. Tacking, even when introduced, for centuries made little progress. The clumsy, tubby ships, all superstructure and square-backed to the wind, were ill fitted for it. Even Lord Nelson's ships of war could do little by way of beating up. The beautiful clipper ship, streamlined as we should say, the fore-and-aft rig of the deep-draught yacht, making almost four points into the wind, these triumphs of sail came only as the swan's song of a vanishing epoch. Sail only came into its own when its own was over.

But Cartier at least knew, from the very obstacles encountered, that he had found a great river, a waterway to the interior. He sailed all round the Gulf, which he named with its river in honor of St. Lawrence. He noted the appealing misery of the harmless savages he saw, left them a great cross set up on Gaspé to hold them till he should come again. He noted in passing the fertility, the sanded shores, and the beautiful forests of our Prince Edward Island. Cartier mistook it for the mainland, but he knew at least that this was not part of the land given to Cain and would do for the King of France. The voyage was only a reconnaissance, but it promised much. As living witness Cartier carried back two Indians with him to France.

[6]*Cartier's Voyages* (Champlain Society. H. P. Biggar).

Cartier's second voyage (1535–36) was the famous voyage from which dates the true discovery of the St. Lawrence, of the indefinite region called Canada, and the discovery of the Indian settlement of Hochelaga. From the commanding elevation of Mount Royal, Cartier was able to divine the course of the inland waters and to speculate on the wealth and wonder of the "Kingdom of Saguenay" which was supposed to lie beyond. All that Vasco da Gama found at Calicut Cartier thought he had found in this vast emptiness.

This great voyage of 1635–36, the discovery of Hochelaga, and the tragic winter at Stadacona that followed it have been so often narrated in full detail that it is needless here to attempt more than a summary.

King Francis gave to Cartier three ships—the *Grand Ermine* of one hundred and twenty tons, the *Petite Ermine* of sixty, and the *Emérillon*, called also in the English books the *Merlin*, or the *Sparrow Hawk*. The ship's company were men of heart and courage as the sequel proved. It has been stated, and denied, that there were criminals among them. The practice of the time would have sanctioned this. For Cartier's later and fruitless voyage his commission gave him the right to take sixty criminals from jail, and the commission to his associate and superior, Sieur de Roberval, allowed him to open the jails and help himself. But if the men who stood by Cartier in the tragic winter that was to come at Stadacona were criminals, then we need more of them in Canada. It is disputed also—scholars will be scholars—whether Cartier carried priests with him. Probably not; that roll of honor begins later.

Till its close in the tragic winter just mentioned this same voyage of Cartier that discovered Hochelaga was like the voyage of a dream—easy and successful beyond belief. It is true that the passage out (May 19, 1535, Saint-Malo–Belle Isle, July 26) was prolonged and tempestuous and that much time was wasted in fruitless detours around Anticosti. But the ships sailed up the St. Lawrence to the mouth of the Saguenay on September 1, and from then on all was wonder. Here was the Saguenay itself, a river of profound depth issuing from between tall mountains of almost bare rock. There were great fish about its mouth, "which no man," said Cartier, "had ever seen before or heard of." Indian canoes danced in the foam. The Indians came aboard; they spoke in their own tongue to Cartier's Indians brought back with him from France. The Indians explained to Cartier where he was—namely, that this river of Saguenay led to the "Kingdom of Saguenay," a fabulous land of wealth and wonder of which Cartier was to hear more and more. Straight up the main river was the "land and province of Canada," and beyond that, some distance inland, was Hochelaga.

Here enters into the world's record the word Canada, ever since unexplained. In the Huron-Iroquois language Canada means a settlement of lodges. Later on Cartier, or one of his associates, made out a vocabulary which said, "They call a town (*une ville*) Canada." But somehow the word seemed to mean either a town or the whole region; just like the double usage in England by which a man living in a town takes an occasional run up to town (London). Such fanciful derivations as Aca-nada, "nothing there," are merely history's earliest jokes on our unappreciated country, like Cartier's "land of Cain" and Voltaire's "acres of snow."

With a fair wind Cartier's ships moved up the river west, in an enchanted autumn scene of forests hung with grapevines, of islands all cluttered with hazelnuts (Isle aux Coudres), and one so heavy with its grapes that they named it after Bacchus. Later royal geographers made it the Island of Orleans.

Cartier anchored in the north channel off this pleasant island. And here there came to them the Indian Chief Donnacona, the "Lord of Canada," with twelve canoes of his people, with every demonstration of welcome and of friendship. The welcome doubled when it turned out that this was the very home of Cartier's two Indian guides and when they told of the wonder of France and the kindness there received. Astonishment and delight knew no bounds.

Cartier moved his ships up from the island to what was later called the Basin of Quebec, where the St. Lawrence narrows to the smallest width of its course. Here was the high promontory of Cape Diamond, the incoming stream of the St. Charles, in the background the blue Laurentian hills, and all around the colors of the Canadian autumn. Here Cartier laid up his two larger ships to winter in what he called the Ste. Croix River, now the St. Charles. There followed Indian receptions, dances, and, above all, the long harangues that followed the feasts, tedious, says a Canadian historian, "in the Huron-Iroquois language," and adds as an afterthought, "or in any other." We realize with something like awe that we see here the origins of the lunch-club talks of the United States and Canada, now spreading around the world, the Indian's vengeance on his conquerors.

The Indians tried to dissuade Cartier from going farther up the river. There were spirits, angry gods, they said, at Hochelaga. But on these Cartier took his chance. Taking his *Emérillon* and two ships' boats, he embarked on another wonderland journey of thirteen days from Stadacona to Hochelaga in the full glory of autumn. Here, in his mid-journey, the St. Lawrence expands into Lake St. Peter, a stretch of twenty miles. Above it the water was low. Cartier left his *Emérillon* and went forward with his boats only. At last in the dusk of an October evening the boats were halted by the swift St. Marys current where an island (St. Helens) partly closes the river. Here he came to land. He had arrived. He was now, though he didn't know it, inside the present limits of the city of Montreal. But he knew that he was somewhere, for a great concourse of Indians, more than a thousand, he said, came flocking joyously to the shore.

The scenes that followed, Cartier's reception by the Indians, the night of bonfires and singing, the presents given and received, the visit next day to the great stockaded fort of Hochelaga, the bringing of the sick and the infirm for Cartier's touch, the reading of the Gospel of St. John to the Indians, reverent as in God's presence, the ascent of the mountain and the vision from its summit as of a kingdom to come—these are embalmed pages of Canadian history. They are almost sacred in the atmosphere they breathe of piety and mutual faith. No picture in all North American history is more inspiring. At least Montreal began well.

The pages of Cartier's narrative have here been so often quoted that they are part of our history. But no account of the discovery of Hochelaga is complete without at least a citation of certain passages in regard to the great stockade itself and the scene enacted within its precincts.

There are some fifty houses in this village, each about fifty or more paces in length and twelve or fifteen in width, built completely of wood and covered in and boarded up with large pieces of the bark and rind of trees, as broad as a table, which are well and cunningly lashed after their manner. And inside these houses are many rooms and chambers, and in the middle is a large space without a floor, where they light their fire and live together in common. Afterward the men retire to the above-mentioned quarters with their wives and children. And furthermore there are lofts in the upper part of their houses, where they store the corn of which they make their bread.

Our captain, seeing the misery and devotion of this poor people, recited the Gospel of St. John, that is to say, In the beginning was the word, touching everyone that was diseased, praying to God that it would please Him to open the hearts of the poor people and to make them know His Holy Word and that they might receive baptism and Christendom. That done, he took a service book in his hand and with a loud voice read all the passion of Christ, word by word, that all the standers-by might hear him. All which while this poor people kept silence and were marvelously attentive, looking up to heaven and imitating us in gestures.

Early on the morning after their arrival, on a bright October day, Cartier and his companions were led by the Indians up the slope from the river to Hochelaga at the foot of the mountain. The distance through the woods—from the foot of the new Harbour Bridge to the University Club on Mansfield Street, which was (and perhaps is) the central hearth of Hochelaga—was about two miles. But the way was lengthened and enlivened by a pause to light a fire and make speeches.

They came thus to the famous stockade itself, described with a perplexity of detail that is the despair of the historian in histories and school books.

Yet there is a certain mystery about Cartier's Hochelaga which history has all too little investigated. There is no doubt that such a place as Hochelaga existed. The various remains that have been excavated from under the soil indicate that its site was somewhere near the Hochelaga Memorial Stone set up in 1925 at the foot of the grounds of McGill University. The writer of this book had the honor of making over this stone the speech of dedication. He spoke in glowing terms of the vanished Hochelaga. He pictured its fifty great wooden lodges, each a hundred and fifty feet long, the vast stockade thirty feet high that enclosed it, its galleries, its ladders, and the huge open square among its lodges in which uncounted thousands of Indians listened to Jacques Cartier read from the Gospel of St. John.

But he had at the time grave doubts, such as many others must have entertained, whether Hochelaga could have really been a place of the huge dimensions indicated and yet have left so little trace; whether Jacques Cartier could have enacted a scene of such intense devotion and interest and yet, on his subsequent journey past Montreal inland to the Grand Sault, have gone past Hochelaga without a visit, without a word, without a thought, apparently, as to how his Indians were making out with St. John.

Equally amazing seems the silence of Champlain in 1603. The history books all tell us that when Champlain came Hochelaga had vanished. But Champlain doesn't tell us this. He never mentions the place.

The extraordinary prestige of Cartier's discovery of the river and of the wonderful site of the island with the Royal Mountain, the peculiar reverence that attaches to his having thus first brought Christianity to the savages throw a sort of veil of sanctity over the whole episode. Doubt seems to savor of irreverence. Yet it is worth while, perhaps, to look into the facts indicated by the meager and uncertain record and to try to distinguish what is undoubted truth from what is error, or even, to some extent, deception.

We may accept the general conclusion that Hochelaga was somewhere near the spot indicated by the stone. Other localities have been assigned to it. Half a century ago the late Dr. S. Dawson, an eminent scholar and a high authority, placed Hochelaga beside the Windsor Hotel, at that time Montreal's latest pride and more interested, perhaps, in sheltering Hochelaga than since the royal visit of 1939. A French-Canadian scholar, also, once gave grounds for placing Hochelaga out near Ahuntsic on the other side of the mountain. But the strongest evidence indicates it as beside, indeed as in the curve of, the little Burnside Brook that once ran down from the sunken hollow in the McGill grounds. The University Club on Mansfield Street represents, as it were, the central hearth of Hochelaga.

But when we turn from the question of site to the question of size that is quite another matter. The existence of Hochelaga, as a huge fortified stockade with vast wooden houses, rests on one document, the narrative of Cartier's voyage of 1535 (*Relation Originale*). Cartier's narrative was not printed in French for a long time; nor was his own handwritten copy ever found. But various manuscript copies were made of Cartier's manuscript and of his similar story of his first voyage in 1534, in which he found and named the river St. Lawrence but couldn't get up it (*Bref Recit*). An Italian collector of travels (Gian Battista Ramusio) had a translation of the narratives made into Italian and published in a collection (*Navigazioni e Viaggi*) in 1556. McGill University has in its library one of the few extant copies of this book. In it appears the famous picture of Hochelaga as a huge round wooden erection that has been in every schoolbook ever since and remains one of the crossword puzzles of history. It was evidently the product of an Italian illustrator utterly ignorant of the reality and working in a frenzy of either imagination or despair. He has his busy Indians working away with saws on board lumber. His Hochelaga is big enough to reach from the mountain to the river.

But this translated account of Cartier was all that the world had. The famous Elizabethan collector, Richard Hakluyt, had the voyages retranslated from Italian into English and took over the picture along with them. Hakluyt also got somewhere, not from Ramusio, a part of the narrative of Cartier's next voyage, that of 1541, in which he gives Hochelaga the go-by. Later on a French edition of the two voyages was printed from another manuscript (1598) and, much later, manuscripts, but not in Cartier's hand, were found in the French National Library for both the *Bref Recit* and the *Relation Originale*.

The reader must reconstruct for himself the nature of the stockade that is thus described. No two authorities agree about it, and Ramusio's picture, as Dr. W. D. Lighthall has abundantly shown in his Hochelaga monograph of 1932, is not so much a help as a hindrance. If we accept it on its face value it must have taken a powerful quantity of logs and a terrific amount of cutting. The trees available would have been elm and oak, hardwood, with perhaps soft maple, though soft maple doesn't run enough to length. There was no spruce, pine, or tamarack. But even at that the stone tomahawk of the Indians was an instrument of argument, not of carpentering.

Champlain saw later a few Indian axes beaten flat out of bits of Lake Superior copper. But Indians couldn't cut down trees on any real scale. Their canoes were sometimes made from birchbark, but they only prized off the bark; they didn't cut the tree. Most of the St. Lawrence canoes were dugouts, burned-out logs with the ends pointed by alternate charring and cutting. You could have done that with a hoe. But, as a matter of fact, even a hoe would have been far above anything an Indian had. He would have used it to shave with.

Take the number of logs in the Hochelaga lodges, each 150 feet by 30; allowing 15 feet per log, it takes 24 logs to go round once—one course: it takes 20 courses (15 feet) as a minimum of height; that means 480 logs to each house and a total of 24,000 logs. There are still the partitions and the roofs to provide for, and the big stockade itself. Give it a perimeter—or no, don't even give it a perimeter. It's too silly; Hochelaga is like the farmer's giraffe. No such animal.

Now we must admit that Champlain found a pretty big stockade fort among the Onondagas. Everyone recalls how he had a platform made, higher than this Onondaga fence, and had himself (and his musket) carried on the platform for a sort of aerial attack on the Onondagas. But you can pack all this into a very small compass. Even Champlain's own Onondaga drawing does not compare with Hochelaga. One admits, of course, that the Huron mission Indians, massacred in 1649, had hundreds of lodges and that the military expeditions of La Barre and the Marquis de Tracy (1666) destroyed hundreds of Mohawk lodges. But if instead of lodge we read "wigwam," instead of stockade read "fence," instead of "palisade" read "pole," then Hochelaga shrinks back to very different dimensions.

It was evidently there, or thereabouts. Certain relics of it exist. If it had really consisted of 24,000 big logs, no fires, no rot would have wiped it out so utterly. Burned-out cities like pre-Roman London or Troy leave old charred logs for centuries. But call it all poles and sticks, a sort of bird's nest, and you can burn it all up like yesterday's camp. The relics that exist, pipes, stone axes, and so on, are the kinds of things that would have been found, and are found, round any annual squatting place of savages. In this case their location, as said above, points to the University Club as the center of Hochelaga. The little river, the Burnside Brook, that now gurgles itself to death in the sewers ran around the lower side. It is strange to think that it was in the lounge room of the University Club that Jacques Cartier read the Gospel of St. John to the savages. It is a thing that would stand doing again.

But why, then, did such an account come into being? It has been argued that possibly it was what we now call "propaganda." It was made to "sell" Canada to King Francis I of France. Hence the same narrative tells of the "Kingdom of Saguenay," full of rubies and gold and men as white as Frenchmen. But the Gospel was needed also. The ladies of the French court were all set on saving the souls of the Indians. As Francis Parkman said, it was an easy way to save their own. Hence the two motives, wealth and the kingdom of heaven, appear in the words of an old nursery rhyme, "as a pretty dish to set before the King."

It might be objected that Cartier would not have stooped to

write this. Quite so: he couldn't and didn't, because he didn't
write it. In any sustained writing there is always evidence not
exactly as to who wrote it but as to who didn't. No one but an
actual sailor could have written the sea stories of Fenimore
Cooper; no one but a person with all the phrases of the law on
his finger tips could have written the plays of Shakespeare. Yet
here is Cartier, if it is Cartier, muddling up the sea terms that
a Breton pilot would use; here is Cartier writing a windy, ful-
some dedication and urging King Francis to kill the heretics.
This piece of savagery would be just right to say to Francis,
who afterward killed them with great cruelty (the Vaudois),
but it sounds all wrong for the humane Cartier to say it. Cartier
was dead before the book was ever printed in French.

Oddly enough this lying propaganda, if it was such, like so
much that is sinful, succeeded. In fact, we owe Montreal to it.
One of the few things we know from the mixed account of
Cartier's third voyage (1541) is that King Francis was enthusiastic about Saguenay and determined to open it up. He authorized the Sieur de Roberval to open all the jails in France and
help himself to Canadian settlers. The "wars of religion" intervened (piety always comes first), but the story of the Royal
Mountain, or its flock of meek Indians, their rapt faces turned
to the sky, waiting only for the Gospel, became a legend.
"Montreal," long before it was founded, came to mean vaguely
a distant place in North America where the savages needed
Christ.

From the Hochelaga stockade Cartier and his gentlemen and
twenty sailors made the ascent of the mountain which he named
Mount Royal. In the French of the day, "royal" was still writ-
able as *réal*. Montreal carries its name unchallenged. Here upon
the summit—not from any one spot, for the trees forbade and
still forbid it, but from various points of vantage—Cartier viewed
the imposing panorama "of thirty leagues in all," as he expressed
it. The Indians explained it to him—the islands, the enfolding
lakes, the great rivers that here came together. One of them,
pointing to the Ottawa, then touched Cartier's silver whistle and
the gilt handle of a sailor's dagger. Cartier thought they meant

that where they pointed silver and gold were found. And they *did* mean that. But later history, still ignorant, explained away Cartier's error; the Indians, it said, only referred to the silver color of the Ottawa, a flight of fancy quite beyond a Huron. Since the opening of the northern mining district, richer in gold and silver than all Peru, we know better. Perhaps luckily, history remained in the dark.

Cartier came down, impressed with the idea that here was the path to Saguenay. But the season was too late to reach it now. He hastened back, picked up his *Emérillon*, and so came safely to Stadacona in mid-October. Here all the previous good fortune was to change to the record of the terrible winter that followed. It is no part of the present work to follow it in detail. Cartier's men had built a solid log fort and mounted on it the cannon from the ships. It was to stand them in good stead. The winter set in early and intense with the utmost rigor of the Canadian cold. The ships froze in solid in mid-November. Indian friendship changed to Indian treachery. A terrible plague, recognizable as scurvy, struck down the French. In February only ten out of the one hundred and ten were fit for service. Twenty-five men were dead, lying under the snow, unburied. Cartier concealed his losses. His men made a brave show of manning the ramparts against the Indians now gathering for the slaughter. Then came what seemed a miracle, or at least a miraculous remedy, made from a native balsam, which cured the pestilence. The Indians waited, hesitating, as Indians always did, before an open attack. Then came the spring, the melting ice, the open river, Canada's annual deliverance.

Cartier hastened his departure. The ships were rapidly prepared. Donnacona kept up his false friendship to the last, kept up his wonder tales of the gold and silver of Saguenay, heightening the wonder with stories of men as white as the French, of men with one leg and no stomach, and "other marvels too long to tell." In reward for which, as a sort of poetic justice, Cartier carried him, by strategy, off to France, as too good to leave behind. With him were taken ten others—a source of later woe. Sailing on May 6, the ships reached Saint-Malo on July 16, 1536.

The First View of Montreal. Cartier's Visit to Hochelaga in 1535. From an Old Print

And with that Jacques Cartier's career, as far as it affected Canada, practically ended. There was a third voyage, as mentioned above, of which the record is confused and uncertain. In this, if we can believe the broken fragment left of the narrative, Cartier came up the river again and rowed past his Hochelaga without troubling to look at it. There may have been a fourth voyage. But in any case nothing came of it all. The energies of France were being absorbed for half a century in what the irony of history calls the "wars of religion." North American discovery fell asleep again. When it awoke Hochelaga had vanished.

CHAPTER II

Place Royale

The Inland Waterways. Geographical Situation of Montreal. The St. Lawrence Basin. Champlain's Voyages of Exploration. At Montreal Island, 1603. Establishes Place Royale, 1611. Later Journeys.

HERE it may be proper, for the later purposes of this book, to pause a while, as it were, with Cartier on the summit of Mount Royal and view with the aid of modern survey and topography the scene around us. The unusual physical features of this exceptional and happy environment make it one of the chief geographical centers of North America.

Its meaning lies in the confluence of the St. Lawrence and the Ottawa rivers, which here come together with such a great gathering of the waters that no single channel carries it. It forces its way through the higher ground, dividing it into a complex of islands and intervening channels. Down the steeper slopes it gathers into rapids. In the wide hollows that it has itself helped to deepen, the St. Lawrence spreads out into the expansion of Lake St. Louis above the Lachine Rapids and the La Prairie Basin below. On the other side the Ottawa expands into the Lake of the Two Mountains. Of the larger islands formed by these dividing channels there lies farthest south and west, farthest upstream,

Isle Perrot, a rough oblong of a length of about seven miles with a maximum breadth of about three. Immediately below it is the main island, the beautiful island of Montreal, thirty miles long from point to point, shaped in a long oval. Side by side with it and so beautifully wooded that in places the eye does not see the dividing Rivière des Prairies is Isle Jésus. On the other side of Isle Jésus runs the similar Rivière des Milles Isles in a wide concave bow from the foot of the Lake of the Two Mountains down to its junction with the Rivière des Prairies at the north end of Montreal Island.

In all this area it is difficult to indicate the direction of the rivers and the lie of the islands by simple reference to the cardinal points of the compass. The compass lies awkwardly across them. The St. Lawrence River in its passage from Lake Ontario to Lachine is moving virtually eastward. But the great rapids give it a throw to the left, and from La Prairie Basin, past the city of Montreal, the river is moving almost due north. Between Montreal and Quebec it flows about northeast, and below Quebec the river and the trend of the Gulf to which it enlarges is more and more directed toward the east. Readers will find that the north and south of Montreal are now called east and west in the perplexing nomenclature of our streets. Visitors to the city must remember that St. Catherine Street East and Sherbrooke Street East run fairly close to north, and that the south shore of the river lies east of the north shore; this is because the north shore got its name away back in Cartier's days from the geography of its mouth at the Gulf, where it really lies north. All such references as the recurrent historical statement that "the harbor of Montreal lies on the north side of the river," must be taken in this sense. As a matter of fact, the Victoria Bridge in crossing the river from the city to St. Lambert on the south shore runs almost northeast and the new Harbour Bridge due east.

The Ottawa where it joins the St. Lawrence has indeed run a strange course. Its sources lie in the wilderness about 160 miles north of the city of Ottawa. It starts off as if it meant to run westward to Lake Superior but keeps swinging around until by the time it has reached Ottawa it has completed a vast semicircle. Inside this enclosed sweep lie its great tributaries, the Coulanges, the Gatineau, the Rivière du Lièvre. At Ottawa it passes without deflection of its course over the roaring "caldron" of the Chaudière Falls, an imposing, almost terrifying sight as seen by Champlain and the early explorers, but now almost buried under the dams, power sites, and bridges of the capital city.

On its exit from the Lake of the Two Mountains the part of the Ottawa that does not join the St. Lawrence above Montreal Island is turned to an easterly course down the Mille Isles and Rivière des Prairies, and beyond Bout de L'Ile joins the main northeast current of the St. Lawrence.

Now the whole area thus described around the confluence of the two great rivers and the enfolded islands is blocked and guarded by rapids by which nature prevented all further navigation from the sea and gave the site its meaning and its history. Explorers coming up the St. Lawrence and reaching the bottom end of the island system (Bout de L'Ile) would naturally, and as a matter of course if guided by Indians, prefer the main channel, the one on their left hand. But some twelve miles up from Bout de L'Ile their course would be impeded—not absolutely blocked—by the broken water of St. Marys current. This is where the island named by Champlain St. Helens Island lies midway in the stream with shallow, rapid water on one side and on the other this fierce St. Marys current, varying with the season, but at times moving at six miles an hour. Boats and canoes could pass it by vigorous rowing, poling, or trekking. But it was obvious and natural to land at the foot of it, as Cartier did on his first discovery of Hochelaga.

But to pass St. Marys current had, in any case, no further meaning than to attain the sheltered water of the natural harbor under the projecting bank and a little island beside it, the original harbor of Montreal. The passage up the St. Lawrence beyond Montreal Island was barred by the vast rapids variously called the Great Sault, the Sault St. Louis, and finally the Lachine Rapids. In spite of the terrifying aspects and the awful roar of the waters of the Great Sault, of which even Champlain was not ashamed to record his fears, canoes and boats under proper guidance could come down in safety. Champlain himself is the first white man on record to have "shot the rapids." Presently it was found that even large steamers could shoot Lachine in safety. The terror of the explorer became the mock terror of the tourist.

Canoes and boats could come down. But nothing could go up except with laborious portaging and trekking. This was the end of real navigation till the nine-mile canal of 1825 left Lachine on one side.

The upward voyage past Montreal, behind the island by the Rivière des Prairies and the Rivière des Milles Isles, is similarly blocked. There are heavy rapids near the bottom end of the Rivière des Prairies, and halfway up its course is the famous and tumultuous Sault au Recollet. It is so called in memory of the tragic drowning of a Recollet friar in 1625, drowned in sight of his Indian flock, with or without their assistance. The Rivière des Milles Isles is blocked by great rapids beside the Isle St. Jean and Terrebonne.

At the upper end of the island system, where the Ottawa and the St. Lawrence connect, are the famous Rapids of St. Anne. Montreal is thus a full stop.

But it is a full stop, then as now, only for a new start. Even the liveliest imagination cannot readily realize what a concourse of waters, what a multitude of inland waterways are represented by these colossal converging streams. Here was to the acute eye of a Champlain the key to the continent. Nor is it a bygone key to a rusted lock. For the course of North American history has turned a full cycle, and the whole question of the St. Lawrence is up again with the discussion of the continental seaway. This magnificent project, to turn a dream to a reality, is already a matter of international agreement, postponed only by the present war. In the hope of many of us it will stand as one of the huge enterprises of constructive peace that will help to obliterate the ravages of war. Hence the facts behind it are as much front-page matter to us as they were to Cartier, Champlain, and La Salle.

The St. Lawrence River when it reaches Montreal has already drained all the Great Lakes. One of the strangest physical features of our continent is that the Great Lakes, an area of nearly 100,000 square miles, are fed almost entirely by rainfall and snow. The rivers that come into them are so short, the watersheds so relatively narrow, that only six miles from Lake Erie there are streams that start to flow to the Gulf of Mexico by way of the Ohio. The Des Plaines River, bound the same way via the Mississippi, rises only four miles west of Lake Michigan. Even on the north side, where Lake Nipigon drains to Lake Superior, it is only ten miles from Lake Nipigon to where the rivers start for James Bay. Apart from the minor tribute of rivers in western Ontario, the Great Lakes, as said, are fed only by precipitation. Yet their depth is so great, all but Lake Erie reaching far below the bottom of the sea, that this vast unaided reservoir keeps Niagara falling. Strangely enough, modern engineering now sets its hand to correct this unfair competition of the watersheds and to turn the waters from the wasted tumult of the empty North to the broad bosom of the Great Lakes, mother of man's industry. That is a far cry from the Montreal of Champlain but a vital concern to the seaport of today.

Nor does the glory of the volume of the St. Lawrence end with the island of Montreal. Passing down, it receives at Sorel, forty-three miles below, the flood of the Richelieu, the Rivière des Algonquins, which has drained Lake Champlain and all the country south to where the headwaters of the Hudson and the Mohawk dispute to carry it down the Hudson to the Atlantic. All these rivers and lakes, trails and portages connect in the retrospect of history with over two centuries of the dark shadows of conflict and war and with one in the bright daylight of peace and good will.

On the south side below the Richelieu are the lesser rivers, the St. Francis, Yamaska, Nicolet, and Ste. Croix.

The north side pays an even fuller tribute. The St. Maurice, whose sources rise beside the sources of the Ottawa but avoid its western aberration, comes into the St. Lawrence at Three Rivers, thus making with the course of the Ottawa and the St. Lawrence a sort of huge circle, and with it an inner chain of communication, known and used by the Indians, especially when the ravages of the Iroquois endangered the main river sources. Another great river joining the St. Lawrence from the north is the Batiscan. But all that they add to the St. Lawrence is eclipsed by the great flood of the Saguenay. This vast river, whose very name is mystery, has come down 112 miles from Lake St. John that lies north and a little *west* of Quebec. This lake is fed by streams from the north and the northwest that have come down hundreds of miles from where the watershed turns to Hudson Bay and Ungava. Here, straight from the north, is the Peribonka (a river of some 400 miles in length), now a part of the world's literature as the home of Maria Chapdelaine. Westward the huge river Ashuapmuchuan still offers its majestic name to a newer heroine. Some distance below the Saguenay begins the desolate territory and the north shore, Jacques Cartier's land of Cain.

All this vast vision of the waters of the past, the present, and the future—legend, history, and dreams—is spread out before us as we stand on Mount Royal. And now, equipped as Cartier never was, we may come down from the mountain.

A man now comes on the scene of American history in the person of Samuel de Champlain, who did more than any other single person toward opening up these inland waterways of the continent. Exploration and discovery had fallen virtually asleep since Cartier's time, but private interest had kept awake. The fisheries of the Newfoundland coast had greatly increased, with not only Breton and Norman sailors, but with a large English fleet out of Bristol and with Spaniards and Basques from the little port of Saint-Jean-de-Luz, a place older in its people and language than all record, a fishing port for centuries, a theater of war from the days of Henry of Navarre to those of the Duke of Wellington, yesterday a drowsy little watering place, and now again caught up in the fate of Europe.

The fishermen pushed farther and farther into the Gulf and adjacent waters. The furs brought down by the Indians opened a new trade. Tadoussac, at the mouth of the Saguenay, became each summer the gathering place of canoes and ships. But each attempt to make winter settlement as yet meant death in that bleak region. All this trade in fish and furs was carried on as a "free trade" by the private ventures of the merchants and pilots of the ports or by associated groups of them. Many persons of rank and court influence were interested. The fisheries remained an open trade, but monopolies were obtained from the Crown for the trade in furs and merchandise in the "River of Canada" and successively broke down. Such a commission of exclusive trade, on condition of settlement, was given to François Gravé Sieur du Pont, written also as Dupont-Gravé. He made a voyage to Tadoussac in 1600, planned greater things to follow, and in 1603 sent out Samuel de Champlain to search for a better site than Tadoussac.

Samuel de Champlain was of Brouage, a Bay of Biscay port, a sailor from his childhood, a sea pilot of exceptional knowledge for his day. He had made a two-year West Indian voyage, had written an account of it, and enjoyed a rising reputation. He was a devout Christian but a practical man too. There is a passage in his *Narrative of the Third Voyage* (1611), evidently meant for the eye of King Louis XIII, since it argues the need of funds, expressing the hope of "bringing many poor tribes to the knowledge of our faith in order that later on they may enjoy the heavenly kingdom." Meantime he helped some of the Iroquois on their way there with a harquebus.

With this voyage of 1603 begin the comings and goings of Champlain to Canada that extend over thirty years, that took him from the Bay of Fundy to the Georgian Bay, from the Richelieu to Lake Champlain, from New York State to Lakes Ontario and Simcoe. He made in all thirteen voyages out and twelve voyages back, ending his life at Quebec where his remains now lie.

Champlain first landed at Tadoussac where he met a great assemblage of savages, a war party making ready to attack the Iroquois. To these he promised the help of France.

It has been said that Champlain was not the first to offer such an alliance. Yet in this initial error of Indian policy there lay for French Canada the source of as many woes as those which brought down Troy. There is here the key to our North American history, the fate of a continent. For the future settlements, as at Montreal, it meant a half century of ever-present danger and the hideous massacre of the summer of 1689, the "Indian Summer" of Lachine. All of this, of course, was veiled from Champlain, but the historical background is plain enough to us.[1]

But at any rate here at Tadoussac, at the very opening of Champlain's career, we have the first illustration of that extraordinary instinct for geography which made him able, as it were, to divine the secrets of the unseen waterways of America. From his conversation with the savages he was able to plot out the region north and west of the Saguenay. It is strange to realize that the region of the Mistassini country remains almost unknown to the geography of ordinary people even now; or at least it was so till the day of the gold mines and the airplane in Canada. Much of it is shown on the new hydrographic maps to be an inconceivable tangle of thousands of small lakes and islands. Yet Champlain reconstructed its broad features; the course of the Saguenay; Lake St. John, its great tributaries leading to a farther watershed; the distances all estimated: so many portages, so many days . . . "a lake two days to cross" . . . "they can easily make 12 to 15 leagues in a day" (thirty to thirty-seven miles). . . . At the divide, so he was told, they met other Indians. . . . "These said savages from the north say that they are in sight of a sea which is salt. I hold that if this be so, it is some gulf of this our sea which overflows from the north into the midst of the continent; and indeed it can be nothing else."

Thus did Champlain "discover" the Hudson Bay some nine years before he read in a printed book the story of Henry Hudson's final and fatal voyage of 1611.

From Tadoussac, Champlain, accompanied by Dupont, passed on to inland discovery. "On the eighteenth of June," he writes, "we set out from Tadoussac to go to the Sault." This—the Rapid, or the Great Rapid—was the name widely current since Cartier's time for the Lachine Rapids, the great central point of inland intercourse. Champlain passed through and specially

[1]To and from America—1599–1601, 1603, 1604–07, 1608–09, 1610, 1611, 1612, 1613–14, 1615–16, 1617–18, 1620–24, 1625–29, 1635.

noted "the narrows," which the Indians called, as they still call any narrows, Kebek. The French spelling of the word long obscured for French people its Indian origin and for English people its Indian pronunciation. Champlain speaks of a waterfall from the top of a mountain (Montmorency) and of the beautiful trees, but of Stadacona not a word, either of name or settlement. It seems to have vanished.

As Champlain went up the river above Quebec he came to a place which he said was the farthest limit of Jacques Cartier's ascent. In reality he was only at the river now called Jacques Cartier, thirty-five miles above Quebec. Cartier had said that at that point there was a place called Hochelay. The name had appeared with various spellings, Ochelay, Achelay, or Hochelay, in several maps before Champlain's voyage. Champlain at this time knew of Cartier's voyage only by hearsay, and it seems likely that he confused Hochelay with Hochelaga, though he mentions neither. If so this would help to explain why he never looked for the real Hochelaga up above.

All about him in this untroubled summer voyage was the beauty of the St. Lawrence. The farther he went, so he reports, "the finer was the country" . . . "trees like walnut trees" . . . "islands pleasant and fertile." Then came the broad stretch of Lake Peter; at the head of it "thirty small islands . . . with many vines on them." Above the lake Champlain found the incoming of the Richelieu River, called by his guides the River of the Iroquois, since it comes down out of their country. He tried to ascend it but was blocked by the rapids of St. Ours fourteen miles up, now flooded over by a dam. Champlain turned back to the main river, ascended another forty-three miles, noting the beauty of the south shore, the islands, and the beautiful open woods in the lowlands, the clustered fruits, "good and pleasant with many meadows," and thus to the island of Montreal at St. Marys current, where Cartier had made his landing sixty-eight years before. With a fair wind astern, Champlain's boats (a shallop and skiff) passed this current and made their way along the shore to the shelter of a little island close to shore and offering protection against the current out in the river. This little island was later to be called the Ilot Normandin and then Market Gate Island, and the sheltered water between it and the shore was, as already said, the original Montreal Harbour. Later the island disappeared under the quays and the docks of the port. Here they came to anchor and went ashore. Then Champlain and Dupont, with Indian guides, made their way some distance farther up in their skiff and, when that failed, went on foot to the Great Sault (Lachine) and beyond.

From what he thus saw and from what the Indians told him Champlain not only gives an accurate description of the vicinity of Montreal but a marvelous reconstruction of what was beyond and above, all the way to Lake Huron. He writes with no reference to Cartier's voyage, to his "Mount Royal" and his "Hochelaga." He explains it all from the beginning. "There are two large islands, one on the north side some fifteen leagues long and almost as many broad which extends beyond the rapid." This is the island of Montreal. Jacques Cartier had not recognized it as such. It is thirty-six miles at the longest, nine at the widest; Champlain makes it thirty-six miles long, a close estimate; for the breadth, no doubt, he perhaps took the doubled islands (Montreal and Jesus), thickly wooded, for one. Champlain's island to the south is Isle Perrot. Montrealers think of it as west of them, but it lies due south of the upper end of Montreal Island.

Champlain describes, without names, the La Prairie Basin, St. Pauls (otherwise Nuns) Island, and Isle Ronde lower down. He speaks of a mountain (of course Mount Royal) "visible from very far in the interior." He describes the Lachine Rapids with something of a mixture of wonder and awe. Indeed in a later visit, when his companion Louis was drowned there, he says that the sight of them "made his hair stand on end." Beyond the rapids he could not go. He took the latitude as forty-five degrees and some minutes north. "We saw we could do no more," he said; "we returned to our shallop," at the harbor. Here he questioned the Indians and "made them draw by hand." He gathered that beyond this first rapid (Lachine) they go ten or fifteen leagues

to a river in the country of the Algonquins (the Ottawa).
Farther up the St. Lawrence, beyond where the Ottawa comes
in, Champlain traces, with an extraordinary approach to truth,
all the difficult succession of rapids, portages, and open lakes
which lie between Montreal and Lake Ontario. For example, he
indicates Lake St. Francis, the great expansion of the river between Valleyfield and Cornwall; makes it thirty-six miles long
(actually twenty-six), and gives the length of the principal
rapids and whether or not canoes must be portaged or can be
paddled. Beyond all this stretch of river and rapid, he writes,
is a lake that is eighty leagues (192 miles) long; at the upper end
of it the water is far less cold and the winter mild. This, of
course, is Lake Ontario (197 miles long), which Champlain himself was later to discover. At the upper end is Burlington Bay
with water far less cold than in Lower Canada. Beyond this is a
somewhat high waterfall, continues Champlain, where but little
water flows. This is evidently a confusion of what the Indians
said. Niagara at times runs dry, and in any case the crest of the
falls looks flat beside Lachine. Beyond this is another lake—Lake
Erie—sixty leagues long (144 miles; actually 250), then a strait—
our Detroit. Beyond that, the Indians said, was a great lake, but
they had never seen the other side of it, a lake "so vast that they
will not venture to put out into it."

This was, surely, Lake Huron, where the knowledge of the
Canadian Indians ended. They said that the sun in summer sets
north of it and that "the water there is very salt like that of our
own sea." This "salt" no doubt was a mistake, arising from the
salt of Hudson or James Bay connected by river and portage
with Lake Huron. But Champlain naturally says, "This makes
me believe that this is the South Sea. Nevertheless," he adds, "we
must not give too much credence to this view."

It is a strange thing, as already indicated, that in none of these
discussions does Champlain mention Hochelaga. He doesn't say
that it had gone. He just ignores it.

Champlain's first voyage thus ended with information that
made him eager to pursue inland discovery. But for a time other
tasks absorbed him. His next journey (in 1604) was taken up

with the exploration of the Bay of Fundy and the adjacent coasts and with his foundation of Port Royal, near by the present Annapolis, a lost paradise of peace and plenty, embowered in orchards and gardens, enlivened in winter by the food and merriment of the "Order of Good Cheer"—too bright to last. Then came his foundation of Quebec, 1608, and with it the first permanent settlers in French Canada and a strategic center on which turned the fate of North America. Yet Champlain's famous "habitation of Quebec" remained for years rather a fort with a winter garrison than a real colony. Not till 1617 appears the record of Louis Hébert, the first settler to bring out a family. Even at that the number of French wintering in New France, down till Champlain's death in 1635, was only about a hundred. New France for its first century was little more than a vast project which, to the very end, its limited population rendered futile.

The foundation of Quebec was followed by Champlain's participation with his Indian associates, Algonquins and Hurons, in their war against the Iroquois, now spreading their ravages far and wide. As has been said, this ill-chosen policy was to bring evil results for Montreal and for French Canada. For the moment it meant the temporary discomfiture of the Iroquois by a handful of Frenchmen using firearms.

Champlain had never lost from his mind the Great Sault (Lachine) and the lake and river route these opened to the South Sea. But it was not till 1611 that he was able to attempt a definite establishment at what we now call Montreal. He left France (Honfleur) early in the season (March 1611) but merely learned thereby the full meaning of the St. Lawrence ice. It took two months and a half to reach Tadoussac. From there in a shallop (longboat) he made his way up the river to Montreal Island, to the little harbor behind the island disclosed in his first visit. At that point a little river, rising in a pond or small lake near Lachine, ran down the sunken hollow that later was to hold the Lachine Canal. It fell into the main river just opposite the little island already mentioned (Ilot Normandin—Market Gate Island). Close to its mouth it was joined by little streams that then ran down what is now Craig Street, and from the mountainside flow streams, such as the Burnside of James McGill, that now sparkle and murmur but a brief moment to fall to the dark pollution of the city sewers.

Round this pleasant meeting place of forgotten waters was a stretch of smooth and fertile meadowland where once the Indians of Hochelaga had grown their winter corn. The inroads of war had long since returned it to desolation. Here Champlain laid out his settlement, Place Royale, as he named it. Champlain was fascinated with the place. "There are fine meadows," he said, "which would feed as many cattle as one could wish; all the varieties of wood which we have in our forests of France with vines and butternuts, plums, cherries and strawberries . . . and an abundance of fish . . . and game birds." Champlain ordered trees cut, a building to be erected on the little island, and fields prepared. He tested the clay of the ground for brickmaking and built a wall (an embankment or levee) ten yards long, four feet high, and thus twelve feet above the summer water, to see how it would be effective against the flood season. This scientific and experimental attitude appears in Champlain throughout. Especially he took note of the possibility of a walled town on a larger lower island, still called, as he christened it, by his wife's name, St. Helens Island.

Dupont joined him from Tadoussac with a large company of free traders attracted at once by the rumor of a new center of trade. Champlain sent out Indian messengers to summon their companions to the place. On the thirteenth of June (1611) a large concourse of Hurons came down from the Ottawa country. There was the usual tumultuous welcome, shouting and noise of firearms and the inevitable Indian oratory. These Indians gave Champlain a hundred beaver skins and eagerly asked for his friendship.

The Iroquois had now become an ever-present menace. Many savages were afraid to come down to the Sault for fear of them. A rumor had been treacherously spread that Champlain was going to go over to the Iroquois. As for the French traders, the Indians trusted them not at all; they rightly saw in them reckless, adventurous men, looking for gain, with no common purpose.

Champlain reassured the Indians; he would ask the King for fifty men equipped with firearms; he would protect them if they were willing to show him their country. He hoped to find, with their help, the way to the South Sea. "I had much conversation with them," he said, "regarding the source of the Great River" (the St. Lawrence), ". . . the rivers, falls, lakes and lands." Some of the Indians claimed to have seen a great sea to the west, far away, difficult to reach. Champlain remained at and around Place Royale from the twenty-eighth of May till the eighteenth of July. It was during this sojourn that Champlain's companion, a servant of De Monts called Louis (we have no other name for him), was drowned in the Lachine Rapids, frequently henceforth called the Sault St. Louis, either in his memory or in honor of King Louis XIII. Bands of Indians kept coming down, but the distrust and the fear of the Iroquois hindered trade. Champlain, promising to return, left on July 18; his shallop flew with the wind and current in a single day from Place Royale harbor to Three Rivers, seventy-seven miles below. Such were the varying fortunes of travel, for a week's voyage perhaps a day's return, or for a day a week. Champlain reached La Rochelle September 11, 1611.

This was to all intents and purposes Champlain's last connection with Place Royale. In his journeys of 1613 and 1615 he came and went to Montreal Island but never found time to prosecute the development of the fort and settlement he had planned. Had he done so the history of Canada might have received a forward development of far-reaching consequences. But Champlain's mind was set on exploration. While in France in 1612 he heard the news of the discovery of the great inland sea, since called the Hudson Bay. This, we must remember, was a one-sided discovery, not of a closed sea locked in with rugged shores, as it turned out to be, but apparently of a great sea all open to the west. Hudson's men who marooned him and came home had seen only the eastern side. Not till the voyages of Captains Fox and James (1631) was the sea known to be closed.

Champlain, therefore, on his next voyage went past Montreal Island up the Ottawa on a fruitless search for this great sea.

After that there came the most famous voyage of all, which took him up the Ottawa, hence to the Georgian Bay, Lake Simcoe, and central Ontario and brought the discovery of Lake Ontario itself. On this journey again Champlain pursued his fatal policy of attempting to lead his insignificant forces and his doubtful allies against the Iroquois. He abandoned exploration for war, crossed Lake Ontario, and, in the Iroquois country itself (New York State), led an attack against the stockade at Onondaga, near Oneida Lake. The attack failed. Champlain was successfully carried away, wounded. He wintered in the lodges of the Hurons, in the Lake Simcoe and Lake Huron country. He meant to strike out west to the great sea in 1616. Indian war prevented this. He came down past Montreal and so to Quebec July 11, 1616.

It is said in defense of Champlain's war on the Iroquois that he found this policy all set on his first arrival at Tadoussac in 1603; also that he would have succeeded and driven out the Iroquois forever if the King would only have given the soldiers for the work; one regiment would have been enough—nothing as beside the army of France. This plea Champlain continued all his life.

When the English took Quebec in the war of 1629—it was held by only a starving garrison of sixteen men—Champlain became a prisoner, was taken to England, released at the peace of 1632, to return to Quebec in 1633, and there to die on Christmas Day, 1635.

CHAPTER III

Ville Marie de Montreal

Foundation of Montreal by Maisonneuve in 1642.
The Missions in the Wilderness. The Association
of Montreal. The Mission Settlement of Ville Marie.
The Fort. The Hotel Dieu. The Attacks of the
Iroquois.

DURING the thirty-one years that elapsed between Champlain's survey and preparation of his Place Royale (1611) and the foundation of the mission city of Ville Marie de Montreal by Maisonneuve in 1642, there was no definite settlement, no all-the-year-round establishment at the place. But the locality was henceforth a well-known rendezvous for traders who came up the river and Indians who came down from the inland waters. The name Montreal, taken from that of the mountain and used by Champlain only in its original sense, was presently widely used both in Canada and in France to indicate not a mountain or a city but a locality in general.

Meantime New France was expanding not in numbers, but in the extent of its reach. When Champlain died there were, as said, only about a hundred white inhabitants. Even when Maisonneuve came from Quebec to Montreal, New France only contained about three hundred French. But meantime the arrival of priests and nuns from France led to the establishment of those missions in the wilderness that were to become the spiritual glory of New France. If there was in the end no crown of empire there abides the crown of martyrdom. Priests, as said, may have come with Cartier. They certainly came over with Champlain, at first certain Recollet friars, a branch of the Franciscans, and in 1625 the Jesuits, whose record and whose suffering are graven on the monuments of our history. The Jesuits, as part of their mission, prepared reports and wrote letters home to their order, and in these half-hundred volumes of the *Jesuit Relations* we have a principal original source of Canadian history. At the time of which we speak Jesuit fathers were making their way up to and beyond Montreal, up the Ottawa to the Huron country (Lake Simcoe), later to be the scene of the great massacre and of the martyrdom of Father Brébeuf and Father Lalemant. This they did in spite of the ever-present danger of the Iroquois raids. No trail in the woods was safe from ambush; no still lake or murmuring river but might echo to their sudden war cry. These dangers of New France were braved by a small band of devoted women who came thither in response to this higher call. We cannot understand the full meaning, the sacred meaning of the founding of Montreal without appreciating the terrible danger —never seen but ever present—which surrounded its foundation.

Along with the coming of the priests and nuns the government of New France had been changed from a basis of random adventure, a privileged trade, to a definite organization. The master hand of Cardinal Richelieu had been turned to the task. A Company of One Hundred Associates had been formed to take over New France and colonize it. A feudal system of land grants was established, the famous seignorial tenure which lasted till 1854, with certain incidents only terminated in 1940. Henceforth there was a regular governor at Quebec and a Father Superior (presently a bishop). A convent of Ursuline sisters was established at Quebec in 1642. The whole population was still a mere handful with outposts at Three Rivers above and Tadoussac below.

Few if any people think of Montreal today as a sacred city. Yet such it was in its foundation. We think of it now as a great commercial metropolis: McGill University is one of the great schools of the world; St. James Street, like Wall Street, carries in its name all the awe and the obloquy of high finance. But the Ville Marie de Montreal, founded under Paul de Chomedey de Maisonneuve in 1642, belonged to the Kingdom of the Spirit.

The quarrels of the Reformation and the wars that followed had set up in France a new ferment of religion. This shows its dark side in Europe in the cruel fury of persecution but in America its bright side, as the propagation of the light of the Gospel. The pages of early Christianity were rewritten in Canada, and nowhere more than in the foundation of Montreal.

The new movement of faith in France had inspired many ladies of the French court and of the French châteaux with a desire to aid in the conversion of the savages. Many nobles and soldiers were inspired also to take part in it. To such people the name Montreal, still inexact, indefinite, came to mean a place in the wilderness where there was dire need of Christ. There began what we might call in our current language a "Montreal movement." This presently took on all the aspects of the miraculous. As we read of it in the devout contemporary pages of Dollier de Casson[1] and in the later work of the Abbé Faillon it breathes the atmosphere of Scripture. Visions were sent to people who had never heard of Montreal, calling them to the work. Such a vision came to Jean de la Dauversière, a burgher of Laflèche, a good citizen, a man of family, but an ascetic who scourged and beat himself that grace might be granted to him. Such a vision came also to the Abbé Olier, a priest from Paris, whose name is inscribed on one of the humblest of our Montreal streets. He had just founded (1640) in Paris the Seminaire of St. Sulpice and the order which later established the Seminaire at Montreal and became in 1663 the feudal holders of Montreal Island. Olier and Dauversière had never heard of one another. But coming together by chance, their eyes met; their countenances were

[1]Dollier de Casson, *Histoire du Montréal*, 1672.

lighted up with recognition. They clasped hands and talked of Montreal. Yet neither, we are assured, had ever heard of it except in a vision.

Others joined. An Association of Montreal was founded. Money was supplied by pious ladies eager to save the distant souls of the Algonquins and the Iroquois. There were to be three religious orders—one of priests, one of nuns for a hospital, the third of nuns for a teaching order.

Neither Olier nor Dauversière was in a position to lead forth the mission. But the hour brought the man. The noble figure of Paul de Chomedey de Maisonneuve appears on the scene of history. His monument stands in our Place d'Armes at Montreal, and no name in our history better deserved one. Nor must one confuse it with the random mention of a Sieur de Maisonneuve, a trader of Saint-Malo, casually mentioned as meeting with Champlain at Place Royale on June 17, 1613, thirty years before. Maisonneuve was a soldier but also a man of the inner light, inspired. "I would go there," he said when they spoke of the Indian terror, "if every tree were an Iroquois."

The ship's company were marshaled at Rochelle. With Maisonneuve were forty soldiers to serve as a garrison and a working body of farmers and servants, all in one. The chief of the hospital was Jeanne Mance, of Nogent-le-Roi, a woman not in religious orders but who had, since her childhood, devoted herself to religious discipline. She too had received a divine call to Montreal. She journeyed to Paris, thence to La Rochelle to join the Montreal expedition. On meeting Olier and Dauversière she knew "their most hidden thoughts" by miraculous intervention. Pious friends supplied her with ample funds. Henceforth her lifework was at Ville Marie de Montreal. This name was selected by the Associates in a ceremony of consecration after the departure of the ship.

They sailed in 1641 but reached Quebec too late to make a further ascent of the river. They therefore spent the winter at Quebec, now fortified and secure, but still a population of only a handful. In the spring they made the ascent of the river. The craft used by the traders from Quebec to Montreal at that date were not ocean-going ships but very large open boats, flat-bottomed, of little draft, carrying mast and sails, but capable of being rowed. These are the *barques* and the *chaloupes*—the longboats and shallops—of the narratives. Larger still were pinnaces which could have more than one mast. Small boats called *skiffs* (*esquifs*), propelled with oars and poles, were brought along to go in water too shallow for the bigger boats. But skiffs could be bigger than the little rowboats now so called. They might hold half a dozen men.

Maisonneuve's river boats were built beside Quebec in the winter and early spring. Here was a pinnace with three masts, two shallops, and also a big barge with sails, a *gabare* probably much like what is called a scow, with sails added. They sailed from Quebec on May 8, 1642. The ship's company included Maisonneuve; M. de Montmagny, whose duty it was to hand over the island of Montreal as from the Company of One Hundred Associates to the Associates of Montreal; Father Vimont, the superior of the mission at Quebec; Father Poncet, who was to remain at Montreal, and several Jesuit priests. There was also M. de Puiseaux of Quebec, together with soldiers, the sailors of the boats, and other artisans—in all some fifty people. The women present were Jeanne Mance and Madame de la Peltrie who, with her maid, Charlotte Barré, left the Ursuline convent at Quebec to share in the foundation of Ville Marie.

A week was spent in the ascent of the river. At length on May 17 they came in sight of Montreal Island, glorious with the sunrise of a May morning that bathed its meadows and its mountainside with light and touched the soft colors of the budding leaves. They landed on Champlain's ground, just under the shelter of the tongue of land beside the little river (the Pointe à Callières). Maisonneuve no sooner landed than he fell on his knees, and all the company as they came ashore kneeled in prayer and joined in hymns of thanksgiving. They had no sooner landed their first stores than they raised an altar, decorated by the women with spring flowers, and here was celebrated the first Mass of Ville Marie. Then Father Vimont spoke. "What you see," he said, "is only a grain of mustard seed . . . but it is so animated by faith and religion that it must be that God has great designs for it."

All day they labored, landed stores, and arranged their camp for the night. When darkness fell there was no oil for a lamp, so the women caught fireflies and put them in a glass and therewith illuminated the altar. Then night fell. Beside them, as they went to rest, was the murmur of many waters, whispering of unseen danger. Only faith and courage could find sleep beside it.

The next day the Governor and his attendants left downstream for Quebec. The colonists set busily to work, their first task to protect themselves. Round their camp they made a ditch and some sort of palisade with stakes; with this began the building of a chapel of bark—prayer and defense, the signs of their allotted task.

Their situation indeed afforded little safety from attack. Montreal offers but little natural facility for defense. In Roman times the flat mountaintop would have made an admirable *castra*, but these were other days and other arms. Down below the mountainside there is little protection. Such as there was lay in the watercourses. The St. Lawrence covers one side, and for the Ville Marie and the Montreal of the French Regime till the conquest the sunken hollow that is now Craig Street was a marsh and river, offering a certain cover from behind. This stream, presently called Ruisseau St. Martin (St. Martin's Brook), ran parallel to the St. Lawrence but in the other direction. It made a turn and emptied into the little river already mentioned (the St. Pierre). The first camp and the first fort were on the downstream side of the St. Pierre. But when the colonists presently built their hospital and houses they moved across the St. Pierre to the higher ground a little farther upstream and thus had water on three sides of them.

This later gave the plan of defense of the walled town. Luckily for Maisonneuve's settlers who were armed soldiers, the Iroquois, who were now armed like themselves with firearms, seldom found what is rudely called "the guts" for a direct attack. Their method was stealth, ambush, death by night. A few resolute armed men might face and defy them. But the danger was present enough. Within a few weeks the Montreal settlers were to learn what it meant. And here perhaps one may pause by the waters of Ville Marie to speak of the Indian terror of which they murmured. It is necessary, as the key to the next half century of the history of Montreal, to understand the Indian situation and the Indian danger.

The Indians of North America had migrated, long before memory and history, from Asia and were thinly scattered over the continent. They perhaps numbered, in what is now the United States and Canada, something over a million. Here and there they lived in clustered lodges, on the Pacific coast (then all unknown) probably in still larger groups. But mostly they wandered. Their languages are numerous, about seventy-five in all, but show them all of one family. Even the Eskimos are Indians in the historic sense.

Of the Indian tribes east of the Mississippi the most widely spread were the great family of the Algonquins. They occupied the country north of the Great Lakes, the Ottawa valley, the lower St. Lawrence, the maritime coast (Acadia), and the Atlantic seaboard of New England. They included such tribes as the Montagnais, a northern tribe of the "Kingdom of Saguenay"; the Ojibways (otherwise Chippewas); the Micmacs; the Narragansetts, and the Delawares. Their language is easily recognized by such sounds as Kebek, Mikmak, Shediac, and all that spells New Brunswick. The Algonquins were largely a nomadic race, hunting and fishing and moving with the game and the seasons.

Over against these, in the space between the Great Lakes, the St. Lawrence, and the Hudson River, were the Huron-Iroquois, tribes of one family but divided later by the dissensions that brought on the wars of extermination. Their language is seen in the softer sounds of Hochelaga, Stadacona, and Niagára (pronounced as it is in Indian). The Iroquois, like the Algonquins, carry their Indian name. But "Huron" is a French nickname from *la hure*, the boar's head, a metaphor suggested by the peculiar tufted appearance, the particular fashion in scalp locks, of the shaven Huron head. Huron in Indian is Wyandot.

The Hurons lived along the lakes and the St. Lawrence. The Iroquois filled the gap between the Hudson and Niagara which proved the key point of American strategy. There were five nations of them, known always by the English version of their Indian names. The Mohawks lived, as one might expect, on the Mohawk River. The French called them Agniers. West from the Mohawks ran the Oneidas, the Onondagas, the Cayugas, and the Senecas. Apart from the Mohawks they all were similarly named in English and French. But the transcription of their names into the two languages is so varied as to be almost unrecognizable. It is hard to believe that the French for Seneca is *Tsonnon-chouan*. This last nation, the most foul and savage of the five, if comparison is possible, lived between where Rochester and Buffalo now stand. They were the left flank of the Five Nations. The Mohawks on the right had as their war trail the descent of the beautiful waterways by Lake George, Lake Champlain, and the Richelieu. The traveler of today over the Delaware and Hudson Railway line may reconstruct, if he will, amid the beauty of the woods and water that he passes, the ambush, the massacres, and the savagery of the Indian war, the agonies of Father Jogues in the wilderness, and the butchery of Fort William Henry.

To the left the Seneca and Onondaga country can recall the expeditions of Denonville and Frontenac. Holding this central region, the Iroquois Five Nations, ferocious beyond all record, conquered to the verge of extermination their neighboring Indian enemies one by one and for a century and a half played off England against France and turned the tide, literally, of the world's history. For had they sided with France, what then?

These Indians were savage beyond belief. To say that they burned their prisoners alive is to say the least of it. No one wishes to dwell on the horrors of torture, the remembrances of a cruelty long gone and passed to its account. But, to be done with it once and for all, one must speak of it here in order to understand the history of Montreal for its first sixty years, in order to know what were the warnings whispered by the moving waters beside

Ville Marie. These Indians not only burned their prisoners but burned them with slow and studied tortures that kept pain alive and life not yet extinct. They unbound them from the stake to drag them, mutilated and bleeding, along the trail for torture renewed every evening and all night, dragged them to their home lodges so that their wives and children might assist in the final scenes, might heap with hideous childish merriment burning coals in patches on the torn bodies dying in the ashes. Nor this to their fighting enemies alone; they stuck little children on spits of wood to burn slowly to death before a slow fire. They forced women to burn their husbands to death with flaming brands of resinous wood. Nor was death the end. These unspeakable creatures chopped up the dead and tortured bodies of their enemies, to boil and roast them for their cannibal feasts. The choicest portion, the brain, fell to the share of the chief. "They ate men," a contemporary witness wrote, "with as much appetite and more pleasure than hunters eat a boar or a stag." It was Father Vimont who wrote that, the priest who celebrated the first Mass at Ville Marie.

Imagine such scenes of horror, and imagine among them the torn and tortured priest, Father Jogues, crawling to reach out his mutilated hands into the flames to baptize with a few drops of water the dying victim in the name of Jesus Christ.

Horrors are well to avoid. But no one who does not know of these things can understand the lights and shadows, the horror and the glory of Canadian history.

Maisonneuve's colonists were soon to learn of them at first hand. In the middle summer of the year, August 2, 1642, Father Jogues, a Jesuit of the Huron Mission, was coming up the river from Quebec to Montreal, carrying with him renewed supplies sent out from France for his work—sacred vestments, chasubles, vessels for the altars, bread and wine for the Eucharist, and such holy and necessary things. With him were three French companions, two associated with his work, one a boatman, and a band of Huron converts, and others waiting baptism in the faith. In all they filled twelve canoes. Their journey brought them to a place in the river at the western end of Lake St. Peter, where the swift current and broken water forced them close beside the shores under the woods. Here two hundred Iroquois, hidden in the leaves, armed with firearms, motionless and without sound, waited for them. They were Mohawks who had come down by the Richelieu for this ambush. At the chosen moment, with the shriek of their war whoop and the discharge of their muskets, they fell upon their victims. The Huron made little fight; those who could escaped, as did one Frenchman. The others were killed or taken.

The Frenchmen stood their ground to be torn down by the savages. Jogues had remained unresisting, baptizing his dying Hurons. The savages turned on him. They beat him senseless and, when revived, chewed and lacerated his fingers with their teeth. . . . Twenty-two Hurons had been taken. Some of them were burned alive forthwith for the immediate enjoyment of their captives. Others with Father Jogues were dragged back along the Mohawk war trail to endure sufferings such as those described above—beaten, mutilated, burned—to end their death in fire. Jogues alone was kept alive. For months the savages held him to witness and to share the torments inflicted on each new group of captives taken on the warpath. At length the Dutch contrived to rescue him. They sent him on a ship to France. He arrived at the College of Rennes, house of his order, ragged, mutilated almost beyond recognition. There he was restored to life.

It has been finely said that there is no suffering that human cruelty can inflict too great for human fortitude to bear. Jogues returned to his mission work in New France, once more to labor, to suffer, and to die under Indian torment, his flesh cut into strips, a tomahawk smashed into his brain.

Such was the news that spread from the fugitives of the massacre to the settlers at Ville Marie in that late summer of 1642. Although a few more colonists were added to their number that August, they scarcely dared go beyond the shelter of their palisades. What we think of today as the upper part of Montreal, its beautiful squares, its tall hotels, its crowded streets, its embowered university, its spacious cathedrals, its roaring stadium

—all this was forest. In it at any moment might lurk the Mohawk. Settlers who ventured too far might pay for it with their lives.

The settlers at Ville Marie for the opening years of their settlement had no better shelter than their palisaded camp beside the river. Their first real building was the Hotel Dieu (finished 1644) higher up on the bank, its site indicated today by the intersection of St. Paul Street with St. Sulpice Street (formerly St. Joseph). This was to be the hospital for the ministrations of Jeanne Mance and those who followed her to the mission. It was a large wooden building, protected with a palisade and serving also as the first church of these days. Burned in 1695, rebuilt to be burned again in 1721, again burned in 1734, it was rebuilt in the building used until 1861, when its place was taken by the building still occupied on Pine Avenue West.

The building of the Hotel Dieu was followed by the construction of a real fort, with solid walls and enclosed buildings, set on the tongue of land between the little St. Pierre River and the St. Lawrence. A cannon brought from Quebec was mounted on the fort. Beside it, on the tip of the tongue of land, was laid out the first cemetery, soon abandoned as the spring floods of the river gave even the dead no rest. Later on the fort also was abandoned and demolished, and M. de Callières, Governor of Montreal and, after Frontenac, of Canada, built a fine house on its former site. Hence the place was presently called the Pointe à Callières.

For Maisonneuve was built (1652), in a clearing of the woods between the Hotel Dieu and the fort, a large three-story wooden structure, something like a French chalet, and protected also with palisades. A rough track that later became St. Paul Street ran from the Hotel Dieu to this house, then turned and went over a little bridge to the fort. When the Sulpician priests came to Ville Marie (1650) they lived first in Maisonneuve's house, which was remodeled to become (1661) their first seminary. It must be remembered, of course, that up to this time they were present at Ville Marie only as priests serving on mission. The feudal proprietors were still the "Compagnie de Montreal." It

was not till March 9, 1663, that the Compagnie transferred, with
the consent of the Crown, its obligations and rights to the Seminary of Saint Sulpice at Paris. It was in 1712 that the Sulpicians
moved into their "new" seminary, the one still occupied. But
even before this they had constructed their outside fort in the
woods (Le Fort des Messieurs), of which two corner towers still
stand on Sherbrooke Street West.

TABLET ON THE FROTHINGHAN AND WORKMAN COURT OFF ST. PAUL STREET

> *Upon this foundation stood the first manor
> House of Montreal built 1661, burnt 1852, rebuilt
> 1853. It was the seminary of St. Sulpice from 1661
> to 1712. Residence of de Maisonneuve, Governor
> of Montreal, and of Pierre Raimbault, Civil and
> Criminal Lieutenant General.*

Pierre Raimbault lived in the house after the Sulpicians moved
in 1712 into their "new" seminary, the one still standing.

Another pious foundation of the earliest days of Ville Marie
was the Church of Notre Dame de Bonsecours farther downstream than the other building. It owes its foundation to the
saintly labors of Marguerite Bourgeoys, who came to the mission
in 1653, one of the most distinguished and devoted of the women
who gave their lives to Ville Marie. Her labors were chiefly in
the work of teaching. But she is remembered also for having
brought out from France a miraculous statue of the Virgin and
the funds to erect a chapel where it might stand in full sight from
the river and serve as the guardian saint of approaching sailors.

Such, then, was the situation of the mission post of Ville Marie
in the early years of its history, the Indian peril ever close at
hand. Some Algonquins came about in the summer of 1642, but
the Iroquois only learned of the settlement in the summer of
1643 when they kept it under watch, roving the forests in bands.

On one occasion (it was June 9, 1643) six men who were cutting wood less than a hundred yards from the fort were attacked by a band of forty savages who rushed upon them from behind the trees. Three of them were killed outright, the rest carried off for a worse fate. One, it was said, escaped later.

Maisonneuve forbade all wandering out. Work must be to the sound of the bell, all leaving the fort together. Some of the more reckless of the French, chafing at this captivity, urged Maisonneuve to go out and fight. Their importunities, month after month, wore out his better judgment. He ordered thirty men to get ready and come out with him to fight. This was at the end of March (1644), with deep snow still in the hollows under the leafless trees, before the return of the birds to the forests. All was silent as they entered the woods. Then the hidden savages, a band of eighty Iroquois, rushed toward them. The French stood firm, firing from behind trees, learning the new strategy of the American woodsman. . . . Some fell. The others, under orders, moved back, tree to tree, toward the fort, Maisonneuve the last. The Iroquois, seeing who he was, tried to rush him, to drag him off captive. Maisonneuve turned at bay, fearless. As the Iroquois chief approached he fired; the pistol missed; his second pistol shot the chief dead. While the Indians clutched for the fallen body Maisonneuve escaped. The French, carrying some of their wounded, reached the fort. Three lay dead in the woods. Two were carried off and burned at the stake. After that no one ever questioned Maisonneuve's courage or his commands.

This heroic conflict is one of the treasured memories of French Canada. The exact scene of the actual struggle is a matter of argument among antiquarians. We know at least that it was in the heart of the financial district of Montreal, near by the present struggles of the Stock Exchange.

Such scenes and such dangers marked the life of Montreal for its first three years. To safeguard its existence the Governor General of New France was ordered to build a fort at the foot of the Richelieu to block the Mohawk warpath. The Indians (two hundred) ambushed the French soldiers at their work. But they seized their arms just in time. After a fierce fight they beat off their assailants at odds of two to one. The Iroquois never had much heart for fighting man to man in the open.

Even at that the fort was of little service. The French were still to learn that against an Indian raid one fort was of little value. They carried their war canoes around it. There must be at least two and a stretch of protected water to make the portage long and hazardous. Hence another fort was presently built on the Richelieu beside the Chambly Rapids. Visitors to Montreal, at no greater sacrifice than a pleasant motor drive of twenty miles, may view the old fort at Chambly and study Indian strategy on the spot.

Maisonneuve's historic fight had taken place at the end of March 1644. All through that year and well into the next there was no safety. The Iroquois seemed to swarm in the woods. Their war parties roved over all Montreal Island till there was no place safe except the fort itself. A small reinforcement of soldiers was sent out to New France by the Hundred Associates in 1645, sixty men to be divided along the river at Quebec, Three Rivers, the Richelieu fort, and Montreal. But their numbers, as with all the little detachments sent out at intervals in the next twenty years, were hopelessly few for adequate protection.

Yet their presence helped to induce the Iroquois to offer peace, which marked the close of what some historians care to call the First Iroquois War. But it closed only to open again more deadly than ever in the fall of 1646. The Iroquois war, or rather the series of raids and massacres, was to last, with only casual cessations, for twenty years.

Maisonneuve was absent when the war broke out; the momentary peace had allowed him (1646) to return to France for his personal affairs and for those of the Association of Montreal. He did not return to Ville Marie till 1648, when the danger was at its height. The raids never stopped. "At Montreal," so wrote from Quebec the Jesuit Superior, "there are barely sixty Frenchmen, twenty Hurons, a few Algonquins, and two of our fathers." "It is a marvel," said the *Jesuit Relation* of 1651, "that the French of Ville Marie were not exterminated by the frequent surprises of the Iroquois bands. The Indians broke into the settlement again and again, sneaking among the trees or along the sunken ditches. Often ten men or less fought against fifty or eighty." Here belong the heroic episodes of such fights as those of Charles le Moyne. At heavy odds he drove off a band of Iroquois from Point St. Charles, leaving them dead with only four French wounded. Here belongs also the heroic fight for the Hotel Dieu itself. This building was now armed with two pieces of cannon and with swivel guns in its windows. Early in the morning of Tuesday, July 26, 1651, a band of two hundred Iroquois swarmed against its palisades. Lambert Closse, the major of the garrison, whose figure stands as one of those on the Maisonneuve monument, with sixteen men fought off the attacks that never ceased till evening. There was need of courage. The terrible massacre which had already overwhelmed the mission of St. Louis among the Hurons on what is now the Georgian Bay, with the martyrdom of Father Brébeuf and Father Lalemant, showed what might befall Ville Marie. Maisonneuve, going again to France to seek help, was almost in despair, ready to recall the colony.

The crowning episode of glory was found in 1660 in the voluntary sacrifice and death of Dollard des Ormeaux and his sixteen companions, a story that can be read beside that of Thermopylae. To save Ville Marie by going out to meet the Indians, Dollard and his companions, their sins confessed, their death accepted, fought off behind a rude stockade at the Long Sault on the Ottawa River the assaults of eight hundred savages. Only after eight or nine days did their heroic sufferings (wounded, sleepless, and without water) end in death by extermination. Dollard's name is also written, as by Francis Parkman, as Daulac. Such confusion of spelling was natural in a colony where spelling was a rare art.

Meantime in these troubled years settlement and trade struggled on as best it could. Ville Marie in 1652 still had only something more than a hundred inhabitants. Parties of Algonquins, arriving for shelter, brought furs, as did even the Iroquois in the pauses of open war. But the place as yet was in no way self-supporting. It was carried on with the original subscription of seventy-five thousand livres collected for the Association of Montreal and with later contributions; Madame de Bullion, a wealthy lady who withheld her name at the time, supplied Jeanne Mance with twenty-two thousand francs, and other sums later, to carry on the work of the hospital.

But indeed it was impossible for the colonists entirely to support themselves since they were for several years almost prisoners in their little settlement. We learn that for their first seven or eight years they all gathered at night for shelter in the fort. Only as the Indian menace lessened did they venture to build separate houses. It would seem that by 1651 about half of the settlers had moved into buildings of their own. Some fifty-five still remained in the hospital and in the fort, anxious, we are told, to get back to France.

The old maps show a straggling row of these houses along a track among the trees past Maisonneuve's house and the hospital. This track presently became St. Paul Street. Farther back were other bush tracks, at first only eight to twelve feet wide, that led to another little cluster of houses. All were connected by a road and bridge over the River St. Pierre to the fort. A little lower down on the shore was a windmill. As a protection to the north (downstream) a "citadel" was constructed on a little hill about fifty feet high, where they set up ramparts with trenches, protected by the wooden stakes, pointed and interlaced, that are called in French *chevaux de frise*. This citadel, all shoveled flat later on, stood near Dalhousie Square. There were no real "fortifications" for another generation.

Thus lived and labored those at Ville Marie till the institution of direct royal government in New France ended its first existence as a mission and began the career of Montreal as a colonial outpost of defense, an inland emporium of trade.

CHAPTER IV

A Half Century of Struggle
1663–1713

The Priests' Farm. The New Royal Government. The Sulpicians as Feudal Seigneurs of Montreal. Growth of the Town. Arrival of De Tracy and Defeat of the Iroquois. Feudal Life around Montreal. The Outside Seigneurie. Lachine. Longueuil. Frontenac and the Indian and English Wars. Treaty of Utrecht.

IN THE heart of the English residential district of Montreal there is, or was till yesterday, a beautiful open space of trees and meadows, some three quarters of a mile across, like an oasis of verdure in a desert of brick and stone. It was called by the attractive old-time name of the Priests' Farm. Through the gateways of the tall stone wall which hemmed a large part of its circuit one caught a glimpse of old gray stone buildings, of wide orchards, gardens neat as Normandy, and pleasant avenues of trees where reverend Fathers might walk in quiet meditation. From this beautiful open space of verdure the surrounding city breathed in fresh air and health, as the pious order of those who founded, owned, and occupied it breathed in the inspiration of their high calling. For this was, and still is, a part of the property of the Sulpician Order (Les Messieurs de St. Sulpice), whose seminary still stands in the heart of Montreal. To them was committed, when the original missionary Association of Montreal came to an end, the seignorial control of all Montreal Island.

Much of the Priests' Farm is gone now. Its outward glory is departed. Necessity compelled the commercial sale of ground coveted as real estate. Apartment houses sprawl upon its higher slopes and cover the "sites" that once were meadows framed in old willow trees. Its bygone silence is lost in the traffic of new streets and driveways that pierce its very heart. Commodious villas rise, neat with new grass and nodding tulips, to blend a strange novelty with what still remains antique. Their beauty is all too new—the rich inheritance of broken fortune.

Yet not all is gone. There still stands at the foot of the slope in the angle of Sherbrooke Street and the Côte des Neiges Road, the widespread school and dormitory buildings of the famous Grand Séminaire, the Collège de Montréal, where generations of Canadian youth have had their training. One sees through the main gates two old stone towers, built in 1694, that stand well inside the present wall. These are said to be among the oldest, if not actually the very oldest, surviving buildings in Montreal. They are in reality two adjacent towers remaining out of the four that marked the corners of the great wall that surrounded the original building that stood here. This was the fort, a sort of outlying protection for Ville Marie de Montreal, called Le Fort des Messieurs. Inside stood a stone château built out of his own personal fortune by a priest of St. Sulpice. The towers were for protection but were used also as schoolrooms where the children of the converted Indians were taught by the saintly Marguerite Bourgeoys, who was attached as an externe to the Sisters of the Congregation of Troyes and whose name is second only to that of Jeanne Mance in the record of good works at Ville Marie.

Higher up the slope of the Priests' Farm stands the more modern building of the Seminary of Philosophy, the training college of the priests. About it are still many of the old trees, the quiet

walks, the gardens, and the long pond of years gone by. Yet
midway between the Seminary of Philosophy and the College
of Montreal below, on land sold to save them, the handsome
premises of the Badminton Club mock with the merriment of
battledore and shuttlecock antiquity on the right and philosophy
on the left. But for the land that is left the title deeds are still the
grant in the name of Louis XIV to the Messieurs de St. Sulpice,
whose history at the period we now reach becomes the history of
Montreal itself.

We cannot, however, understand the position of the Sulpician
Order and their control of the town and land of Montreal without explaining the general change now made in the administration of the whole colony of New France. The government was
dissatisfied with the slow progress made by the One Hundred
Associates. The company was wound up and replaced by government under the Crown. There was henceforth at Quebec a
Governor General of New France, a Superior (presently a
bishop),[1] and a Council appointed for life, subject to the King's
continued pleasure. With these there was a new official, the
Intendant, who acted as representing the King's "business interest," his steward, so to speak. In case of conflict these authorities must wrangle it out—and did. There was also created a new
"Company of the West Indies" to manage all North American
colonial trade, but it proved ineffective and was terminated in
ten years.

Thus the government of New France was henceforth carried
on under peculiar conditions. During the whole winter there
came no word—there could be none—from France. There was
no such thing as the overland mail, which in later days reached
British Canada from the Atlantic colonies and after that from the
United States. "When the river freezes," said the great Frontenac, "I am King." This meant for a strong man a sort of
sovereignty, for a weak man confusion. A further consequence
of this was the peculiar situation of Montreal under the superior
authority of the Governor General of New France. It is true
that a royal decree of 1647 had associated with the Governor of

[1] Laval, 1659, Bishop of Patræa in Partibus.

New France a Governor of Montreal along with a Superior at Quebec as the Supreme Council of Police, Commerce, and War. But as the Governor of Montreal was normally absent from Quebec and the Superior, by reason of his duties, frequently so, this made the situation worse instead of better. On the other hand the grant to the Governor of Montreal, by this same decree, of 10,000 livres a year and free transport (yearly from France) of 30 tons of freight, with the obligation to maintain a garrison of 30 men, helped to make his position financially independent of Quebec, where the Governor General received 25,000 livres with 70 tons of free transport.

This position became more and more anomalous as between two centers, each of which overtopped all other settlements, one being the center of government but the other rapidly becoming the chief emporium of trade and a rival center of population. The friction between the two authorities began with Maisonneuve's first winter in Quebec before Ville Marie de Montreal was even founded. It never ceased till the conquest.

The population of New France was still, in 1663, only about 2500. Royal government brought in immigrants, and the population in the twelve years, 1663–75, more than trebled (2500–7800). Among the immigrants Normans predominated (about one fifth); those from Poitou were nearly as many; those from Paris about one seventh, Brittany much fewer, the rest scattered. There is no lack of statistics. Little colonies love to count themselves as youth loves a mirror. A census of 1667 showed the French population of New France as 4312; Quebec and the settlements hard by, 1011; Beauport, 123; and Côte de Lauson (south shore), 113. At Three Rivers the settlement that grew up to meet the fur trade from the interior had 666 people. Montreal had 766. Beyond these was nothing. The settlements clung for their life to the river. Yet around these central points agriculture was struggling into existence. There were 11,448 arpents (9000 acres) of grainland, 3000 cattle, and 85 sheep—counted, apparently, to the last one.

At Montreal settlement had been slow and precarious. The population was estimated to have reached 525 in 1665; 766 in

1667, as just said; and 830 in 1672. An old plan of Montreal in 1672 shows a considerable addition of houses. There is a windmill beside the river a little way upstream from the fort. The original bush track parallel to the bank now appears as a regular road that was later to become St. Paul Street. There are houses on both sides, and in this same year Notre Dame Street was laid out by survey.

Royal government, after a brief period of rule by the incompetent M. de Mézy, sent out as Governor, began in earnest with the arrival of M. de Courcelles and with him, as the first Intendant of New France, the famous Jean Talon, the first in the long line of the commercial statesmen of Canada. Although only six years in the colony (1665-71), "his power of organization and creative genius," says Sir Charles Lucas, "left a lasting mark on New France." With them, and set over both them, arrived a veteran general of France, the Marquis de Tracy, whose commission of 1663 made him lieutenant general of South and North America (*L'Amérique Méridionale et Septentrionale*).

It was known that De Tracy's business was to exterminate the Iroquois. From the ships that reached Quebec just before him there landed four companies of the famous Carignan-Salières Regiment. Others followed later in the summer, in all about twelve hundred men. These were veterans of the war of Louis XIV against the Turks. Some of them afterward returned to France to be reconstructed and to remain till the Revolution as the Regiment of Lorraine. But most of them remained in Canada after their service in the Indian war and settled on land grants along the Richelieu near Montreal. Many families of today trace from them their descent.

There came also with M. de Tracy to Quebec a glittering troop of young nobles and of gentlemen of fortune attracted by adventurous prospect of the approaching campaign in the wilderness. Their coming made a great stir, and the arrival of the soldiers sent a thrill of joy through the settlements. For by this time the audacity of the Iroquois was surpassing all bounds. On April 25 of this very year (1665) they had made a surprise attack at Montreal on the Hotel Dieu itself. Before they could be beaten off they had killed one guard, wounded another, and dragged off two unhappy victims for death in the flames. Early in the same summer they had succeeded in capturing, while he was hunting on Ile Ste. Thérèse, one of the most notable of all the Montreal colonists, Charles le Moyne. This man was to give eleven sons to the service of New France. The eldest of them, Charles le Moyne, was Governor of Montreal (1724–33) and Administrating Governor of Canada (1725–26). He was created Baron de Longueuil by the French Crown (1700), a title recognized by the British government after the conquest and still existing. His son Charles, the second baron, held the same offices: Montreal, 1749–55, and Canada, 1752–55. Another son of the founder of the family was Pierre le Moyne, Sieur d'Iberville (1661–1706), a sailor from the age of fourteen, who made history by fighting the English on Hudson Bay, both overland and by sea. With his brother, the Sieur de Bienville, he founded Louisiana. The family seigneury of Longueuil, across the river from Montreal, once seemed almost to rival the island seigneury itself. Fate passed it by, a suburb with little left but the pride of history.

This first Charles le Moyne, undaunted by his capture, carried it off with a high hand, threatened the Indians with the coming of the French soldiers to burn their lodges. The Indians were so impressed that they brought Charles le Moyne down to Quebec and gave him up unharmed, as a sort of token for peace. But the situation had gone too far. The French knew that they must make war first.

Meantime in Montreal the rejoicing over the new sense of security was tempered by the news that Maisonneuve was to go. The Marquis de Tracy, with that peculiar politeness known only to a Marquis, wrote that "he had permitted M. de Maisonneuve, Governor of Montreal, to make a journey to France for his own private affairs." A successor was appointed for his absence, and "this as long as we shall judge convenient." Marguerite Bourgeoys, the famous teaching sister already mentioned, wrote that Maisonneuve "took the order as the will of God and went over to France not to make complaint of the bad treatment he had received but to live simply and humbly an unrecognized man."

This intent he carried out. He reached France in 1665, twenty-three years after his first coming to Canada. For his remaining eleven years he occupied the second floor of an apartment in the Fosse St. Victor, where a single servant ministered to his old age. He died on September 9, 1676. This temporary oblivion of his name and fame was to be redeemed later on, after his contemporaries had gone long since to graves mostly forgotten. The monument of Maisonneuve in the center of Place d'Armes at Montreal is beautiful as art and sculpture, but still more beautiful in what it commemorates.

After the arrival of the New French troops under the Marquis de Tracy, the departure of Maisonneuve, and the opening of the campaign against the Iroquois, New France entered on the half century of conflict, now with the Iroquois, now with the English, now with both, which only ended with the Peace of Utrecht in 1713. During this period Montreal gradually lost its aspect as a mission settlement. In a certain sense the good work was carried on and has lasted until today, as witness the Seminary of St. Sulpice still existing in the heart of the city, and the work of Marguerite Bourgeoys still carried on in the vast and beautiful building of the Sisters of the Congregation, built in 1908 on Sherbrooke Street West. But from this time on Montreal appears less as a mission than as the organizing center of war, of western exploration, and more and more the emporium of the fur trade, the economic basis of the life of the colony. There are few national annals that so stir with danger, adventure, and heroism as this half century of history; few if any that offer so wide, so picturesque a scene of conflict in the wilderness of forest and lake and stream. This history has been turned into a part of the world's literature by the genius and industry of Francis Parkman. His detailed pages quicken the past into new life. In them we seem to hear the whisper of the forests and the murmur of the waters and to see the morning mists of the lakes rising to reveal the war canoes of the savages. From such volumes alone

can we get a real picture of our Canadian past. But these annals
are rather those of Canada as a whole than of the city of Montreal by itself. For our present purpose we can venture nothing
beyond a summary.

As the most striking part of this moving panorama, as the
lurid colors of the foreground, we see the march of war. The
fierce war with the Indians (1657–66) only dies down to be
renewed as a struggle against England and its Iroquois allies
(1683–1701). War itself brings extension of territory by the
building of forts and the wider hold on the country. In the
pauses of war in the twenty years of something like Indian peace
(1666–83) trade multiplies, especially the trade in furs which
spreads farther and farther into the interior. The *coureur des
bois* is added to the missionary priest. With this goes exploration,
wider and wider, in part as an adjunct of trade or mission, in
part as an end in itself, by an instinct as old as humanity and as
young as everybody's childhood. The period ends with the
desperate struggle that opened the eighteenth century, Queen
Anne's War, and that ended in the disastrous Treaty of Utrecht,
foreshadowing the fall of France in America.

War came first. A chain of forts was at once built to protect
New France and to facilitate attack on the Indian country; a
fort was built at Sorel at the mouth of the Richelieu, one higher
up at the rapids at Chambly, one at Ste. Thérèse, and one at the
north end, the foot, of Lake Champlain. The French struck at
once, in the heart of that very winter. The expedition under
Courcelles passed up Lakes Champlain and George and so to the
valley of the Hudson and the Mohawk, ground of which every
mile is now connected with the memories and the monuments
of war. But this first war "failed to connect." The French found
to their surprise that the Hudson Valley had now become English. The Dutch, after their war with England, had ceded New
Netherland. In its place was now New York, a proprietary
colony under Charles II's exiled brother, James, Duke of York.

The French, not being at war with England, wisely retired
and went home. But the next autumn they came again under De
Tracy himself, this time to the Mohawk Valley, and laid it waste

with fire and sword, burning the lodges and destroying the winter corn. The Mohawks fled. They had learned a lesson. New France was free from them for nearly twenty years.

The interval of relative peace and security which now ensued and lasted for nearly twenty years gave to Montreal its first real opportunity for growth, expansion, and trade. Immigrants now began to come in larger numbers and to include many women, either married or looking for marriage, so that the number of established households grew apace. The vertebrate structure of the old town can still be seen in the financial district of the present Montreal. The original surveyor selected the highest land which lay in the area between the St. Lawrence and St. Martin Brook (Craig Street) and which was already built over here and there. About in the center of this were the grounds and buildings around the Hotel Dieu, already nearly twenty years old. Just behind these grounds, that is, farther from the river, was the highest line of ground, and here at that time a new church, the Parish Church of Notre Dame, was already being built. Hence a long, straight street, christened the Rue Notre Dame, formed the basis of the survey by which the town, after 1672, was laid out into definite streets. The work was done by Bérigne Basset, the first surveyor of the colony, acting under the direction of the famous Dollier de Casson, the Superior of the Sulpicians and the first historian of Montreal. This notable man, who came out to Montreal at the time of De Tracy's expedition of 1666, in which he served, played a large part in the history of Montreal until his death in 1701. He represents the type of the soldier-priest that comes down from the Middle Ages with the Crusades, that appears in homelier form in the Friar Tuck of Robin Hood, and finds a later reincarnation in the Confederate general, Bishop Leonidas Polk,[2] who fell fighting in the American Civil War. Dollier de Casson was a man of gigantic stature and of a physical strength maintained by strenuous activity. He had been a captain in the French army under Marshal Turenne, had become a Sulpician priest, a member and presently the Superior of the order at Montreal. Many legends run of his vast strength, his ability to

[2] *Leonidas Polk, Bishop and General*, W. M. Polk, 1915.

hold up a man seated on each hand or to handle a couple of Iroquois like Indian clubs. He became the historian of Montreal, extolling all brave deeds but his own.

The Rue Notre Dame was drawn past the church, parallel to the river, from end to end of the settlement. The direction, as already explained, splits the cardinal points of the compass, being much nearer to a north and south line than to an east and west. Then and long after Notre Dame Street and the ones made parallel to it were spoken of as running north and south, nowadays as east and west. At its upstream end (south) Notre Dame ended in the cross street of St. Pierre, laid out in 1673 and still there; at the north end was Bonsecours Street. Just beyond Bonsecours the town ended at the Citadel Hill already mentioned, for which a fortified windmill had been built in 1656. The Notre Dame Church, the Séminaire, and the Place d'Armes were all laid out as now existing, but the buildings have since been replaced. The rough road already in use since 1645 on the riverside of the Hotel Dieu now became St. Paul Street, not lying quite in a straight line but beginning at a point on the little River St. Pierre (Lachine Canal) farther upstream than Maisonneuve's fort, running at first straightaway from the little river, and then north, shifting its course a little as it went and edging always nearer to high ground, so that Notre Dame Street, when drawn out to its north end, is just about to meet St. Paul when it stops. Somebody once wrote some clever verses to show that the original street of every great city was once a cow track and still carries curves in its course where the original cow stepped aside to graze. The deviating course of St. Paul Street still shows where the cows of Ville Marie once wandered along the old track or paused a moment to graze beside the Board of Trade. The little paths among the settlers' houses became the earliest cross streets, the oldest, older than the survey, St. Joseph (later St. Sulpice), passing through the center, with the Hotel Dieu on one side and the new church on the other. Maisonneuve's house, afterward the first seminary, has already been described. The streets St. Pierre and Bonsecours, as said, were at the ends of the town. Between St. Joseph and St. Pierre was St. François Xavier

(1678), between St. Joseph and Bonsecours were St. Gabriel (1680) and, north of it, St. Charles (1677).

In 1678 there was laid out another street quite close to Notre Dame, running parallel to Notre Dame from St. Gabriel to St. Pierre, so that it bounded the Place d'Armes on the inland side. This street, Rue St. Jacques, of small significance in its early days, was to come into its own in the British Regime as the main street of Montreal and later to rise to all the pomp and majesty of high finance as St. James Street. Our later city has drawn away, as cities do, from its moneyed quarter. It works there by day, but it prays still down below on Notre Dame Street, and lives, sleeps, and makes merry upslope round Hochelaga, and its last sleep is farther away still, with the mountain hollow as its pillow. Here lies, in this old plan of 1673, the venerable origin of some of the familiar jokes upon our city: of the one about the Scotchman and the Irishman who both took off their hats in our Place d'Armes, the one to the Notre Dame Church and the other to the Bank of Montreal; and the one about the old French-Canadian woman from a country parish, come up to worship in La Grande Paroisse, and was found kneeling beside the teller's wicket in the bank.

Not only was the city laid out in streets along which a great many new houses appear between 1673 and 1687, but it was now fortified all round. A royal engineer, Daniel du Luth, commissioned under the governorship of M. de Callières, encompassed the town with strong palisades thirteen feet high, with curtains and bastions. The original fort on the St. Peter River was now demolished, and the St. Lawrence protected the town on the south. A canal let the water from St. Martin Brook and the St. Pierre River down to a flour mill.

During this period the government of Montreal was a very simple matter. In military matters the command lay with the Governor as head of the garrison, with power, definitely expressed in a royal ordinance of 1669, to call out as militia all the able-bodied men of the town and the outlying settlements. Indeed necessity called them; it was do or die. For the very simple functions of civil government the Seminary of St. Sulpice named the officers. There was a civil judge for the whole island and a *procureur fiscal*, or crown attorney, who brought cases to him as a jackal to a lion. A recorder (*greffier*) kept the record. There was in addition, for the daily care of the town, a sort of town manager, called a syndic, who was chosen for a three-year term in a general meeting of the townsmen. He represented the only touch of democracy, as yet pure and primitive, for he got no pay. Even at that, the office of syndic proved in a colonial environment too democratic for the royal government at home, and its powers were reduced presently to practically nothing.

The administration of property, and especially of property in land, was much more interesting. This too is not only as a matter of history but of current concern. For it may well be that our community settlement of the future may borrow a few pages from this old feudal record. The occupation of the land in Montreal and in all the country round rested on the old feudal system of seignorial tenure, which lasted unchanged till the British conquest, continued with modifications till its abolition in 1854, even then left certain traces in land taxes, etc., not finally obliterated till 1940. This system, like everything else, worked admirably in its proper place. It would have been as needless as unpopular in the peaceful pioneer settlement of Ontario, household by household and farm by farm, or in the vast homestead settlement of men and machinery in the West, with neither man nor forest to fight. But in old French Canada, a forest country with savages in the woods, the feudal system came into its own as at its first establishment in the devastated France that was remade out of the wreck of the Roman Empire. As in old France, a thousand years before, each seigneurie in New France became, as it were, a point of strength, a redoubt in the wilderness. With its houses of stone, its enclosed farm buildings, its protecting walls, its forge, its mill, it combined the community of a little village with the security of a fort.

The earliest concessions of land in and close to Ville Marie were made by Maisonneuve himself. But the extension and order of the feudal regime show the master hand of Talon. The system was organized as follows. The Sulpician Order (Les

Messieurs du Séminaire de St. Sulpice) were the feudal lords of the Seigneurie of the island of Montreal as they were later of various holdings elsewhere. Their holdings by the end of the French Regime amounted to a quarter of a million arpents (200,000 acres). In this capacity as feudal seigneurs they granted in the town itself plots for building and land for gardens and orchards. Each holder of such a lot paid ten sous, ten cents, a year. The present city taxes on many of these lots would be about fifty thousand times as much; it seems almost worth being scalped for. Outside the town the Seigneurie granted larger pieces of land, thirty to forty arpents, to be cleaned and cultivated, with an annual tax of half a cent an acre. These little grants were held *en roture*, simple direct tenancy under the seignorial lords. A higher stage of holding was seen in grants of land on Montreal Island, in the quality of subfiefs, *arrière-fiefs*, the feudal tenant here becoming the "boss" of smaller people settled on his fief. The concessions were made without any purchase price, but the tenant was under obligation to clear land and settle people on it. He must pay also half a cent a year per acre as his feudal tax and as a mark of homage must give to the seminary every year a bushel of wheat and two fowl for every hundred acres.

More serious taxes, called *lods et ventes*, were levied on any sale of feudal property, though not on its inheritance, amounting to one twelfth of the price received. From the modern point of view such a tax would cripple all movement of real estate. But that was exactly what it was meant to do. In any case it appears that if the transaction was approved the tax was omitted. That distinguished scholar, M. Camille Bertrand, the archivist, tells us that as a consequence of this there are a great many French-Canadian families still living "on the land of the first ancestor." Higher up still were larger grants of land on Montreal Island which became, by joint consent, *fiefs nobles*, that is to say, made practically independent of the feudal control of the Messieurs de St. Sulpice, though still rendering homage. The advantage to the seminary and to Montreal was that the new seignorial houses, well built and well defended, acted as a protection to the whole island and were so located and spaced as to do so. The first of these grants was one made on December 20, 1665, to Philippe-Vincent de Hausmenil, of land beyond the St. Pierre River to the southeast. With the next one is associated the name Lachine, which echoes down our Canadian history as undying as the sound of its many waters. This was 420 acres granted on January 11, 1669, to the famous explorer of the Mississippi, Robert Cavelier de la Salle. As is well known, La Salle's Seigneurie acquired the name of La Chine by way of a joke (on exploration), one of those cherished by fond repetition, too good to lose. Later history mistook it for earnest. It passed from a nickname to a legality, and in the older English translations of French books, such as La Rochefoucauld's *Travels in North America*, it appears quaintly enough as "China." But the original Seigneurie, which was called the Fief St. Sulpice, was not on the site of our present Lachine. It lay on Montreal Island above the rapids, close to the present Canadian Pacific Railway Bridge. The remains of an old mill still mark the spot. Part of the town of La Salle is built on what was the site of the Lachine, on which was to fall the massacre of 1689. The rapids are two miles below; the present Lachine, at the junction of canal and river, is two miles above. Another three hundred acres, granted in 1671 to Zachary du Puys, the major of the garrison, correspond to the present Verdun.

Beyond these the chain of semi-independent holdings (*fiefs nobles*) extended over Montreal Island. At the lower end of the island was (1671) the Fief of Picotte de Bellestre, which is represented by our Pointe aux Trembles. Two others were on the "Back River" (Rivière des Prairies). But the upper end of the island was the real bulwark against the descending war parties. Most notable of all, perhaps, was the Fief of Boisbriant, on the Lake of the Two Mountains, more fully discussed in a later chapter. Near by and at the extreme upper end at the conflux of the rivers, at the very point of danger, was the Fief of Bellevue, our Ste. Anne de Bellevue. History records its name in Indian ravages and near-by massacres. Its chapel was long the outpost of prayer in the wilderness. Tom Moore's ear was later on to catch its faintly tolling evening chimes warning the rowers of the falling night. Today all around and beside Ste. Anne's breathes the soft atmosphere of the orchards, meadows, and gardens of the Macdonald Agricultural College, where the gentle voices of the female classes of teachers in training echo back the murmurs of the river.

Even more imposing in location and in history are the great outside seigneuries granted by the Crown, independent of Montreal but forming a part of the same general scheme of regional colonization. The chief ones are those in Longueuil, the seigneury of the celebrated family of Le Moyne already mentioned. With it are the historic seigneuries of Boucherville, Varennes, and Verchères on the south shore of the St. Lawrence; Chambly and Sorel on the Richelieu; and Châteauguay above Lachine, all names famous in our history. Others later extended inland.

We can realize how admirably this seignorial system could work for the mobilization of the infant colony in time of war and a guarantee of ample sustenance in peace. The only difficulty was to keep the settlers, especially the younger men, on their allotted holdings. The temptation of life in the woods, the profits of the illicit fur trade, carried on without license or permission, were too much for them. These wandering coureurs des bois became a standing perplexity of New France. Even the penalty of death for a second offense, as authorized by King Louis XIV and announced by Frontenac, mattered little to men who didn't propose to be caught for a first.

But during this period the town shows not merely an increase of population but a change in its character. Here begin to appear the arts and professions of peace. The first Montreal notary seems to have hatched out from the scriveners (*tabellions*), the recorders, and the secretaries of the seigneurs. The mass of the people in the colony being entirely unable to read and write, and there being no printing press in Montreal till Benjamin Franklin brought one in 1776, the ability to write things down for other people became of itself a sort of learned profession. The medical profession was likewise born from the casual chirurgeons (surgeons), whose task of necessity follows the ravages of war, and some of whom now find a permanent place as doctors, intermixed, we are told, with quacks. Painting and sculpture are represented by a few odd people who had brought their talent and its preoccupation with them from France, a pursuit at least free from all taint of commercial profit. History, the muse for which a wilderness is paradise enough, never fails. One thinks of Lescarbot in Acadia and Dollier de Casson in Montreal.

Not only the expansion of the fur trade but the expansion of exploration itself centered upon Montreal in this interval of peace and even during the war period that followed. From Montreal went out the expeditions (1673) of Joliet and Marquette, discoverers of the upper Mississippi; of Father Hennepin, who reached the Falls of St. Anthony; of Greysolon du Lhut, who himself lived many years in Montreal, the site of his house beside the Place d'Armes now marked with a tablet. Most notable of all is the expedition of La Salle (1670–80) from his seigneury at Lachine in that search for the Western Sea that gave it its nickname and led to his discoveries on the Mississippi. All this, however, belongs to the general history of North America rather than to the annals of Montreal.

Such was the situation and such the growth of New France during the period, all too short, before the renewal of Indian war. M. de Tracy and M. de Courcelles and Talon the Intendant were all back in France in 1671. In their stead ruled as Governor (1672–82) Louis de Buade, Comte de Frontenac, commonly regarded as the most impressive figure in the history of French Canada. Under Frontenac as Governor of Montreal, and later of Canada, was his able lieutenant, Louis Hector de Callières, whose regime witnessed the progress described above. But we are now to turn again from the annals of peace to those of war.

Frontenac was a truly great man, born to rule, aggressive and overbearing, looking and dressing the part. The savages knew him by instinct; they came to heel like whipped dogs. So great a historian as Sir Charles Lucas has defamed Frontenac's memory by speaking of "his barbarous methods." "At Montreal itself by his orders," he writes, "the French compelled wavering Indians to burn Iroquois prisoners to death." This is not true. They permitted their allied Indians, on at least two occasions, the hideous treat of burning Iroquois. We may take here the testimony of the young officer, the Baron la Hontan.[3] He tells us that Frontenac sent word to the Iroquois that they must stop burning Frenchmen alive or he would burn their people if he got them. The savages disregarded the warning. Frontenac received two Indian prisoners at Quebec. He gave them to his own Indians to burn, as one throws a bone to dogs. The ladies of his little court protested: "Monsieur de Frontenac, you cannot do this." Frontenac could and did. The Indians went to the flames, one singing, one collapsed with fear. Some people might judge it among the best things Frontenac did. It is said also that four Indians were burned in Montreal in 1696 by whites and Indians, with six hours of cruel tortures. But these retaliations did more to check Indian cruelty than a century of preaching. This is the only way to meet the barbarity of a sunken nation. We know that now.

Frontenac understood Indian war. The time to stop it was before it started. So he at once built Fort Frontenac at Cataraqui at the lower end of Lake Ontario, our present Kingston. This covered Montreal and put fear into the hearts of the Senecas, at the inside end of the Iroquois chain. Frontenac did great things for New France, encouraged the fur trade and restrained the unlicensed trade of the coureurs des bois. It has been often claimed that he took a toll out of trade for himself to help repair his own damaged estate; if so, it was part of the morality of the time, a system of baksheesh, known long after in Egypt and Turkey and not quite lost anywhere. Frontenac was like Admiral "Jacky" Fisher of our own day; he thought there was nothing like "favoritism," meaning the power to push a good man ahead, especially if he is your friend. Hence he made enemies, and particularly with the Jesuits, since there is no room for two

[3] *Lahontan's Journal*, Ed., R. G. Thwaites, 1901.

despotic authorities at a time. Yet by an odd contradiction of character Frontenac planned a sort of representative government in Canada, something like the meeting of estates in France and the old parliaments (courts of registration) of the French provinces. This may have been sheer conservatism and not a democratic leaning, the desire to put the old country into the new. Extremes meet. We see such things again and again in the history of Canada, the "seigneurs" of New France, the "titles" (never given) of Simcoe's Upper Canada, even our royal societies and our Usher of the Black Rod and such. It's a sort of nostalgia, a longing for things of the old home.

Frontenac's parliament scheme of "estates" fell through. King Louis XIV struck it out. Frontenac was only King when the ice was there. With the spring ships, the rule of Louis XIV came back. Nor was ever any king more industrious or more watchful. He read all the dispatches from Canada. He made little notes on the side: "The King thinks this. . . . The King wishes that." And what he wished was done. Our English history, as full of the odor of prejudice as an old cask, presents us a Louis XIV as a butterfly among ladies all in silk, slowly turning to a crooked old man among ladies all in wigs. In reality Louis was industry itself, sagacity. He knew men like Colbert and Frontenac when he saw them. But with peace established, complaints from New France reached the King right and left, and Frontenac had to go.

But Frontenac's successors were men of no account, and the Indians knew it. The Iroquois had been playing back and forward with the French and English. Some had sided with the French, turned Christian, and became in time the "praying Indians," those who founded our Caughnawaga beside Lachine. But now they all joined in a great council (1684) at Albany and allied themselves with the English. This time there was no Frontenac to oppose them, nor even Fort Frontenac to cover Montreal, for it had been abandoned. The Governor, De La Barre, moved soldiers and Indians to occupy it again; illness broke up his camp; he moved across Lake Ontario, threatened the Indians, like a schoolmaster who calls angrily for order, and then retired to France, glad to be gone. After him came Denonville, who took an army into the Seneca country, burning crops and wigwams. But this was like knocking down a wasps' nest. They all came back.

With that the Iroquois prepared to wipe out French Canada. All the old danger was back again. In the middle summer of 1689 the first wave broke on the settlements around Montreal. Montreal itself they could not now so easily reach. For the plan of fortification carried out under a French royal engineer had put a wall of palisades and ditches all around it. But the outlying places were open. In the dead of night of August 5, 1689, amid the roar and glare of a Canadian summer thunderstorm, the Iroquois fell upon the settlement at Lachine. The massacre that followed is one of the terrible pages of our annals. Eighty soldiers, there on guard as an outpost, and with them two hundred inhabitants, men, women, and children, were butchered without mercy on the spot. One hundred and twenty were carried off, some to be burned forthwith at the stake, others to die by torture in the Indian lodges.

Frontenac came back to Canada that autumn, and a people wild with distress turned to him with joy as to salvation. He brought it. He chose strong men. He had with him De Callières, who was made Governor of Montreal, and such men as Greysolon du Lhut and Nicolas Perrot, coureurs des bois who knew the Indian country. By New Year's he was among the Mohawks, giving them back their own. He rebuilt Fort Frontenac and carried war into the Indian country above. But the French power had sunk so low, the Indian danger had spread so wide, that not even Frontenac could at once restore safety. To protect one place was to invite an attack upon another. Witness, for instance, as a part of the history of the Montreal vicinity, the sudden attack on the fort at the seigneurie of Verchères, twenty miles down the river from Montreal on the south shore, in that meadowland which Champlain had so much admired. The garrison had been drawn off along with the seigneur himself, needed elsewhere. The defense of the fort by the girl Madeleine de Verchères, in command of three and a half men (one man was over eighty), is part of our schoolbook history. The motor tourist and the passenger on the passing ocean liner still gaze with awe and inspiration at this consecrated spot.

Hence it took Frontenac four years to beat the Indians down. But he did it. By 1696 he was able to set out from Montreal up the St. Lawrence with an army of two thousand men. They went by Fort Frontenac and Lake Ontario and laid waste all the country of the Onondagas and the Oneidas. When peace with England came, the Peace of Ryswick, in 1698, the Five Nations were glad enough to be, as our present slang has it, "included out" from both sides as neutral. Frontenac's work was done. He died at Quebec on November 28, 1698. There he lies buried as Champlain before him and Montcalm to come.

But Frontenac, before he died, had broken the power of the Iroquois forever as far as wiping out French Canada was concerned. Henceforth they were just the devil allies of the British, the French having their own attendant devils too but not so good.

When Callières succeeded Frontenac as Governor of Canada a great peace was made between the French and the Iroquois (1701). When war broke out again with England, the War of the Spanish Succession, North America had to pay the price of ravage for the question as to which prince should inherit the throne of Spain.

But this time, fortunately for Montreal, the tide of war turned to the Atlantic coast and the St. Lawrence. The great military episodes of the war belong to the general history of Canada rather than to the present survey. The war ended with the Treaty of Utrecht, which gave to Great Britain the possession of Hudson Bay, Newfoundland, and Nova Scotia, but left to France its mainland Acadia (New Brunswick), its islands, Cape Breton and St. John, together with New France and the vast inland empire which it might include.

CHAPTER V

The Old French Regime
in Montreal
1713–63

The Château de Ramezay. Montreal at the Time of Charlevoix's Visit. The New Fortifications of 1723. Life in Montreal. Social Distinctions and Classes. Slavery Under the Old Regime. Peter Kalm's Visit of 1749. His Happy Picture of French Canada and Montreal. The Lot of the People as Compared with Later Times.

THE CHÂTEAU DE RAMEZAY, once the home of M. de Ramezay, a Governor of Montreal under the old French Regime, and later the residence of various British Governors, stands by itself in the lower part of the town in a beautiful isolation that time and courtesy have spared. It is at the faraway end of old Montreal, so far from the hotels and shops of the modern city that it seems to be, as it is, a part of another world. It is a fine old stone building, low and long, untouched, it would appear, by the hand of time, and looking just as it did two centuries ago. Its iron palings guard it; its cannon are still there

73

in case the English come. Its row of poplar trees along the palings, diminished and vanishing, still rustle and whisper of Normandy. All around it and behind it is the open sky, a landscape effect impossible for modern cities. Broad, open spaces surround it as if the newer buildings instinctively drew back, respecting history and a lost cause. It is quite a distance across from the château to the great buildings of the City Hall and the Law Courts, or, shall we say, of the Hôtel de Ville and the Palais de Justice, buildings where taxpayers anguish and murder argues for its life. Their voices must not come across to the château. More space still is added by the open Jacques Cartier Square on this the hither side of the château, with the Nelson Monument by which, in a sort of paradox of history, Jacques Cartier seems congratulating Lord Nelson on Trafalgar.

This is the only site remaining where the remnants of old French Montreal have the opportunity of such isolation. All the rest of its past is intricately mixed with what is new. Maisonneuve still stands on his monument in Place d'Armes, looking across at Notre Dame Church and telling it what he thinks of the Iroquois. But the buildings of two trust companies look down upon them both. The streetcars make of the Place d'Armes a crowded turning point, and from a near-by street the skyscraper tower building of the Royal Bank looks down on Maisonneuve from such a height that it can hardly see him. Nor does it need to; under Maisonneuve's management the site of the bank was only worth ten cents a year. They do better now.

Look through the palings of the château and you will see from the signboard that it is preserved thus as a museum. Anyone entering, on some empty, silent day, its spacious old wainscoted rooms finds them just as they were when filled two centuries ago with the soldiers and ladies of New France. It seems as if a whisper could bring them back, as if the creak of one of the old boards beneath their feet might make them turn to look. It is seldom that one gets a chance to bring the past so close. We always think of the people of past centuries in an unnatural way, stuffed and dressed and artificial, rendered romantic by the very thing we called romance. Here in these unaltered rooms they turn to people like ourselves, merry or sad, and, to those of us grown old, all young. One stands here in this old château, the prize of conquest, to muse, perhaps, upon its vanity. What right has it to be, this seizure of sovereignty, this forced allegiance by the power of arms? French Canada, we are always assured, is now a part of the British Empire; a "loyal" part was once the Victorian word, though we never use it now. One wonders. Can it be that there are no regrets, no backward glances? At least the reflection of what was here and what is should give to us in Canada a renewed understanding of our French compatriots and a new forbearance if ever needed.

The château was built by Claude de Ramczay, a Governor of Montreal (1703–24). He came to Canada as a young officer in 1685. He served in Iberville's expedition against the English in Hudson Bay and led a Montreal force in Quebec in 1690 to aid Frontenac in his defense against Phipps's vessels of war. He married and settled in Canada and built the château in 1705. It is a very common mistake to suppose that the château was the home of the French Governors. Indeed, De Ramezay had expected the King of France to buy it for this purpose. This was never done, and in the last years of the Old Regime it became the storehouse of the French West India Company. In those days the château looked across into the beautiful gardens of the Jesuits. Beside it on the town side, standing flush along Notre Dame Street, was a heavy old stone building, the house of the Baron de Bécancourt. This later became the warehouse of James McGill, founder of the university, and while still standing was commonly called the Old McGill House. It is all gone now.

Under the English Regime the château became Government House and remained so until Lord Metcalfe's occupancy. It was used also by Benedict Arnold, though not by Montgomery, at the time of the American occupation of Montreal during the invasion of Canada. It was the headquarters of Benjamin Franklin and his colleagues on their mission to Montreal. After Lord Metcalfe the château was turned into offices, then into law courts, then into a normal school, then into offices again, and at last, in 1894, found a fitting repose as a museum.

There it sleeps. From such a vantage ground we may well review the old French Regime which it so well typifies.

It was the good fortune of the town of Montreal to enjoy an unbroken peace, or what was then regarded as such, from the Treaty of Utrecht until the final war, the Seven Years' War (1756–63), which ended in the cession of Canada. It is true that war between England and France broke out again and that military expeditions were sent against western Indian tribes, but the town itself enjoyed an undisturbed existence. We enter here upon a period of peaceful and happy growth, not as idyllic in its simplicity as its sister colony, the Acadia of *Evangeline*, or as energetic in its forward movement as the British Montreal of a hundred years later, but a place of relative comfort, of Old World manners and courtesy, of conservative custom, and, if not of wealth, at least of no great poverty. Much that was to be lost in France in the turmoil that came later was here retained in Canada and Montreal, and much that was in the Montreal of the Old Regime exists here today as the basis of the life of our French compatriots. In looking at the old town we are viewing not the bygone past but a section of the past carried over and preserved in the present.

We are fortunate in having Montreal depicted for us as it was only eight years after the Peace of Utrecht, in the happy pages of Father Charlevoix, whose name is for all time connected with the history of Canada. Pierre François Xavier de Charlevoix, who became a Jesuit priest at the age of sixteen, was sent out while still only twenty-three for four years as a teacher at Quebec and became henceforth a historian of New France and of America at large. He visited Montreal in 1708. Later on he was sent out (1720–22) to make an extensive tour in New France and the English Atlantic colonies, in the course of which he visited Montreal again in 1721 and wrote an extended account of it. His *Histoire et Description Générale de la Nouvelle France* (published in 1744) became and remains a firsthand authority for our history.

Charlevoix, in his first journey (1708), came up the river in summertime and noted, as did all travelers from Cartier onward, the beauty and fertility of what one may call the Montreal district—the country from the head of Lake St. Peter upward—as compared with the rugged and forbidding north shore from the Gulf to Tadoussac. His second journey (March 1721) offered the contrast of winter travel in a cariole, along the ice at the edge of the river and lake. His itinerary as between Quebec and Montreal gives us a view of the conditions of winter travel in French Canada, practically unchanged all through the Old Regime and long after, indeed until the coming of the railway. It runs as follows: Quebec to Three Rivers (about eighty-three miles), March 4 to March 6, three days; Three Rivers to the mouth of the Richelieu (about forty-seven miles), less than one day; thence to Montreal (about forty-nine miles), one day and part of another. The custom of thus breaking the journey to Montreal with convenient stopovers was usual both in summer and winter.

Winter travel by land was, of course, vastly superior to land travel in summer. New France, apart from the military highway from the St. Lawrence to the Richelieu (Montreal to Chambly), was, till 1733, roadless—at least in any large sense. It was, indeed, a part of the obligation of the seigneur and of the habitant to open roads from one riverside farm to the next. But as every settlement was connected with every other by water, these sidetracks were of little account. In 1733 the surveyor in chief, M. Lanouiller de Boisclerc, traced and connected a complete road from Quebec to Montreal, thenceforth a post road. When a regular mail service was thereupon set up from Quebec to Montreal the carriers went through without the stopover of the customary traveler.

"Montreal," writes Charlevoix, "has a very pleasing aspect." One notes at once that Charlevoix calls the place "Montreal," the name "Ville Marie" having by this time dropped out of ordinary use. Similarly, along with the official name New France, he uses "Canada" as an alternate, a usage becoming so general that it appears in official correspondence. "The beauty of the country," he continues, "and of its prospects, inspires a certain cheerfulness of which everybody is perfectly sensible. It is not fortified, only a simple palisade with bastions, in a very indifferent condition with a sorry redoubt on a small spot which serves as a sort of outlook and terminates in a gentle declivity, at the end of which is a small square. This is the place you first find on entering the city from the direction of Quebec."

The old plans of Montreal (after 1723) show the fortifications as constructed by De Léry just after Charlevoix's visit, the old palisades being demolished in 1722. One can recognize this north end of the city, of which he speaks, by the "windmill" (it was built in 1656) and the redoubt. The outlets through the wall show the St. Lawrence Gate, one of the five gates piercing the wall and leading out of the city toward the suburb of St. Lawrence in the direction we now call north. The main gateways in the direction up and down the river give us at the upper end the Porte des Recollets (corner of the present McGill and Notre Dame), through which Amherst's victorious soldiers entered in 1760, and through which the defeated American General Hull and his fellow prisoners, 375 in number, were brought in 1812. One notes that one of the two roads which branch apart on leaving the gate is marked "Chemin de la Montagne." People who write to the Montreal papers at recurrent intervals to say that our "Mountain" Street is called after Bishop Mountain (the first Protestant bishop) will do well to study this map which was made before the bishop was born. The gate at the same end nearer the river is the Porte la Chine, recalling again La Salle and his seigneurie. The other two main gates were the Harbour Gate (Porte du Port) and the Porte St. Martin on the lower end of the town, leading out of it toward Quebec. This naturally acquired the name the Quebec Gate. There were also lesser, or postern, gates.

"The seminary and the parish church," writes Charlevoix, "the convent of the Recollets, the Jesuits, the Daughters of the Congregation, the Governor, and most of the officers dwell in the upper town." By this he means St. James and Notre Dame Street. Of these buildings the Seminary of St. Sulpice (to which the seminary moved in 1712) is the only one still standing, though of course the beautiful grounds, reaching all the way to St. Paul Street, are practically all gone, nothing left but an embowered garden, so walled in, so lost and forgotten, that most Montrealers are unaware of its existence. The parish church of Notre Dame is still there as rebuilt in 1824. A tablet on the corner of Notre Dame and St. Hélène streets (north of McGill Street) reads: *"Here stood until 1866 the church and monastery of the Recollet Fathers (1692), in which the Anglicans from 1764 to 1789, and the Presbyterians from 1791 to 1792, worshipped."* This also, through all the French Regime, had spacious grounds and gardens.

The establishment of the Jesuits at this date was only a large church and one small house, but their beautiful gardens occupied the north end of Notre Dame Street where it met the Rue St. Charles, a space which is now represented by the Court House, the City Hall, and the Champ de Mars, with Jacques Cartier Square opposite. Nothing in the present Jesuit establishment in Montreal (Collège Ste. Marie) and the beautiful Collège Brébeuf behind the mountain corresponds to the site of this earlier foundation. The order was suppressed by the Pope in 1772. After the death of the last surviving Jesuit in Canada, Father Cazot, in 1800, the estates of the order lapsed to the Crown. The papal ban was lifted in 1814, but the Jesuits did not return to Canada till 1839, when their own Montreal premises had been long since turned to other uses.

The Daughters (Sisters) of the Congregation of Notre Dame spoken of by Charlevoix are now the great teaching order whose schools for girls extend over North America. They date from Marguerite Bourgeoys (1653) and the foundation already described. In Charlevoix's time, and long after, their establishment was at the junction of Notre Dame and St. Jean Baptiste with spacious grounds adjoining those of the Hotel Dieu on St. Paul Street below. In 1853 they bought the beautiful country property of "Monklands," for a brief time previously the residence of the Governor General of Canada and the scene, as told below, of Lord Elgin's tribulation at the time of the Montreal riots (1849). From that they moved into the spacious abode on

Sherbrooke Street West, built for them in 1908. "In the lower town," writes Charlevoix, by which, of course, he means St. Paul Street, "are the Hotel Dieu, the royal magazines, and the Place d'Armes." By this Charlevoix does not mean the Place d'Armes of today. At the time of his visit the old Market Place was also called the Place d'Armes, as appears on the map of the royal engineer, M. de Catologne, of 1723. It opened off St. Paul Street on the riverside between St. François Xavier and St. Joseph (St. Sulpice) streets. "Here also," he says, "is the quarter in which the merchants for the most part have their trade." These merchants represented, overwhelmingly, the fur trade, and oddly enough the fur trade, such as it is, is there still after two hundred years, strung out in dingy but venerable old wholesale houses surviving on St. Paul Street.

The Hotel Dieu was still in the same location as the original Hotel Dieu of Jeanne Mance, but the first building had been burned in 1695. There was still standing Maisonneuve's house, occupied after his departure by the Sulpicians. It lasted until destroyed in 1852. The (old) Market Place just mentioned was not only a market but a grim theater of justice where stood the gallows, the pillory, and the jail. Here executions were held. Here (in 1752) a criminal guilty of a revolting murder was put to the terrible death of being broken on a wheel. His body was buried outside the town, under what is now Guy Street. The spot was marked with a cross. When Guy Street was made the cross was moved into the grounds of the Grey Nunnery beside it.

Such relentless "justice" was rare in the colony. As a rule pity intervened. The Negress who set fire to the town in 1734 was sentenced to be burned alive; instead, they hanged her and burned her dead. Let it be recalled that at a date, almost as late as this, in New York Province a man was burned alive by sentence of law.

Beyond the Market Place again, and across the little Rivière St. Pierre, there stood the house built by Callières in 1672. Near by was the General Hospital, a work of piety at large, founded in 1688 by François Charron for the care of the sick and the infirm and for the instruction of youth.

"There has been for some years a project," says Charlevoix, "for walling Montreal around. But it will not be an easy matter to bring the inhabitants to contribute to it." The fortification began next year with the demolition of the old palisades and works and the construction of a stone wall all around the city. The walls were eighteen feet high, four feet thick at the base and three at the top. The gates and sally ports were protected by bastions. But the opposition of the townspeople toward paying a contribution of six thousand livres (francs) toward the cost of fortification was far more reasonable than Charlevoix realized. They were a generation bred to war and knew all about it. The proposed fortifications were of a kind to repel a direct attack of savages, the height of the wall and the projection of the bastions rendering it easy to guard the gates. But the townspeople were now too numerous and too well armed to fear Indian attack. Against attack by artillery the walls were useless. The event was to prove it forty years later.

It was just after Charlevoix's visit (June 1721) that a great fire swept the lower part of the town. Accidentally started in the Hotel Dieu, it not only destroyed that edifice itself but with it about 126 houses, or half the town. In a sense the fire, as is so often the case in rising cities, was a blessing in disguise. It encouraged the building of stone houses, though Montreal remained mostly of wood till the conquest; it led to attempts to straighten and widen streets and to adopt some rudimentary fire protection. The inadequacy of this was shown, however, when a second fire, that of 1734, destroyed the newly built Hotel Dieu and with it a large part of the lower town, forty-six houses. The Hotel Dieu built at the first settlement (1644) had been burned down, it will be recalled, in 1695, so that the building now erected and occupied until 1861 was the fourth occupied. The Hotel Dieu of today, on Pine Avenue, replaced it in 1861.

The fire of 1734 was started, as said above, as an act of vengeance by a slave woman. We so seldom connect slavery with French Canada that it is with surprise we learn that slavery was perfectly legal and that there were slaves there all through the French Regime, and for a generation into the British. The French government wisely prevented any general slave trade of import from Africa, as they thought slave labor unsuited to the colony. But people, rich enough, brought in Negroes as house servants, and there was a certain importation of "Panis" (commonly written Pawnees), a peculiar race of Western Indians captured and sold to the French outposts and, by an exception among their race, soft enough to work. The Iroquois wasn't. Like the British he "never, never" would be a slave.

Not only was there slavery,[1] but Montreal, all through this period, was a place of class distinction and social inequality. French historians who speak of the colonial simplicity of New France are speaking of it only in a relative way, as compared with the social setting of Versailles, where noble birth was estimated in quarterings and noble blood by the quarter pint. Longfellow, in his *Evangeline*, has given a picture of the other New France, that Acadia on the Bay of Fundy, where "even the richest was poor and the poorest had in abundance," and where class distinction was unknown. This may have been true of Acadia. It was not true of Montreal. Almost, if not quite, in its earliest days social distinctions appeared. It is true that in the mission days of Ville Marie there was the common equality of prayer, the common devotion of the spirit; and there was, in the Iroquois wars, the common equality of danger, the brotherhood of combat. But as danger passed and security grew, social distinctions reasserted themselves. There was nothing in the spirit of the time to stop them. The distinctions of birth brought from France were maintained, so too the distinction of wealth as brought out by individual colonists; the whole seignorial system was one of class, the holder of a seigneurie outranking the holder of a fief noble, and both of them above an arrière fief, and all far above the peasant (en roture) on a plot of land. If one adds to this the new inequalities that came with fortunes of expanding trade, we can easily see that New France was not a place where

[1] Ida Greaves, *Slavery in Canada*, 1927.

everybody was as good as everybody else. Indeed such places, even in America, were still hard to find. New England had its gentle and simple; even Pennsylvania had its degrees of piety, and in Virginia inequality grew as easily as tobacco.

There was added the existence of a governing class, since there was no popular election. The Governor General, visiting Montreal from Quebec, the Intendant, the Governor of Montreal, and the military officers were at the top. With them were a number of appointed officials, people with many functions but no real authority, what the French call officials à façade, like a big shop front clapped on a little shop. All these people, seigneurs, Governors, officers, and officials ranked above the people still called "the vulgar."

Yet here, as in all North America in early days, the poor had at least the escape to the land and to the woods. In a new open country, with land still free and the woods empty, industrial poverty can never take so cruel an aspect as it later assumes. When the land is gone and the woods are closed industrial poverty becomes a prison. There is no way out. Most of all was such escape ready and easy in Montreal. For the fur trade was at the door and the woods beyond, and the adventurous might go forth, or the "habitant" turn to a coureur des bois, or even the idle "go Indian."

Apart from the slaves the population of French Canada was almost entirely French. A few British drifted in, chiefly as prisoners of war who stayed on after the peace, Roman Catholics who found the environment congenial. These married French girls. Their unpronounceable English names were converted by current convenience to the sound of flowing French. Ordinary people couldn't spell. The notaries wrote the new names by ear. The language of these incomers disappeared in their family, and in the course of generations nothing but tradition connected them with British descent. It seems doubtful whether all the "Sylvains" of Montreal today (there are about sixty of them) are aware that their name is Sullivan.[2] A good many of the two hundred "Phaneufs" may not know that this name began as Farnsworth,

[2] C. Bertrand, *Histoire de Montréal*, 1935.

in the person of an ancestor prisoner of war in about 1700. The French Canadians from the beginning until today may be reckoned as a singularly unmixed stock.

The fur trade represented the chief, practically the only "business," the main economic support, of New France and the mainstay of Montreal as its chief emporium. It was carried on partly by direct trade into the city and brought with it the perplexed problem of the Indian and his firewater. There were, as usual, stringent regulations which avarice, as usual, sought to circumvent. Other trade came down from outlying posts as far back as Michilimackinac. Its speculative nature and the life of adventure that the fur trade involved gave it an irresistible attraction. It drew the young men from their settlements to the woods and thus, while seeming to enrich, in reality impoverished the colony and undermined its existence. French Canada had rich farmlands that it never used, not only along the Richelieu but in those eastern townships hard by, the richest land of the province of Quebec, untouched till the days of the Loyalists. Higher up the St. Lawrence was the still more fertile Upper Canada (Ontario) with the garden territory of the Niagara district and the western peninsula, which the military power of France, if really exercised, could easily have seized and held, to make it a land as luxuriant as France itself. Nor was farming all. Beside Three Rivers was iron ore from which a feeble and halfhearted operation produced rude instruments. For shipbuilding all the material was at hand. Shipyards such as those established by the English a hundred years later could have proved the salvation of both old France and new. A few ships indeed were built, but the models were unsuitable, the timber was ill chosen, and for lack of patience and experience the shipbuilding of New France proved a failure.

This misdirection of economic life was clear to the wiser of the French themselves. There is preserved a report of Raudot, an Intendant of 1706, in which he says, "The English do not leave their homes as most of our people do; they till their ground, establish manufactures, open mines, build ships, and have never yet looked upon the fur trade as anything but a subordinate part of their commerce."

With the fur trade of the period went the continual exploration that was at once the guiding star and the will-o'-the-wisp of French Canada. The sequel showed the country utterly inadequate for the support of its vast and imposing claims on the territory of North America. But to these French explorers still belongs the honor of their achievement. The chief name is that of Pierre Gaultier de Varennes de la Vérendrye, whose family belonged to Three Rivers but whose enterprises, in which his sons participated, were conducted from Montreal. Their discoveries of the western prairies of Canada and the Rocky Mountains of the United States, like so many other achievements of the French, only allowed others later to reap where they had sown. Vérendrye himself died in Montreal in 1749.

Seen in the light of this misdirection of effort of which it was the center, the picture of old French Montreal is not without a touch of pathos. Here were vast schemes for reaching the Western Sea, journeys through empty desert in pursuit of a mirage of trade and fortune that had no existence, the empty glory of maps and names—all this on the part of a community that in reality had wealth lying at its feet. Yet even such failure carries its peculiar credit and honor. It appeals to us in the same way as the likable quality seen in individuals whose careers have failed or whose achievements never got started.

We have spoken of this period as one of peace. This is true of Montreal but of course does not apply to England and France and to North America at large. Just as the question of a successor to the throne of Spain convulsed North America from 1702 to 1713, so the ravages of war must spread again (1744–48) over the question as to the succession to the throne of Austria. This time Montreal was entirely spared, and its district was almost so. An expedition under Rigaud de Vaudreuil in 1745 made a ravaging foray into the Mohawk Valley and Massachusetts, a second raid being made in 1746. This led to ravages by small Mohawk parties in which a few settlers were killed or captured at Châteauguay, at Isle Perrot, and Ste. Anne's. The main brunt of this war fell on Acadia, where Louisburg was captured (1745) by an expedition from New England aided by the royal navy. The only other military features of Montreal in this happy period were the expeditions sent out, with success, in 1728 beyond Fort Michilimackinac against the Indians of Green Bay (the Foxes), as a means of striking the Indian peril at its source.

During the old French Regime we can hardly think of Montreal as a seaport in any proper sense or with any meaning more than that there was continuous water communication to the sea. Quebec was the ocean port and also the port at which shipbuilding, such as it was, was carried on. Even below Quebec there were no proper charts to the sea until the famous Captain James Cook charted the St. Lawrence below Quebec for Wolfe's expedition. Between Quebec and Montreal the natural channel as yet unimproved offered no greater depth in certain stretches than eleven feet and was rendered difficult for ships under sail by shallow currents and below Three Rivers by the tide. Navigation in the French Regime had no heavier cargoes to provide for than the carriage of persons, personal goods, and the export of furs. For this purpose canoes, boats, and large boats under sail easily sufficed. References to "ships" refer to these large *bateaux*. "The bateau," writes Mr. Lawrence Tombs in his admirable *Port of Montreal*, "was a large flat-bottomed skiff, sharp at both ends, about forty feet long and six to eight feet wide in the center, and capable of carrying about five tons of cargo. It was provided with masts and lugsails, with about fifteen feet hoist, an anchor, four oars, and six setting poles shod with iron. The bateau was manned by a crew of four men and a pilot."

Little, therefore, could be done to improve the position of Montreal as a port from below. But already in those early days people planned its improvement from above so as to make it easier to bring the fur trade down the St. Lawrence and carry goods up. Hence the project, and to a certain extent the actuality, of a Lachine canal is among the first public enterprises of the colony. It will be recalled that the rapids of the Great Sault (Lachine Rapids) block the river above Montreal. More than that, the course of the river at the rapids is swung off so as to make it a long way round to Montreal even if one hazards the risks of shooting the rapids and incurs the labor of trekking and portaging at the side. The distance by the path of the river from the quieter water above the rapids themselves and via La Prairie Basin to Montreal is about fourteen miles down the rapids. But a straight cut across the land is only eight and three quarter miles. Moreover, the straight cut, the present bed of the Lachine Canal, is largely a natural sunken hollow very easy to turn into a watercourse. The amount of fall from the water above the rapids varies with its flood and volume. But the fall of the ground itself may be reckoned from the fact that the Bonaventure Station is forty-eight feet above sea level, Lachine Station eighty.[3]

We have seen that a little river, Rivière St. Pierre, originally ran down this hollow and emptied into the St. Lawrence under the Pointe à Callières behind the Ilot Normandin (Market Gate Island). If one follows this river up for five or six miles one finds its source in a body of water that was a marsh or a big pond or a little lake, according to water and season. The old maps show it as Lac à l'Outre. Between this water and Lake St. Louis there is no great rise of land, and to cut a canal would be no great matter, except that in part the rise of land is rock. With such a cutting made, with the pond made permanent and the River St. Pierre deepened and cut straight, an easy passage by canoe would be substituted for an arduous effort and a dangerous risk. Hence it was that as far back as the days of Dollier de Casson (he died in 1701) efforts were made toward a canal, or at least to improve this watercourse. A system of locks to let large boats up and down was too expensive, but it was thought that even with the natural flow of water boats might go both up and down, with a minimum of portaging. A certain beginning was made, but lack of funds left the project still incomplete at the conquest.

And here we may pause a moment in the narrative, as happiness pauses on the brink of disaster, to view in some little detail the old French town of Montreal as it was in its last years of peace and allegiance, before it was overwhelmed in the British conquest.

[3]*Altitudes in Canada*, Commission on Conservation, 1915.

Strangely enough, the circumstances of our present city offer a peculiar opportunity for such a retrospect. The lower part of it, the "business section" of Montreal, corresponds very closely to the area covered by the old walled town. Now this "city" shares with the "city" enclosed in London the peculiarity that many work yet almost none sleep in it, so that it falls on a Sunday to a silence and emptiness unknown elsewhere. This is true most of all in the heart of winter when the harbor is frozen over and the port deserted, the warehouses along the water front closed and tenantless, the water front itself overwhelmed in snow. At such a time the place has turned, as it were, to a ghost city of the old French Regime, whose outline it still bears, and whose old stone houses are still to be seen here and there built in and built over in its crooked streets.

On such a Sunday morning the silence seems to fall all the deeper with each successive snow that blocks the narrow streets, buries the signboards, and mantles in frozen billows, ready to fall, the edge of every roof, the projection of every cornice. On such a day the footsteps of the rare passengers seen here and there upon the streets fall noiseless on the snow. They too seem ghosts, moving, as it were, nowhere. There is no sound or movement except that at each successive service the deep bells of the Notre Dame parish church echo the hours, and the parishioners flock to and fro across the Place d'Armes to the office of the Mass. Yet somehow they too—as different from the businessmen of the weekdays as the Iroquois themselves, wrapped and muffled against the cold—have taken on the air of old French Canada itself, as if a part of the ghost picture.

To make it still more real there stands Maisonneuve's statue in the Place d'Armes in front of the church, its pedestal and its pedestral figures half buried in snow. The crouching form of Major Lambert Closse, his pistol ready to fire, looks out, more vigilant than ever, from under his canopy of snow. Here projects from under its white mantle the treacherous arm of a buried Iroquois, there the sickle of a habitant settler.

In such a place and in such a company we can build up again the town that was. Here, still plain enough, is its plan and outline.

This St. James Street—the Rue St. Jacques—still runs its full length along the upper side of the town. Notre Dame is still there just below it, and St. Paul, broken with many crossings and intersections and little squares punched out of it, still staggers its unsteady course lower along the slope. But the values of these streets are all reversed. St. Jacques was the least of them. Notre Dame, the first street really laid out with a surveyor's line (1672), was the main street, the street of quality and fashion, the chief road of entry by land. St. Jacques was a smaller, later street which there was just room to squeeze in between Notre Dame and the sharp slope of the hill behind, where the land fell to the marsh and river.

In the old French town on the Rue St. Jacques we should have found ourselves close beside the fortification wall, looking down into the hollow and across it to the snow-covered gardens and woods and mountainsides above. St. Paul, of course, was the oldest street in another sense, for it was the first pathway, the track through the trees, that connected Maisonneuve's fort (on the other side of the Rivière St. Pierre, the Lachine Canal of today) with the buildings by the riverside, Maisonneuve's own house, the Hotel Dieu, and those built later. Presently the fort was demolished, the town itself built along St. Paul and Notre Dame streets, and the old French town of which we now speak, the fortified wall with its bastions and river gates, passed along just below St. Paul. Hence St. Paul too had a grandeur of its own, looking down on the Common (Commune) along the riverside, on the landing places, and across the river, and having on it the Château de Vaudreuil, the residence of the Governor General of New France when in residence. In front of this residence was the aristocratic grandeur of the Marine Parade. Thus St. Paul held the water gates while Notre Dame held the main entry by land.

We can thus see the plan and scope of the old town in this frozen, ghostly outline of silent stone. Yet perhaps it would be better if we could somehow wave a magic wand over it and see it, not in the death of winter of today, but in the warm life of the summertime two hundred years ago. Such a wand by good fortune we possess in the description of Montreal and its sur-roundings that was written in the summer of 1749 by Peter Kalm, a visiting Swedish naturalist. We open the pages of the English (1771) edition of Kalm's *Travels*, its very print and its form giving a sympathetic touch of antiquity, and in a moment (for Mr. Kalm possesses the unconscious art of interest) we are transported to a place so different from our ghost city that we realize we have substituted a skeleton for a living being. This is no longer a stone city cramped behind its narrow fortifications. This is a large, spacious place with trees and gardens everywhere. The place seems too large if they ever·had to defend it. And this town is not built of stone. There are indeed beautiful stone houses like the château that M. de Ramezay built or the Château de Vaudreuil itself, but most of the houses are still of wood. Mr. Kalm will presently tell us that this is very different from Quebec, where most of the houses are of stone. Indeed the differ-ence ran all through the French Canada of 1749, all through its rows of farms that now reach along the St. Lawrence from Quebec to Montreal, and along the Richelieu, and from the Richelieu to Montreal, and all around the islands of Montreal and Jesus. Wherever these river courses could reach there were now the seigneuries and the river farms of New France. But beyond that were only forts—that of Cataraqui (Kingston), a fort at Niagara, and the Fort Rouille that was to give place to Toronto. Of these houses some were built of stone and some of wood, and this—Peter Kalm guessed it as cleverly as we do—was because they built with whatever came best to hand. But all the houses ran to the same ground plan, the flat front, the small windows, and the tall pointed roof.

But let us, however, view Montreal with Peter Kalm's own eyes. It may be explained that Kalm was a Swedish naturalist, de-scribed as a Professor of Oeconomy (whatever that is; certainly not Economics) at the University of Aobo in Swedish Finland (wherever these are). He was mainly interested in studying plants and gathering seeds, and his journeys took him to the British provinces of North America and into and through New France. Kalm's London editors of 1771 seem to think he showed an anti-

British bias which they correct in meticulous footnotes. It is hinted that he was peeved at the British ownership of the once Swedish colony that became New Jersey.

But as that conquest had happened a hundred years before and was made by the Dutch, not the British, such peevishness would seem extreme even in a professor. Kalm's picture of New France is certainly idyllic. But he saw it under idyllic circumstances, in the glow of a Canadian summer and in the halcyon days of Canadian autumn, a scene as peaceful as ever contemplated by a kingfisher on a bough. For the latest final peace, that of Aix-la-Chapelle, had come in 1748, and all North America smiled like a garden. Especially for Peter Kalm, for when the Governor of Quebec (M. de la Galissonnière) and the Governor of Montreal heard of Kalm's garden mission, they insisted that he must be the guest of the King of France, paying for nothing. Royal government is able to do things in a royal way.

Far different was the country that Peter Kalm saw around Montreal from what Father Charlevoix had seen a generation before. There had not, it is true, been that extraordinary transformation that a hundred years later changed all the best of Upper Canada from wilderness to farmstead within forty or fifty years, for that was the work of many hands, when dense forests fell before axes that multiplied every year, working in peace and security. But even in New France the change is notable. Beautiful it all seemed indeed to the traveling Peter Kalm in 1749, arriving with certain fellow Swedes by the Lake Champlain route. He was rowed across on a July morning from La Prairie, the walls and houses and spires of Montreal visible all the way over. They landed below one of the water gates. "We found," he writes, "a crowd of people at the gate . . . very desirous of seeing us . . . because Swedes were a people of whom they had heard something but whom they had never seen." This was flattering, but still more so was the arrival of a captain to take Kalm to the house of the Governor, the Baron de Longueuil. "He received me more civilly and generously than I can well describe and showed me letters from the Governor General at Quebec, the Marquis de la Galissonnière, which mentioned that he was to supply me with whatever I should want, as I was to travel in this country at the expense of His Most Christian Majesty."

After this first visit to Montreal Peter Kalm went down to Quebec, where he was received with equal courtesy by M. de la Galissonnière. He came up the river again, still the guest of the King of France, in a boat with six rowers, what sailors would call a gig, with a canopy over his head to keep his precious brains from the Canadian sun. Everyone in Canada seems to have greatly appreciated Kalm's horticultural mission as a benefit both ways. He was in Montreal again for a month that autumn, so that much of his description of the town is made after his return and compares the two localities of Quebec and Montreal.

Kalm notes the fine buildings surrounded with beautiful trees and ample gardens. "Some of the houses of the town," says Kalm, "are of stone, but most of them are of timber though very neatly built. Each of the better sort of houses has a door toward the street with a seat on each side of it for amusement and recreation in the morning and evening. The streets are broad and straight [Kalm is here thinking of city streets in the Europe of 1749] and divided at right angles by the short ones. Some are paved but most of them are very uneven."

Peter Kalm's pictures of the life of the town are of special interest, preserving for us what no maps or official records can recall. "Every Friday is market day, when the country people come to town with provisions . . . the only market day of the whole week. On that day likewise a number of Indians come to town to sell their goods and buy others. . . . There is not anything, however dear to them," says Kalm, "that they would not sell for brandy."

Peter Kalm, for all that he is a professor and a naturalist, has a keen eye for the ladies of French Canada and devotes several pages to them, attempting to classify them as only a naturalist would. He distinguishes the French ladies from France and those native to Canada; the later are subdivided into ladies of Quebec and ladies of Montreal. Class I (French ladies) "possess the politeness of the French nation." Class IIA (Quebec ladies) "are equal to the French ladies in good breeding, having the advantage of frequently conversing with French gentlemen and ladies." Class IIB (Montreal ladies)—some of these, indeed, seem to have laughed at Peter's French. Having no opportunity to hear bad French, an opportunity grown larger in Montreal with the centuries, it sounded funny to them. Kalm takes his vengeance when he says that "they are accused of partaking too much of the pride of the Indians and of being much wanting in French good manners." Kalm's picture of Montreal and its environs is one of peace and plenty. There are bountiful gardens, fruit in abundance, and all about the town the wheat fields, as his visit drew on, bathed the landscape in yellow. He visited La Chine (so he spells it), a "fine village with a fine church of stone and farmhouses lying along the river about four or five arpents from each other." An arpent then, as now, was a French measure either "long" or "square"; as length, 192 feet, hence as surface (roughly), four fifths of an acre. Kalm tells the familiar story of how "M. Salee (La Salle) talked of nothing but his new short way to China," and hence, "the place got its name, as it were, by way of a joke." This is the sole joke in Kalm's three volumes. He visits also the Sault de Recollet, a little settlement where even the church is built of wood, but with cornfields, meadows, and pastures all around it, but the old people said they remembered it as all forest.

Kalm left New France in 1749. He saw nothing of the Canadian winter. Nor could he have realized how the peace and relative plenty all around him in that golden autumn were to change to the carnage, the distress, the desolation of ten years later.

For people of curious mind and for economists, we may here attempt to form some idea of how the economic side of life under the Old Regime in Montreal and in French Canada may be compared with that of later times and of today. Were the people, the plain people, better off than those of today? It is very difficult to give a tabulated answer since life in those days depended greatly on barter, on exchange of services, and on self-support. The people, says Peter Kalm, "all seem poor." But elsewhere he notes that "it is easy for anyone to set up as a farmer and live well at small expense." The daily drink of the plain people was water. Kalm tells us that they brewed no beer. The glory of John Molson was yet to come. The rich drank imported wine, none being made in the country. Indeed the only manufactured drink was the seasonal spruce beer.

It is very hard to give any adequate notion of money and prices. The nominal scale of money[4] was based on the livre. This in origin had meant a pound weight of silver but had gone down and down by the depreciation of French coinage, so that it presently reached practically the same level as a quite separate unit called a franc, and the two words became interchangeable. A livre was divided into twenty sous. Three livres made an *écu*, a word commonly translated as crown but not really equal to it. Compared with foreign money, the British pound of those days was supposed to equal twenty-two livres. The shilling in England, where it existed as a coin, went at twenty to the pound sterling. The great unit of New World trade was the Spanish dollar. At this time the amount of silver in a dollar made a pound sterling worth four dollars and forty cents. But in the American provinces there were no shillings as actual coins but only as a way of counting. In New York Province and in North Carolina they counted eight shillings to a dollar (the "York shilling" of old-time Ontario that some of us still recall); in New England and Virginia, six shillings; in Pennsylvania and elsewhere, seven and sixpence. Hence a penny, the twelfth part of a shilling, was about the hundredth part of a colonial dollar; hence the use of "penny," still current in the United States for a cent, or "centavo." Thus, in summary, twenty-two livres, or two hundred and forty sous, were worth a pound sterling, or four dollars and forty cents; roughly a sou was two "cents"; a livre or franc was twenty cents. A New York shilling, being worth twelve and one half cents or pennies, was equal to six sous.

All of this by way of account. French Canada had no circulating coins except a few sous and battered pieces of mixed metal.

[4]A. F. Dodd, *History of Money in the British Empire and the United States*, 1911.

Circulating money was paper. The Intendant issued government bills to pay for government purchases, in sums down to as little as one livre or less. These passed from hand to hand. In October, before the last ships went out, all who wished cashed these bills in with the Intendant for bills on France to buy goods for import. The government also at various times printed "card money" and other issues. The whole currency was a mess till after the conquest.

Using these units as best we can, we find that in Montreal at the close of the regime current wages of plain labor stood at thirty to forty sous (sixty to eighty cents) a day; skilled labor, four livres (eighty sous). Servants' wages seemed very high to European visitors; a footman received one hundred and fifty livres a year, a maid one hundred. In spending these wages fifty livres (twelve days' skilled work) bought a cow; in 1880 it would have taken at least twice as much; one hundred to two hundred livres bought a horse; six livres bought a sheep; a hog was worth, live weight, one tenth of a livre, or two sous a pound; a day's plain labor was worth twenty pounds of live hog (in 1880 about ten pounds). Eggs sold in Montreal at three sous a dozen, a pound of butter at fifteen to twenty sous, a minot of wheat, the old term for a boisseau, or bushel, sold at forty to sixty sous. No cheese was made. People smoked their own tobacco. They made their own maple sugar. They largely made their own shoes, clothes, candles, and moccasins. Anything that they didn't have they went without. Things not yet invented they never missed. Judging by the conditions as remembered by the author of this book of farm life in Ontario in the 1870s, they were better off.

The profits of trade it is difficult to compute. At its uninterrupted best it would mean greater opportunity than now. But it was never uninterrupted. Montreal sold to the Indians muskets, powder and shot, coarse white cloth, blue and red cloth for fancy petticoats, hatchets, knives, needles and steel for flints, kettles, earrings, vermilion to paint their faces red and verdigris to paint them green, looking glasses, burning glasses, and glass beads. In return they brought down all sorts of furs, and in particular beaver, elk, deer, bearskins, otter, foxskins (black and gray and red), muskrat, marten, and a list that seems interminable. All these had prices attached in Montreal (beaver, three livres; fox, three; otter, five; bear, two, etc.), but with the Indians they went as trade. If an Indian exchanged, as he did, a black foxskin, which with us might represent hundreds of dollars a skin, for a few glass beads worth with us about ten for a cent, it is hard to make any commercial comparison. Each party to the bargain got a lot for a little.

The rich lacked only the opportunity to buy. Kalm quotes a price of 250–300 francs a hogshead (sixty-three gallons or, roughly, a livre a bottle) as representing an extreme wartime price for French wine in Montreal.

Such is the picture of Montreal in the last years of the French Regime, a picture not without its shadows, but with bright and happy tints that only needed peace and good will to deepen them to enduring color.

It was not to be.

Within a few years the colony was to be racked with the war that ended with the capitulation of Montreal and the cession of Canada.

CHAPTER VI

The Capitulation of Montreal
1760

Vaudreuil Surrenders Montreal. The Close of the Seven Years' War. The Capitulation. Military Government in Montreal. General Murray and the King's New Subjects. Civil Government in 1764. Conflicting Elements. The Quarrel between Britain and America. The Quebec Act.

ON A SEPTEMBER EVENING in 1760 the Marquis de Vaudreuil, Governor and last Governor of New France, sat with an assembled group of officers in the beautiful old house that was his official residence in Montreal. The house was the Château de Vaudreuil, and it took its name from his father who built it and who had been a former Governor of Montreal. The King of France having contributed one thousand livres toward building it, this house ever since had been placed at the disposal of the Governor General of Canada whenever he might come to Montreal from Quebec. It stood with its grounds and gardens at what was then the corner of St. Paul and St. Charles streets. This would mean on the map of today the corner of St. Paul

Street and Jacques Cartier Square. It faced the water, overlooking the Military Parade, the Quai, and the river beyond. The house was not as beautiful in design as the Château de Ramezay, which was situated near by, but it seems to have been taller, with something more of grandeur. We know it only from its pictures, for the house has been gone for more than a century.

The Marquis de Vaudreuil, round whose memory centers all the pathos of a lost cause and of a vanished regime, was a handsome man of sixty-two, with the characteristic appearance of a soldier and a nobleman. History has made of him one of its scapegoats, for history must have its characters, its heroes, its villains of the piece.

We must admit that Montcalm wrote home of him as "tame and rather weak," but Montcalm's standard was wild and strong, and even he admits that Vaudreuil had good sense and "knew the country." He ought to have known it. He was born there (Quebec, 1698), had spent much of his life and service in Canada, and married a Canadian widow. Toward officials and officers sent out from the mother country he felt that mixture of antipathy and jealousy which was felt by both British and French Canadians almost until today. They called it then *le préjugé colonial* and now the "inferiority complex." This had colored all the relations between Vaudreuil and Montcalm. Yet even Francis Parkman, who darkens Vaudreuil almost beyond washing, admits the industry and zeal of his service.

It is true that when Vaudreuil went home to France he was indicted along with fifty-four other officers and officials for embezzlement, inefficiency, and misgovernment, and as many other things as the indictment could think of. History seems to forget that Vaudreuil was acquitted. Vaudreuil, it says, was full of gasconade and bluster, tall talk and loud threats. So was Frontenac, only Frontenac succeeded and Vaudreuil failed. Frontenac, history whispers, was crooked and smiles the accusation away, then shouts out loud that Vaudreuil was crooked. But some of us like to connect the memory of this last Governor of New France with the wistful, affectionate phrase that he used of Canada when he said good-by to it—"vast and beautiful country."[1] That is so much nobler than the snarling sour grapes of the "acres of snow" that comes down in history beside it. Little good is left of the Governor's name except a parliamentary county and, perhaps better, the neat little railway station of Vaudreuil, at the upper end of the island system of Montreal where the railways join the mainland, and even these, with the usual hard luck of the Marquis, are not from his name but from his father's.

So the Marquis sits that evening in the candlelight of his salon to discuss with the officers what he must do. He and they and a diminished French army of some twenty-four hundred are in Montreal, but in the night outside the British armies are gathering thick as autumn leaves all around them, in size such armies as America had never seen before. The fires of their camps and bivouacs are strung out in the fields and orchards southwest of the town, from what we now should call Notre Dame de Grace, all the way to Lachine. This is General Jeffrey Amherst's army that was assembled up above on Lake Ontario and has come down the St. Lawrence in hundreds and hundreds of boats, leaping the foam of the rapids in such a flock, one right on the other, that French skirmishers along the shore were powerless to impede them. Right across the river on the south shore is another army under Captain Haviland, moving down by the Richelieu. Their hold on the river shore is extending to join hands with the great fleet that has carried the third army up from Quebec, a fleet with hundreds of bateaux crowded with men, and also of actual vessels of war. The British ships hold the river all the way to Quebec; they hold Quebec itself and the river and the gulf below to where it reaches Cape Breton Island and the conquered fortress of Louisburg, conquered the year before. From the sea there can be no help.

For the Marquis de Vaudreuil and those who sit with him this is the last throw in the game for North America in the great war for the destiny of a continent that had begun six years before. It is the last throw, and they hold no cards. It is the end.

[1] Letter to the Minister at Paris, September 1760.

Some of Vaudreuil's officers, with the Chevalier de Lévis to lead them, passionately beg for permission to throw themselves with their regiments onto St. Helens Island, the only ground left to them, and fight it out to the end. But this is not a real proposal, only a gesture of courage and despair. Montreal itself is of no avail to them. When Amherst's cannon open on it, it cannot last an hour; they are prisoners on it, not defenders. "We were pent up in that miserable place," wrote afterward one of the surviving French officers, "without provisions, a thousand times worse than a position in an open field, whose pitiful walls could not resist two hours' cannonade."

But it is not only the military situation that is hopeless. The state of the country all about them is hopeless too. The war has stopped all import of supplies, has stopped trade. Even malignant nature has not played fair and has thrown hard winters and scanty harvests into the scales of war. In this land of plenty of Peter Kalm ten years before the people are starving: they are eating the horses off the farms; their clothes are worn, their fields unplanted. Their men have been drawn into the fighting militia for every season and every raid and conflict from the fight at Fort Duquesne in 1754 till this autumn itself, seven years of it. There is no village street, no river row of farms in all French Canada that has not its desolate homes, its unreturning men, its children working in the fields. In some places, as in the environs of Quebec, their misery had reached its depths. "Their houses," wrote an eyewitness, "are burned, their cattle taken away, their goods pillaged. Our poor women may be seen emerging from the depth of the forest, dragging their little children after them, eaten by flies, without clothes, and crying with hunger." Nor is the affliction of the Canadian habitants yet over. General Amherst has warned them that if any of their men leave home again to fight their houses will be burned down, warned them and made the warning good. Vaudreuil has sent messengers to warn them that if there are any of them who do not leave their homes to fight their houses will be burned down, has warned them and will make good when he can. Those who wonder why the peasantry of French Canada accepted so

A Quaint Scene on the St. Lawrence, with Montreal in the Distance, in the Days before the River Teemed with Great Vessels.

quietly the British conquest, why they were content to get back to their river farms and wayside crosses, will find the answer if they will read these inner pages. The outer pages of history, all drum and fife, all fire and smoke, move these "Canadians" around, like pawns upon a board, beside the "regulars" and the "Royal Americans," and the other pawns. But these pawns had homes to be burned.

History always speaks as if the Seven Years' War that decided the fate of North America was settled on the Plains of Abraham by Wolfe's victory over Montcalm on September 13, 1759. This is not so, or at least it is only so because it turned out to be so. In spite of increasing exhaustion and in spite of odds, that need not have been the end.

The case stood thus: The war had been going on, so it must have seemed, for ever so long; to be exact, for already six and a half years, since the so-called Seven Years' War lasted (from the first shot fired till the pen and ink of peace) nine years. It was not a fight of England and France for Canada, as Canadians naturally like to suppose. The English didn't want Canada. They had already given it back once and might have done so again. This was a war for the Ohio country; in other words, for the vast inland America now seen in its true light. Both English and French had extended their trade inland over the mountains and up the lakes inland till they reached the region where the two great rivers, the Allegheny and the Monongahela, unite to form the Ohio. This, "La Belle Rivière," then flows westward through a country of endless beauty of woods and meadow, looking for the sea.

Both nations wanted the Ohio territory; hence there came the building of rival forts, where actual fighting went on without actual war. Then came the French establishment of Fort Duquesne at the great river junction. The real war began with Braddock's defeat in trying to seize it. It took the English seven years to make it Pittsburgh. Even for the motor tourist today it is a far cry from Pittsburgh to Cape Breton Island and Louisburg. Yet the war roamed and ranged all over that territory. The English from the start had the advantage of potential numbers,

their 1,500,000 colonists against 65,000 French. But the French
had the temporary advantage of despotic control as against
colonial apathy, and of the master generalship of Montcalm.
The war for the Ohio turned on attacking Canada chiefly by the
Lake Champlain route, where today every town and every railway station seem to recall in their names and local traditions the
mingled glory and savagery of the war. The other path of attack
was by Oswego and the St. Lawrence. The French, on both
other routes, as at Duquesne itself, at first beat the English back.
But at last the British sent over, and recruited, armies of such
size as America had never before seen. By June of 1758 they had
15,000 men at Lake George; Montcalm a quarter as many. The
French government, hampered in Europe, never could, or at least
never did, send troops adequate for the task. The French perforce
abandoned their posts on the Ohio and at Ticonderoga. They
drew back into Canada itself. A great fleet came up the St. Lawrence; the skill and instinct of its Admiral Saunders and his captains (James Cook was among them) brought it right to Quebec
and past it. The surprise attack and the victory of General
Wolfe by way of the high ground above Quebec changed, so
we are told, the destiny of North America. But this was not the
inevitable end; the cause was desperate but not yet lost.

The end came a year later with what we are witnessing now
with the Marquis de Vaudreuil and his officers in the Château
de Vaudreuil. The Battle of the Plains of Abraham by which
Quebec was captured had taken place a year before: a strange,
swift battle, practically without artillery or cavalry, fought and
all over in one short crisis, to be measured in minutes, as between
two sets of infantry moving like toy soldiers on a table. It gave
the English Quebec but not Canada. The British fleet sailed away
from the St. Lawrence in October 1759, bearing with it the
embalmed body of General Wolfe. A British garrison remained
in Quebec. The French were still outside, still held all the banks
of the river, still held Montreal. The winter froze the river; sea
power was off; the big ships were gone. In the spring the French,
under the brilliant leadership of the Chevalier de Lévis, fought

a second battle on the Plains of Abraham, sometimes called the Battle of Ste. Foye, and turned the tables. The English were driven into Quebec with the river still frozen. They had lost a thousand men. The French losses were even greater and included two hundred Canadians. Yet we are told that joy ran through the colony as the news of Lévis' victory spread from parish to parish. As the ice honeycombed and broke and began to drift out, the fate of Quebec, not for ever but for then, turned on which fleet might come. The French of those days were not beaten off the sea as after Trafalgar. They built better ships than the English and had fine sailors. Thirty years later the French, under D'Estaing in the American war, gained the temporary mastery of the Atlantic coast and made possible Washington's coming victory.

This time it was not to be so. The British fleet appeared in the river, and the British resumed their mastery of the St. Lawrence. The French perforce withdrew to Montreal. Three British armies gathered for the enveloping attack: yet there was still hope. The armies had to come long distances by separate ways up the St. Lawrence from Quebec, down from Oswego and Lake Ontario, and down from Lake Champlain and the Richelieu. If not timed to arrive together, the three armies might have been beaten one by one, a strategy as old as schoolbook Roman history. Lévis might have effected this, for it is said that he was a better strategist than Montcalm. But the chance never came. The ordered movement and the timed arrival of the separate armies, separated by hundreds of miles of wild country, have been much extolled. Hence Montreal, with a total garrison of about 2000 men, had to face the army of Amherst from the St. Lawrence, 10,170 men; Haviland from the Richelieu, 3400 men, and Murray's army of 2200 converged in a fleet of thirty-five bateaux, three frigates, and three gunboats.

This was the situation over which the Marquis sat in council that September evening. With Vaudreuil were a group of officers, veterans of years of war, some whose names were yet to make history. There was the Chevalier de Lévis and Bourlamaque, who had commanded on the Richelieu.

One in especial deserves mention: Bougainville, a captain of dragoons, then thirty years old, who had been aide-de-camp to Montcalm. Later he was to become celebrated as a sea captain, an explorer, a Pacific navigator who gave to France its possession of Tahiti and to the gardens of Europe the lovely flowering bougainvillaea that bears his name. He lived to a great old age, the fires never dying down: as an old man he begged Napoleon to let him back into naval service to avenge Trafalgar. He died, full of years and honor and a senator of France, just in time (1811) to see nothing of the ensuing downfall. Montreal may well feel proud that the name of Bougainville belongs in its history.

There was indeed no choice before Vaudreuil and his generals on that fateful evening of September 6, 1760. The end had come. All that they could hope to do was to obtain honorable terms of capitulation. Vaudreuil had drawn up and showed to his generals a long list of articles (fifty-five) which became presently the basis for the capitulation of Montreal, one of the charter documents of Canadian history. Most of these provisions, in regard to persons and property and in respect to the departure and transport of French officers and officials, soldiers and civilians leaving for France, were such as the British could readily accept, for although the surrender included not only Montreal but all the remaining inland territory and forts, and thus ended the operations of war, the capitulation was not a final treaty of peace, and General Amherst was not concerned with the cession of Canada in any real and final sense.

Two points, however, created difficulties over which messengers went back and forth during the day (September 7) following the council of war. One concerned religion. Vaudreuil asked for the free exercise of the Roman Catholic religion. Amherst would grant it only "as far as the laws of England would permit." On this he was inflexible; yet in the sequel the modified clause proved the stronger instrument, bending where the other would have broken. Inflexible he was also on the "honors of war" which Vaudreuil had claimed. This signified the right to march out with colors flying, the regimental bands playing, and the men fully armed, their cannon with them. This to the officers meant everything. It was the honor paid, in more chivalrous days than ours, by the victors to the vanquished in tribute to the gallantry of their defense. Amherst refused all military honors on account of the "infamous part the troops of France have acted in inviting the savages to perpetuate the most horrid and unheard-of barbarities in the whole progress of the war." It may be left to impartial history to judge the facts in the case. At best it seems a pot-and-kettle accusation. It is true that Amherst had, on the eve of the capture of Montreal, forbidden Sir William Johnson's Indians to torture French prisoners. But a last-minute conversion is easy. The allies of the Senecas could wear no mantle of purity, and one recalls the "inciting of savages" and the massacre still to come, in the Revolutionary War, in the Mohawk Valley and in Wyoming Valley of Pennsylvania. But Amherst refused all pleading. In vain De Lévis and others begged Vaudreuil's permission to occupy St. Helens Island and fight to the death. The gesture was noble but chimerical. There was no real hope in it. For by that time—the afternoon of September 7—they could see the British army from the Richelieu encamped across the river and now in touch with Murray and the ships. The town was held fast on all sides.

Early in the morning of the eighth Vaudreuil signed the capitulation and Amherst occupied Montreal. "Colonel Haldimand," writes Amherst in his dispatch, "with the Grenadiers and the Light infantry took possession of one of the gates of the town." On the ninth the French army—2132 of all ranks—surrendered themselves and their arms on the Place d'Armes. No flags were surrendered. Vaudreuil said he had none; he did not add that De Lévis had burned them all the day before. On the eleventh a glittering parade of Amherst's united armies, again on the Place d'Armes, received Vaudreuil as a personal honor. Here present were men whose names remain a part of the history of Canada—Generals Murray, Burton, Gage, and Howe, all of them later military Governors of Montreal; Colonel Fraser, whose Highlanders settled among the habitants, their descendants presently talking nothing but French; Colonel Haldimand, a French-speaking Swiss, later Governor of Canada; and, most notable of all, Sir Guy Carleton, a veteran of the last war, a victor of the next, later as Lord Dorchester to be the Frontenac of British Canada. More dubious presences were those of Sir William Johnson, leader of the Iroquois, and Captain Rogers of the Rangers.

Thus entered a British garrison into Montreal to remain a feature of its civic life, with the brief alternative of an American garrison in 1775–76, until after the Confederation of Canada (1871). A happy omen of its entry was Amherst's general order forbidding "the least appearance of inhumanity or any unsoldierly behavior in seeking for plunder." Thus the entente between French and English in Montreal begins on the day of its occupancy with the friendly personal relations of Amherst and Vaudreuil and the peaceful intercourse of soldiers and civilians, old subjects and new. Many of the French soldiers asked and obtained leave to take the oath of allegiance and remain in Canada.

The French troops left Montreal on September 22, 1760, embarking for Quebec and thence for France. There left Canada in all 185 officers, 2400 soldiers and 500 sailors, domestics, women, and children. By permission the ships sailed under a flag of truce, for it was still wartime at sea. Vaudreuil, with 142 officers and civilians and their families, left. After the French were gone the organization of the government of Canada was a very simple matter since it was regarded as only an interim arrangement. Amherst still commanded in America but left for New York, his headquarters (October 5, 1760), and never saw Canada again. His attention was soon diverted from Canada to the new Indian danger, occasioned by apprehension of absorption under British rule, that presently led to the rising (1763–66) known as Pontiac's War. Montreal fortunately was far from this conflict.

Under the military rule which lasted from September 1760 until April 1764 there was a Governor at Quebec, one at Three Rivers, one at Montreal. After civil government began there was a Governor at Quebec and a military commandant at Montreal.

The first military Governor of Montreal was General Gage, who left in October 1763 to serve in the operations against Pontiac; after him, until civil government, Colonel Ralph Burton. Under the military government, based on Amherst's departing orders, recognizance was made of the organized militia; its officers and the seigneurs were appointed, along with British officers, to settle civil disputes as under the customary French law. Military courts tried criminals. The church was let alone. The "laws of England" were conveniently stretched to allow Roman Catholics on juries and in various offices.

A few words are needed here for the proper chronology and geography of the Peace of 1763 and the thirteen year interim which followed. The Peace of Paris was signed on February 10, 1763. George II had died during the war, October 25, 1760. George III had been proclaimed in Canada (at Quebec) on January 27, 1761, the day after the news reached that city overland from New York. Civil government was provided by a Royal Proclamation of October 7, 1763. It did not go into force until eighteen months later (April 1764), to allow time for Canadians to leave Canada if they wished. The name of the new province was Quebec; it remained so till 1791. Both General Murray and General Carleton had reported that it was impossible to find out the extent of territory called Canada. But the word Canada was the common designation of the country from now on.

The boundary of the province of Quebec of 1763–74 was peculiar. On its south and east sides it was much as now, but with the adjacent territory still called Massachusetts, there being no New Brunswick till 1784 and no Maine till 1820. It crossed the St. Lawrence River in latitude 45° (present southern boundary). Then it struck off on its own account in a beeline for Lake Nipissing, then a beeline to Lake St. John (northwest of Quebec City), then another beeline to the sources of the River St. John (of the north shore), and down this to where it met the St. Lawrence north of Anticosti Island. These "beelines" were never drawn and were forgotten after 1774. They passed through country, some of it little known and some of it not known at all. No one then knew where the headquarters of the St. John were, and

it is tribute to the vastness of our country that even now, or as
late as the official map of 1940, nobody knows it. It is filled in
with little dots, unexplored. Few people even in Canada have
ever heard of this St. John (St. Jean) River. But it is there, about
the same length as the Thames.

Much has been said about the exodus from Canada at the conquest, including those who returned to France immediately after
the capitulation of Montreal, and those leaving as permitted
within eighteen months after the final signature of peace in 1763.
The legend grew into our history that all the "best" people abandoned French Canada after the conquest, leaving behind only
the lower town classes and the peasantry. Even accepting the
word "best" in the dubious use here made of it, it hardly seems
that the legend has support. In the first place there is no doubt
that a great many of the "worst" people went away in the persons of Bigot the Intendant and his pack of fellow crooks, Cadet,
Pean, and company, the officials whose rapacity had impoverished the country. The trials that followed in France acquitted
the Marquis de Vaudreuil of any personal guilt but sent a number of his subordinates to prison.

In the next place it seems to be shown that a substantial majority of the seigneurs of the colony remained in Canada. The
French-Canadian authorities themselves differ on this point. But
the Harvard historian of the seignorial system, Professor W. B.
Munro, finds that the exodus was "in all probability not so great
as historians have usually supposed." Above all, the clergy remained at their post. The late Judge Baby of Montreal made a
painstaking survey of the case and concluded that 130 seigneurs,
100 gentry, 125 traders of mark, 25 lawyers, and 25 or 30 doctors, with the great majority of the notaries, remained in Canada.
The number of seignorial holdings before the conquest is put
at 218, but at any given time the number of individual seigneurs
would be less.

What further complicates the matter is that after the conquest
British-owned seigneuries came into existence. General Murray
granted two before the final treaty: Murray Bay to Captain John

Nairn, and Mount Murray to Captain Fraser. Many seigneuries also were bought by British officials, officers, and presently by rich merchants. Sir John Johnston got Argenteuil; General Burton bought three or four; Haldimand had Sorel, and presently Simon McTavish had Terrebonne. Montreal, of course, remained as it was under the Sulpicians, and it seems certain from the list of seventy-four names compiled by Judge Baby that practically all the prominent French merchants remained in the town.

Unhappily the British garrison was not the only British element, so called, which took up its quarters in Montreal at this time. It was a misfortune for the town, and it gave an unhappy turn to its history, that the first English-speaking incomers were birds of a poor feather. In those days every army on the march drew to it a miscellaneous assortment of "camp followers," "traders," "sutlers," and miscellaneous hangers-on who followed its march as birds follow a ship. Victory brought them like vultures to a corpse. The people here concerned, no doubt with many honorable exceptions, were rather birds of prey than patriots. Yet, being "old subjects" of King George and being Protestants, they were able to represent themselves as on an entirely different footing from alien "papists" newly taken over. Moreover, the proclamation of civil government had authorized the summons of an assembly as in the other provinces. The recent summons of an assembly at Halifax (1758) seemed to point the way. But such assemblies consisted solely of Protestants elected by Protestants. Such an election in Quebec would be as impolitic as it would be unjust. The common sense of the military men would have none of it. But the traders clamored for it, noisy as rooks.

General Murray was round in his denunciation of such people. Murray, like most of the British officers and soldiers now left in Canada, got along admirably with the French Canadians and especially admired the plain people of the colony, their simplicity of life, their sincere religion. He resented the disturbance occasioned by the newcomers, the trickery of their trade, their clamor for privilege and favors, their attempts to introduce the

British practice of imprisonment for debt as an adjunct to their dealing with their local debtors. "Most of them," he wrote home, "were followers of the army, of mean education, or soldiers disbanded at the reduction of the troops. All have their fortunes to make, and I fear few are solicitous about the means when the end can be obtained. I report them to be in general the most immoral collection of men I ever knew, of course, little calculated to make the new subjects enamored with our laws, religion, and customs, far less adapted to enforce these laws and to govern. . . . Magistrates," he continued, "were to be made and juries to be composed from four hundred and fifty contemptible sutlers and traders."

Murray's denunciation of these rapacious and unscrupulous traders has passed into history. With it goes the warm and affectionate words in which he speaks of the French-Canadian people, the "King's new subjects," as the phrase of the moment had it.

"Little, little," wrote Murray (October 29, 1764), "will content the new subjects, but nothing will satisfy the licentious fanatics trading here but the expulsion of the Canadians who are perhaps the bravest and best race upon the globe, a race who, could they be indulged with a few privileges which the laws of England deny to Roman Catholics at home, would soon get the better of every national antipathy to their conquerors and become the most faithful, the most useful set of men in the American Empire."

Murray's intemperate language betrays itself. It is like that of the lady in Shakespeare who "doth protest too much." It has been criticized and overcriticized by the historians. One even calls it "childish," forgetting that out of the mouths of children comes truth. And the truth is that Murray shared with most gentlemen of his day the feeling of class, the liking for aristocracy, for military officers as opposed to men in trade, and the desire for a lower class, lowly and submissive, as even the rubric of the church could wish them. Yet his language is truth stated in hyperbole. When we say that our friend is the best fellow in the world we know exactly what we mean, and equally so of our opponent as the lowest skunk out of jail. Murray spoke and wrote that way; there are many of us who still do and can understand him. He meant that the French Canadians were a mighty decent people and that a lot of the new traders were crooks.

But in reality General Murray, like Sir Guy Carleton after him, paid the French colony but a sorry compliment. They were soldiers. They dreamed of French Canada as a military outpost of the King, loyal and devoted, with a "stubborn peasantry" ready at any time to leave the harvest field for the field of war, without asking why. The "sutlers" and "fanatics," after all, had a better dream, and it came true.

These latter people who came to Montreal immediately with, and on the heels of, the British armies no doubt were in the main a poor lot. But it is necessary here to make a proper distinction between these early "fanatics," these birds of prey who settled on the conquered country, and the solid British, particularly Scottish, business element which, as it were, presently effected a reformation of Montreal. We can call these newcomers, if we wish, for purposes of humor, the original Montreal "businessmen," but in reality we must distinguish the sheep from the goats, and particularly the first nondescript class who came on the heels of the army, and the people of means, or at least of honorable industry and capacity, who came later. Nor did the distinction always turn on wealth itself.

The truth is that for Montreal the age of commerce and finance, of the Northwest fur trade and the timber and shipping trades, now began in earnest. The conquest brought great opportunities for the expansion of legitimate trade and legitimate profits from the new route to the West now afforded. The fur trade of the Great Lakes, and even of the Hudson Bay territory, could henceforth be reached by Montreal, to say nothing of the now-open access to the Ohio country. But these earliest incomers were attracted rather by the hope of immediate gain on the spot than by the more distant prospect of further enterprise.

Let us take as illustrating the period the two contrasted types of British citizens of Montreal as seen in Thomas Walker and James McGill. Walker's name, long since gone to deserved oblivion in popular memory, filled an undeserved space in the

annals of the day. He was not, however, an impecunious camp
follower but a man of wealth who had come up from Boston to
make hay in the new sunshine. It is said that he brought ten
thousand pounds sterling. He thus commanded influence with
the authorities in London. Money can be seen a long way off.
Indeed it was Walker's influence which presently led to the
petition for General Murray's (undeserved) recall in 1766.
Walker, from his first coming, took the lead in the true-British
ultra-Protestant movement, demanding popular rights and using
his wealth and influence to advance his fortune. This attempt,
which seemed like the exploitation of a beaten enemy, so angered
the officers of the British garrison that presently Walker's house
was broken into, he himself "beaten up," losing part of an ear
(December 6, 1764). Later on, amid great excitement, a group
of officers were arrested, taken down to Quebec, and placed in
custody. The indictment failed for all but one. The affair
dragged for years. But the episode, as said, enabled Walker to use
his influence to get Murray recalled. As the trouble with the
American provinces grew, Walker turned his British coat inside
out and was warm in sympathy with the Continental Congress.
Sir Guy Carleton, who evidently detested Walker, had him
arrested when the "Army of Congress," as will be seen, was pre-
paring to attack Montreal. He put him in irons in a cell for a
month and, when compelled to leave Montreal, he took Walker
along, still in irons, in the hold of a ship. The capture of the ship
set Walker free. We can hardly wonder if he turned rebel in
earnest. Back in Montreal he sat on the right hand of Benedict
Arnold in the winter of the American occupation and as a result
had to clear out when the Americans were forced to withdraw.
Benjamin Franklin, who found himself Walker's fellow traveler
on his Canadian pilgrimage, wrote him down, along with his
wife for good measure, with his usual insight: "I think they both
have an excellent talent for making themselves enemies, and I
believe, live where they will, they never will be long without
them." Walker never returned to Canada.

But compare James McGill, a newcomer of the same period.
Walker's name is forgotten, but that of McGill never will be

while students can still sing. The campus of McGill University echoes with his praise at its every outing.

> *James McGill, James McGill,*
> *He's our father, oh, yes, rather—*
> *James McGill.*

McGill was a young Scotsman who had migrated to North America. He came up from the provinces to Montreal a few years after the cession. He was one of the first of many such young men from his native land, with no great means, looking for opportunity, and bringing energy, brains, and character to offer for it. He throve early and honestly. It was his peculiar lot to be one of the little committee which surrendered Montreal to General Montgomery without a fight. This was plain necessity, Carleton and the soldiers being gone. But McGill threw in his lot with the old flag; he filled a large page in the history of the city, and, dying (1813), left the noble bequest which has made his name known round the world.

This vexed situation lasted for the ten years from the institution of civil government till the Quebec Act of 1774. The fate of Canada was still uncertain, but the reports sent home, as in particular by General Murray, of the fertility and resources of the country were making for its retention as a British colony. This led to suggestions in certain quarters for making it truly British, for setting up Protestant schools. "The intention," writes Dr. Atherton, after reviewing the evidence of public documents, "was precisely to tolerate for a time the Romish religion and gradually to supplant it." Fortunately unforeseen obstacles turned aside the current of events.

But naturally the period was perplexed and uncertain. The military Governors, on excellent terms with both seigneurs and habitants, let the French go their own way. They applied the French customary law, which they found in use, to all controversies over property and other civil matters, applying the British criminal law, as was equally natural, for the punishment of crime. Sir Guy Carleton, who followed Murray as acting Governor of Canada in 1766 and Governor in 1768, shared Murray's views and attitude toward the French Canadians and was equally severe in his general view of the newcomers. Yet in a sense they brought, or helped to develop, a boom in trade. A customs house was set up in Montreal in 1763, and for the first time the harbor assumed the appearance of a real port. The British merchants claimed, as early as 1771, that "they have set examples and given every encouragement in their power to promote industry . . . and carry on three fourths of the trade of this country." This plea appears in the petition sent to England in 1771, signed by thirty-one merchants of Quebec and Montreal, asking for an assembly. Among the Montreal names are to be recognized those of James McGill, Alexander Henry, John Porteous, Isaac Todd, and other fathers of civic history.

As against this there went to London a petition from fifty-nine "Canadians?" praying for the retention of their old laws and customs. Hence imperial policy was locked in a dilemma. To create an assembly, under the existing law of England which shut out Roman Catholics, would obviously be as unwise as unjust. To deny it to British Protestant subjects seemed a breach in the walls of Britain. It was hard to know what to do.

As usual something else happened instead—that "unexpected" which the proverb says always happens. The fate of Canada was tied up with that of the American provinces. The dispute over taxation that followed the close of war in 1763 began as controversy, then turned to legislative action with the taxes of the Stamp Act of 1765, repealed on protest, but with an act of 1766 protesting that it was justified. Then came more legislative acts with customs duties, made and repealed, all except the tea tax, then open resistance and the famous Boston Tea Party of 1773. But as yet, as Franklin said afterward, no one talked of independence, whether drunk or sober.

To punish the provinces the British government passed the Quebec Act of 1774. This act extended the boundaries of Canada (still called Quebec) to take in all the vast, scarcely known country between the Ohio and the Mississippi; this territory would be thus placed out of reach of provincial interference and under the safe control of the Crown. The act declared it inexpedient to call an assembly, thus cutting the ground from under the feet of popular liberty over an area that reached from Labrador to the Mississippi. More than that, the act protected the Roman Catholic Church, giving it not only full freedom of worship but the right to collect its wonted tithe (an agricultural land tax) from its own people. This practically meant "establishment" or something very close to it. The act was, and remains by its continuation through the statutes of 1791, 1841, and 1867, the palladium of the privileges of the Roman Catholic Church. It meant, in the sequel, the retention of Canada by the British Crown. But it was dearly bought at the price of losing the American provinces. The oil thrown on the troubled waters of Canadian discontent was oil on the flame of American rebellion. Controversy was exchanged for war. Within a few months Montreal found itself again occupied by an alien army.

CHAPTER VII

The American Occupation of Montreal

The Old House on Notre Dame Street. The American Revolution. The Invasion of Canada. Ethan Allen's Attempt at Montreal. General Montgomery and the Army of Congress Occupy the City. Benedict Arnold at Montreal. Benjamin Franklin. Close of the Revolution and the Coming of the Loyalists.

THERE was placed on an old house in the business district of Montreal, on the corner of Notre Dame and St. John streets, a tablet to the memory of that brave and honorable man, the American general, Richard Montgomery. He was killed, as all remember, outside the gates of Quebec, in a hopeless attempt at assault, in a driving snowstorm, made late at night on December 31, 1775. This tablet serves to remind us of that peculiar episode in the history of the city, the American occupation of Montreal in 1775–76. Montgomery himself, with his "Army of Congress," was in Montreal for only about two weeks. But after his departure for his attack on Quebec, American forces occupied the city all the ensuing winter and spring, until the change in the fortunes of war compelled their withdrawal.

The house thus marked was a sturdy stone building of 1767, still defiant of wind and weather after almost two centuries of existence. It stood, as we might expect, on what we now call the south side (the riverside) of the street. Notre Dame Street on the other side has long since been rebuilt as the back door of the opulence of St. James Street. But on its lower side it still carries the trace of the old French town. The house disappeared under demolition only a year or so ago.

Richard Montgomery[1] was a very striking man whom both friends and enemies were glad to honor. He was American only in the sense that he had settled in America. Born in Dublin County, Ireland, he entered the British army and served at Louisburg and under Wolfe in the Battle of the Plains of Abraham. A little after the war (1772) he left the army, settled in New York, and married into the famous Livingstone family. His enthusiasm led him to join the forces raised by the Continental Congress. At the time of his Canadian enterprise Montgomery was a fine upstanding man, universally liked and respected. "He was tall and slender, well-limbed, of a graceful address and a strong and active frame." The quotation is from a eulogy pronounced in his memory in Congress.

The situation which had placed General Montgomery in these headquarters at Montreal was this. The Quebec Act of 1774 had blighted the last hopes for conciliation. The Americans of the thirteen colonies saw themselves thereby robbed of the vast inland Ohio territory, which the recent war had just disclosed as a promised land. It was to be handed over to the government under the Crown, without popular rights, with a feudal tenure of land, without the common law or trial by jury. This seemed the eclipse of colonial freedom. Still more could be made, for indignation's sake, and was made, of the privileges granted to the Roman Catholic Church throughout this vast "Quebec" of the Quebec Act (1774). The pulpits of New England thundered against idolatry.

Events moved fast. The colonists called a Congress at Philadelphia. The Congress denounced the Quebec Act in unsparing

[1] J. L. Lemoine, *The Sword of General Montgomery*, 1870.

terms. Both sides, malcontents and military authorities, reached out to seize arms and munitions. This led to the clashes of Lexington and Concord, to the seizing of the key point of Ticonderoga, to the raising of a Continental Army, to the battle of Bunker Hill (June 17, 1775) and the investment of Boston.

An early and obvious move was to invade Canada, not to conquer it but to call it to liberty. As early as May 1775 American revolutionary bands appeared round Lake Champlain.[2] Carleton's attempt to raise local forces to meet the threat showed at once how matters stood. The French Canadians mainly kept themselves aloof from a quarrel between two British factions (*les Bostonnais* [Yankees] and *les Anglais*). The English Canadians, most of them from the provinces, were largely on the side of the Congress. In Montreal on May 4, 1775, a meeting composed of most of the English of the town was harangued by a New England delegate and urged to send two deputies to a new Congress which was to assemble in Philadelphia on the tenth of the month. Carleton wrote to England in June of the failure to induce either habitants or Indians to take up arms.

The first American forces withdrew, but their reconnaissance was followed by a definite invasion of Canada by an "Army of Congress," under General Schuyler, coming by the familiar gateway of Lake Champlain. Schuyler falling ill, his place was taken by Richard Montgomery. The plan included the entry into Canada of a second force under Colonel Benedict Arnold, by a sidetrack through the Massachusetts (now Maine) wilderness. The armies were to converge on Quebec as welcome liberators, its gates to open at their approach. Unfortunately the sympathy of the Canadian seigneurs and the clergy, if not of the mass, had been lost at the start by the fierce denunciation by the Congress of the Roman Catholic religion, as embodied in their "address to the people of Great Britain." They declared that it had "deluged your island with blood and dispersed impiety, bigotry, persecution, murder, and rebellion throughout every part of the world."

With that, and the invective of the pulpits, the invitation to

[2] V. Coffin, *Province of Quebec and Early American Revolution,* 1896.

join Congress (October 26, 1774) seemed like that of the wolf to the lamb, the call to the ducks on the pond. Meantime Sir Guy Carleton remained in Montreal but began to realize that any attempt to gather local forces adequate for defense was impossible. Carleton wrote to England from Montreal (September 21, 1775): "The rebels have been more successful with the habitants and have raised them in great numbers." At the same time his deputy (Cremahé) at Quebec wrote to him: "No means have been left untried to bring the Canadian peasantry to a sense of their duty . . . but all to no purpose."

It was plain, therefore, that neither the French Canadians nor the French-Canadian Indians would take part in the conflict. All turned on the relative strength of the irregular "Army of Congress" and Carleton's available troops. It was soon plain that Carleton's were hopelessly outnumbered. The Congress forces descended the Richelieu and surrounded St. Johns (September 1775). Its fall would leave Montreal helpless. Yet the first attempt to take Montreal, while Montgomery was still investing St. Johns (July 25, 1775), failed utterly. It was made by that strange character, Ethan Allen of Vermont, whose name is in every American school history. He was a great giant of a man, blasphemous and fearless, the leader of the gang called the Green Mountain Boys, who lived in a perennial state of protest and violence against the land claims of the province of New York to their native mountains.[3] Allen, a mixture of mountain bandit and village atheist, was the natural leader of such men. Violence was his trade and profanity his breath. The province had outlawed him; the Revolution made him a patriot. He it was who broke into Fort Ticonderoga on the night of May 10, 1775, driving the frightened sentries in front of him and shouting, "In the name of the Great Jehovah and the Continental Congress." The schoolbooks stop there. They do not record the series of oaths which followed, "so shocking," says Allen's latest biographer, "that his own men listened in rapt wonder."

[3] See anecdote in *Tree Toad*, R. H. Davis, 1935.

Ethan Allen had joined in the invasion of Canada. He was not exactly part of Schuyler's army. He had just "come along." He had no commission and was only "colonel" because the "boys" had made him one by choice at Ticonderoga. Schuyler and then Montgomery let him act as a sort of scout. He went on down the Richelieu, his strange personality gathering forces to join him. He presently had two hundred followers, mostly Canadians, partly armed, and with a commissariat of six hogsheads of rum. He wrote to Montgomery: "I could raise two thousand in a week's time."

In the same district was another leader, Major John Brown, with two hundred men. He proposed to Allen that they seize Montreal. Ethan Allen was all for it. "Montreal," he said, "or a turf jacket." He made his plan: Brown to come from La Prairie and attack the upstream end of the town, Allen to cross from Longueuil and fight his way into Montreal by the Quebec road. Brown's signal that he was ready to assault was to be "three loud huzzas."

The whole attempt was a strange fiasco. Allen's men, when they changed from rum to fighting, fell away at once. Only one hundred and ten got to Longueuil, ninety of them French Canadians. They were induced to stay by a promise of fifteen pence a day and a share of the plunder of Montreal. Allen got his raggedy army across from Longueuil by night in boat- and canoeloads, trip by trip. They gathered somewhere below the city on the Quebec road close to Longue Pointe. The sun rose; day came. There were no "huzzas" or signals, and it is doubtful if they could have been heard anyway (McGill Street to Longue Pointe). Major Brown, from lack of faith or lack of courage, had dropped out.

Word reached Carleton's garrison. A sortie of five hundred men—in part regular troops and Indians—made resistance hopeless. Yet Allen fought. As a piece of tactics he ordered half his men to "outflank" the regulars. They "outflanked" them so far that they were never seen again. Allen sent a second flanking party on the other side. They too flanked for good. Allen and the rest (thirty-one men) fought from behind stumps and in ditches. Many fell wounded, none dead. Then they surrendered.

Indians leaped at Allen to kill him. He grabbed a British officer and used him as a shield. The officers treated Allen with admiration and respect. But at Montreal General Prescott flew into hysterical rage and raised his cane. "By God, sir," said Ethan Allen with his great fist shaking in Prescott's face, "you will do well not to strike me, for I'm not accustomed to it."

They treated him abominably. He was put on board a ship in the river, heavily ironed to a bar eight feet long. Thus he stayed six weeks before being taken to Quebec and thence to England. The story of his brutal treatment makes sad reading but happily does not belong in the present record. Allen remained two years in chains, was exchanged back to America, founded, after the Revolution, the independent republic of Vermont, but died in 1789 before it became a state.

Carleton was sufficiently encouraged by this defeat of Ethan Allen to form hopes of staying on. He gathered, with the help of the seigneurs, a force of eight hundred men on St. Helens Island. The attempt was hopeless. His men deserted at the rate of thirty or forty each night. The fall of St. Johns (November 1775) left no hope except to save the citadel of Quebec. Carleton put what forces he could on ships and bateaux and left for Quebec, taking Thomas Walker as a prisoner, as already said. American forces, operating on the river, captured all but Carleton's own boat. Walker returned in triumph to Montreal. Tables turned quickly in such unstable days.

Montgomery, having taken St. Johns, moved on Montreal by way of La Prairie and across the water to Nuns Island (St. Pauls). Resistance being hopeless, a committee of leading townsmen, chosen in a general meeting, six French, six British, came out to arrange terms of surrender. The French were Pierre Panet, Pierre Mezière, St. George Dupré, Louis Carignant, François Malhoit, and Pierre Guy. The British included James McGill, John Porteous, Richard Huntley, John Blake, Edward William Gray, James Finlay.

They had prepared a long, indeed a windy, list of terms, French eloquence here mingling for the first time with Scottish exactitude—free religion, free this, free that, open trade with

England, etc., etc. Montgomery, with characteristic sense and humor, waved it all aside. The city, he said, was his for the taking. As for these liberties, he had no intention of taking away any of them. The only one he could not offer was trade with England, a thing beyond his power. "Come then, my brethren," he said, "unite with us in an indissoluble union; we will run toward the same goal."

Thereupon Montgomery's Army of Congress marched into Montreal, as Amherst's army had, by the Recollet Gate, at the corner of McGill and Notre Dame. This time, however, there were no Highland pipes, no tossing feathers, no scarlet uniforms —except some that Montgomery's army had taken from his prisoners. The "Army of Congress" was a raggedy lot. The men were dressed mostly in hunting suits, carried rifles and short axes, tomahawks and long knives. The flags they carried were plain crimson cloth, some with a darker rim. There were no stars and no stripes. The stripes appear on Washington's flag of the next new year (1776), a British Union Jack of the day (no Ireland), and thirteen red and white stripes. The glory of the stars only came after independence. The Stars and Stripes never flew over Montreal. Why should they? For the oddity of the whole invasion is that from the beginning to the end all the parties to it were subjects of King George III, some loyal, some disloyal, and most nothing in particular. In any case the invasion was all over (June 14, 1776) before the Declaration of Independence.

Montgomery's own stay in the city, at the headquarters spoken of, was very brief. He left Montreal (November 28, 1775) with his main forces for the real object of his expedition, an attempt to seize Quebec. In this he was to be joined by the force under Colonel Benedict Arnold, the Judas Iscariot of the American Revolution, still serving his first master. Arnold was a dressed-up soldier with a real uniform, with a hat all plumes, and a commission from Congress. Ethan Allen, with a volley of oaths, had put Arnold into his place; namely, none at all, at Ticonderoga. But he has contrived, partly perhaps by his hat and feathers, to impose himself on American history. His march to Quebec "through the Maine wilderness"; that is, by going up the Kennebec River and coming down the Chaudière, has been extolled as a great feat of history. As the Revolution drifted into the past the march became a legend, and heroic accounts were written such as Judge Henry's "Hardships and Sufferings of the Band of Heroes," dictated in extreme old age. Such stories tell how the men upset their food in the river, ate their moccasins, and how a great number deserted. If so, they must have managed very badly. The venerable Canadian historian, Professor Kingsford, who wrote his voluminous pages with the detachment of a mathematician, says that Arnold's expedition "through the wilderness" was much the same as what Canadians now regard as a camping holiday. The season was just right, too late for flies, too early for winter. The route had all been marked out some years before as a blazed trail by an English military officer. There were no enemies and no casualties. They left friendly people on one side of the divide and found friendly people on the other. Kennebec and Chaudière are still there, and anyone can go and make the portage. If he upsets his canoe and eats his boots he is scarcely a hero.

Reaching the St. Lawrence, Arnold made what is called his "unsuccessful assault on Quebec." There was no assault. His men approached the fortress and gave three rousing cheers, expecting a welcome. Instead they roused the discharge of a cannon. Arnold retreated upstream, waiting for Montgomery. While he was waiting Sir Guy Carleton, in a canoe with muffled paddles, slipped past Arnold's forces at night and got into the citadel.

Montgomery arrived. On the night of December 31, 1775, he led his forces in the dead of night in a snowstorm up a sideways road against the main gate of Quebec. They never reached it. A single discharge of a cannon by an alert night watch laid Montgomery and twelve of his men dead. The snow buried them as they lay. The garrison dug them out in the morning. And Montgomery was buried under the bastions. All the world praised him. "The whole city of Philadelphia," says Bancroft, "was in tears." Even in England "the defenders of liberty vied in his praise." "He was a rebel," said Fox, "but all saviors of their country have been called rebels." Arnold's forces remained around Quebec until the spring.

Meantime, Montreal was under the charge of the veteran General Wooster, whose role was that, so familiar now, of the old hero of the last war, no good in this. Things in Montreal went from bad to worse. Overseas trade was gone. The "Army of Congress" brought no ready money except the continental dollar (just issued, July 1775) and Massachusetts bills. Local sympathizers, betting on the wrong horse, subscribed funds at first, James Price as much as £20,000 in all, but such sources soon ran dry. Wooster's rule was of that mixture of lenience and severity which always fails. Many Tories were arrested and fined, a good number sent away to New York Province. In social life the "best" people kept away from the Americans.

The town, by the end of the winter, was in a ferment. Colonel Hazen, who commanded at Montreal after Wooster left for Quebec (March 23, 1776) and till Arnold arrived, wrote to General Schuyler: "The clergy are unanimous . . . against our cause . . . with respect to the better sort of people, both French and English . . . seven eighths are Tories, who would wish to see our throats cut."

Arnold arrived back from Quebec in May 1776. Headquarters had been moved to the Château de Ramezay, exactly the thing for Arnold's vanity. From what we read, he attempted entertainment in fine style, but the people he most wanted stayed away.

There then arrived in Montreal, as apostles of concord, the famous Congressional mission of Benjamin Franklin.[4] The commissioners were men well chosen: Franklin himself; Samuel Chase of Maryland, an honorable and patriotic man, and Charles Carroll of Carrollton, Maryland, the richest man in America. They said he was "worth" £150,000; from all records his heart was worth more. Carroll was a Roman Catholic, and he brought his brother John Carroll, who was a Jesuit priest or had been until the recent suppression (1772). Both the Carrolls spoke French. The mission brought with it a printing press duly in-

⁴*Journal of Charles Carroll, 1776.*

stalled in the basement of the Château de Ramezay with a French printer, Fleury Mesplet, the first in Montreal to work it. The idea was to disseminate light among the French habitants.

The mission on its arrival was entertained with a party of Montreal society in the château. They were lodged in the Besancourt house, just beside the château, as mentioned in the last chapter, occupied at the moment by Thomas Walker, lately rescued from the British and now the leading rebel of the town. The mission from the start was a flat failure. Franklin has left hardly anything on record about it; one may judge that he was ashamed of it. Later on the printing press "in a community where only one in five hundred could read and write" struck him as funny. "We ought to have brought schoolmasters," he said. Yet the printing press turned up trumps, or at least type. When the commission left, Mesplet stayed on. He printed little books, works of devotion, and such. The first book printed in Montreal was *Règlement de la Confrérie de l'Adoration Perpetuelle du Saint Sacrement* (1776). A press brought to Quebec had printed a manual of devotion as early as 1765. Presently Mesplet got out a French newspaper, *La Gazette* (1778), which became bilingual in 1788, and presently forgot its French to become the city's metropolitan English morning paper.

The Carrolls failed also. Not even a Jesuit could persuade people that the Roman Catholic religion would be happier under the Acts of Congress than under the Quebec Act. Carroll's argument reminds one of the famous plea of a later American trust magnate, "Leave the consumer to us." It was equally unsuccessful. As danger gathered down the St. Lawrence the commissioners cleared out, Franklin on May 11, 1776, in company with Walker and his wife; the rest on May 29. Arnold and his "Army of Congress" also cleared out (June 17), Arnold taking with him from Montreal a lot of plundered goods which he sold in Albany.

All this happened before the Declaration of Independence of July 4, 1776.

With the close of the American invasion of Canada, Montreal ceased to be a part of the theater of conflict, and the history

of the long years of war that ended only with the Peace of 1783
belongs elsewhere. Only for one brief period did it look as if
war might come again to Montreal. The entrance of France into
the war as the ally of the United States (1778) put a new complexion on the scene. Already the young Marquis de Lafayette,
coming to America to join Washington "on his own," had
eagerly advocated the invasion of Canada. The French alliance
and the arrival of the French fleet opened a wide opportunity.
Lafayette obtained the warm support of Admiral d'Estaing and a
favoring vote of Congress. He proposed to ask France for five
thousand new troops. He would invade Canada at both ends and
in the middle, striking at Montreal by way of the Connecticut
River. Congress approved the plan. D'Estaing sent to Montreal a
proclamation (October 28, 1778) entitled *Déclaration Adressée
au Nom du Roi à Tous les Anciens Français de l'Amérique Septentrionale*. It called upon the French of Canada to return to their
native allegiance. "You were born French. There is no other
house so august as that of Henry IV, under which the French
can be happy and serve with delight." But the note was wrongly
pitched. Many plain French Canadians, after eighteen years of
fairly fair play and of religious freedom, felt less sure of
Henry IV. But even at that the appeal shook French-Canadian
clerical and seignorial opinion. Sir Fredrick Haldimand, who
had succeeded Carleton as the Governor of Canada (1778–86),
wrote home: "Since the address of the Count d'Estaing and a
letter of M. de Lafayette many of the priests have changed their
opinions." Jesuit missionaries, it was reputed, were seeking to
rouse the Caughnawaga Indians for the Congress. Haldimand
buried himself with defensive measures on the Richelieu to cover
Montreal. But the danger passed. General Washington himself
averted it. To his sagacious mind a French conquest of Canada
would turn back the clock of the history of North America.
There was no invasion. Without it, revolt in Canada was impossible.

But though the war of the Revolution, after its opening
phases, affected Montreal but little, the conclusion of peace

affected it and all Canada a great deal. For it led to a new American occupation which settled the future destiny of the country by the incoming of the United Empire Loyalists. Their migration, which brought forty thousand settlers to British North America within one generation, was on a scale unknown to the world of that day. Even before the peace was ratified they were leaving New York in shipfuls; after it, in fleets. They swarmed into Nova Scotia when a fishing village such as Shelburne became a town, or rather a camp, as large as Boston. The mainland section of Nova Scotia became New Brunswick with twelve thousand settlers in 1784. Other Loyalists made their entry across New York State by way of Oswego and Niagara. Others again came all the way round by river and sea, with Montreal as the great point of distribution. For many this trip took two seasons, the winter spent on the way. Many stayed in Montreal.

The new settlers transformed the country. They brought the English language on their lips and British freedom, as expanded in America, in their hearts. Patterned on their minds were the Massachusetts schoolhouse, free education for all, Thanksgiving turkey, town government, election to office, everybody at least as good as everybody else and perhaps better. This incoming flood broke the mold in which French Canada was cast. Into empty Upper Canada it came, to use a metaphor older than our glass bottles, as new wine to a new bottle, needing all the bottle to itself; into Lower Canada, as new wine into an old bottle, endeavoring to stretch the skin. Hence the clamor from Montreal for the government to open up land that was not seignorial and to divide it into "townships," to make it seem like home. Hence presently the Eastern Townships. Here belongs the famous petition from Montreal (November 24, 1784) asking for an assembly. It carried 246 names, all British except Levi Solomons, and a few odd names difficult to classify. The second name is James McGill. With this from all British quarters came the desire and the demand for British institutions, for government by vote, for separate rule in Upper Canada.

Strangely enough, Lord Dorchester—the title borne by Sir Guy Carleton soon after his return as Governor General of

Canada, Nova Scotia, and New Brunswick in 1786—was luke-warm in the cause of change. He thought it unwise to divide the provinces, argued that the demand for an assembly came only from the commercial class in Montreal and in Quebec, and that the gentlemen and the clergy were still against it. Dorchester was sixty-two years old. Age will have its way. Thus divided councils held action in suspense.

The current stirred not only political life but economic life as well. Here begin for Montreal new industries, of new charac-ter and importance, such as the first attempts toward the export timber trade that presently made the St. Lawrence raft a unique feature of the Canadian scene. Men of brains and energy were attracted by the new Montreal as by a magnet. Here enters on its annals, in 1782, the name of Molson, which henceforth echoes down the history of the city in the throb of the steamship, the tinkle of the bank tellers' coins, the whisper of the college library, and the roar of the college stadium. At its first coming it breathed in a softer atmosphere. Young John Molson, aged eighteen, came out from Lincolnshire, a country where the moist climate of the fens and fields breathes malt with the air and where brewing is a hereditary, domestic art. This art, unknown in French Canada, Molson brought to Montreal. Mr. B. K. Sand-well, the biographer of the Molson family, speaks of young John Molson's opportunity with something like awe. "He found a large, prosperous, and growing population entirely without local supplies of the national beverage." Molson built his brewery a little way downstream from the town, close beside the river. Archaeologists can easily locate the spot as the brewery is still there.

But if the man found the opportunity, the opportunity had also found the man. Within a decade brewing was but one of Molson's many activities. As Henry Ford, exactly a hundred years later, tinkered in his back yard with a "gasoline buggy," so did Molson on the riverbank tinker with a "steamboat." Accen-tuate both syllables instead of one, "steam, boat," as they named the thing yet to be contrived, and the past will rise before you.

Nor was Molson the only man of opportunity, remaking

Montreal. There were dozens of them. Most of all is this true of the fur trade which at this period got the new impetus that created the Northwest Company and wrote history. There are certain trades and avocations dear to the human heart, and certain others repugnant. All the world loves a sailor, suspects a lawyer, and avoids a professor. The fur trade is one that carries a peculiar attraction—the open air, the splash of the canoe, the smell of the pine woods, the campfire, and the lullaby of falling water. . . . This native attraction now joined with new opportunity. Now that England owned all America to the sunset, British explorers could go and search for it, as witness Captain Carver's *Travels through the Interior Parts of North America.* British fur traders could go West by the new route of the lakes and rivers. Exploration and trade went together. We may doubt if such men as Alexander Henry and Alexander Mackenzie knew which they were doing. Henry came first, coming to Montreal at the time of Montgomery's invasion, and entered on the Western fur trade, spending many years beyond the Great Lakes on the plains. On Henry's trail followed a flock of independent traders, every man for himself, striking out from Montreal into the Lake Superior wilderness. Common sense showed the folly, in the fur trade among Indians, of every man for himself, which meant every man for today and no man for tomorrow. The Montreal traders, under the leadership of Henry, joined in an association called the Northwest Company. At this time, there being no statutory companies or company law of incorporation, except by single charter, the company was really a partnership. The headquarters were at Montreal, housed presently in the famous Beaver Hall that stood well outside of the town, southwest of it, on the slope that perpetuates its name in Beaver Hall Hill. At this time, and for another thirty years, the fur trade was the leading commerce of Montreal. Many, if not most, of the substantial men were in it, there being sixteen shares divided as follows: Todd and McGill, two shares; Benjamin and Joseph Frobisher, two shares; McGill and Paterson, two shares; McTavish and Company, two shares; Holmes and Grant, two shares; Walker and Company, two shares; McBeath and Company, two shares; Ross and Company, one share; Oakes and Company, one share.

Among these Montreal traders was formed in 1785 the famous Beaver Club, originally of nineteen members, all of them men who had wintered in the wilds. Later on they let in tamer men, who lived in town, and had fifty-five members with ten honorary members. They held club nights and club dinners, told tales about the bush, mixed hot scotch, and sent an aroma of good cheer down the decades. Their ghosts still walk in the Montreal Curling Clubs.

This new stimulus to trade affected to some extent the character of the Port of Montreal. More ships came up from the sea in what was then an all-British voyage protected by the Navigation Acts. But the number was still trifling. Except with a very special wind, ships had to be hauled up against St. Marys current with long teams of oxen, as many even as forty. The bateaux, as already described, carried practically all the trade, with transshipment at Quebec. The Durham boat, used in the States, does not appear in Montreal till later. The steamboat was too weak to offer a tow—a "tug"—up the current for many years after its invention. It had all it could do to tug itself. But on the lakes up above shipbuilding began with settlement itself.

It had been quite obvious that the government of the province of Quebec (still so called) must be altered, indeed that the province itself must be altered. The American Loyalists and the French new subjects had too little in common to amalgamate. Hence the new Constitutional Act (or Canada Act) of 1791 that cut Quebec in two and set up Lower and Upper Canada. The ultimate wisdom of this may be left to historians to argue. It looked like common sense to people in Upper Canada at the time. There were about 150,000 French and about 15,000 English-speaking Canadians, with rural French Canada still entirely French, as the Eastern Townships were not yet opened, and the new Upper Canada settlements entirely English-speaking.

The new act reiterated the guarantees to the Roman Catholic Church. It set up provincial legislatures at Quebec and at Toronto, each with an appointed legislative council and an elected assembly. Montreal now found itself a parliamentary constituency sending up, or rather down, four members to Quebec, to the Assembly of fifty. Montreal, meaning the district around, also sent two members, being one of the new "counties." With characteristic inanity the government of the day christened the counties of French Canada with English names and divided Upper Canada into German districts. Later on both were painlessly removed. When the first Assembly met at Quebec on December 17, 1792, the Montreal town members included James McGill—nothing was now complete without him— J. B. Durocher, James Walker, and Joseph Papineau. In the new Assembly sixteen members were British and thirty-four French. It was from its cradle bilingual both in speech and record. It met, though it didn't know it, on the very eve of England's entry (February 1793) into the first great war that had already begun and was to last out the lives of many of them. At the moment no such thought troubled them. The British were as slow in realizing the approach of war in 1792 as in 1913 and 1938. In Montreal the new members' thoughts were elsewhere: Papineau's no doubt in his warehouse or on his clever son, Louis Joseph, then six years old and attending the seminary in Quebec; McGill's thoughts on his fur trade; Molson's on steam, and all on the pipe of peace.

Thus shifted noiselessly the scene of history. In place of French Canada was now British North America; the walled French city of Montreal knocked down its walls (1803) and opened its Harbour Gate to the world.

CHAPTER VIII

Lower Canada
1791–1841

A Half Century of Lower Canada. The Great War and the News of Trafalgar at Montreal. The Great Peace. A Rapid Age. Steamboats. Gaslights. City Government. The Coming of the Immigrants. The Cholera Years. Opening the First Railway. The Rebellion. Execution of the "Patriotes."

BY AN ODD COINCIDENCE of Canadian history the half century from 1791 to 1841, like the previous 1713–63, actually means a definite period. It corresponds to the life of the province of Lower Canada, created under the Act of 1791 and expiring in 1841. Read in the false light and from the false angle of history as written, until yesterday, to be learned at school, it seems all fire and smoke, all war, anger, and rebellion. Here first is the shadow of the great war in Europe, beginning in 1792 and lasting with just a little break (1802–03), hardly observable from Montreal, till the city heard in July of 1815 the news of the Battle of Waterloo of June 18. The war is hardly over till we are dragged forward to the Rebellion of 1837–38. In such history any little intervals of quiet seem like boating at Chippewa, above Niagara Falls.

But in reality the period as seen in retrospect by old people in Montreal in 1841 would not seem like that at all. The war to them was something like a shadow that came and went, darkening and passing. An old man might remember the excitement and apprehension that went with the outbreak of the French Revolution, but more likely, as nothing happened, he had quite forgotten it. He might remember having heard people say that Napoleon was going to send a fleet against Montreal. Among the vivid memories that never left him would be those of Montreal in 1812–13, with the streets full of soldiers, with every able man under arms or under a pitchfork, the cheers and shouts when they heard about the battle, right close by, at Châteauguay and how three or four hundred of their own side, they said, had beaten ten times as many Americans. Still more vivid, only yesterday, only three years ago, would be the recollection, brief but lurid, of the Rebellion, of the fighting on the Richelieu, the cruel slaughter in St. Eustache Church, and the hangings in Montreal.

But those pictures, lurid in the foreground, were not the real scenes of life, but only patches of fire seen against a wood as evening falls. Real life, as it came down the years, carried different recollections. If you were to let the old man tell you all about it (a dangerous permission to give) you would find that his main recollection of that half century in Montreal was the terrific change from a period ever so slow to a period ever so fast. It is with all old men. In fact, the old man would admit that he didn't know what the world was coming to. Old men never do. He could recall from his childhood the old French town, all gardens and seminaries and soft with the sound of the church bells; could recall looking forty feet down from the great walls of the fortification (eighteen feet high) at the pasture of the common and the river and the bateaux hauled up on the mud. Why, in those days you took a good part of a week, or even more, to come from Quebec. Ships would lie down there, below the current; they might be a fortnight waiting for a wind. But now, in 1841, a steamboat runs you back and forward over the river or rushes you across to La Prairie to get on a train that whirls you away to St. Johns at fifteen miles an hour—another steamboat and off again—and in less than a week, in a few days, you're in New York.

Think of that sleepy old French town with perhaps two hundred English families in it, and this great city of 1841 with forty thousand people, where you hear English spoken all day, with ocean ships all the way from Liverpool, with this great Lachine Canal where the little river and the marshes used to be, but now steamers up and down from the Great Lakes. Think of the wonderful new gaslight, of this plan for a great bridge to be made across the river, and people talking of this newfangled invention they call a magnetic telegraph that takes a message forty miles through a piece of wire. The old man hopes he doesn't live to see anything of that sort in Montreal. Perhaps he didn't. It came in 1847, but he may have died of cholera first.

The enthusiasm of the opening French Revolution, almost bloodless in its early stage, awoke in foreign lands echoes of sympathy, of sentiment, of silliness. "The greatest event in the world," said Fox when the Bastille fell. British "friends of the people" and "Constitutional Clubs" held gatherings where lords and lackeys met as equals, "in childish imitation," says a British historian, "of what was going on across the channel."[1] In the United States a wave of ultrarepublicanism, with Phrygian liberty caps and songs and demonstrations, swept the country. "The American people," says McMaster, "went insane."[2]

Something of this, accentuated by its French nationality, swept over Montreal also in the early years of the French Jacobin republic instituted after the execution of the King. Our local histories expand the disaffection in Montreal into something like a Jacobin movement. But this is out of all proportion. We have to remember that although Great Britain and France were at war from February 1793 and all intercourse suspended, the United States and France remained at peace. Diplomatic ministers and agents came and went. There was thus an easy access to Montreal, from Vermont, of all kinds of agitators and spies, people with no real connection with Canada, sent in by Genêt,

[1] J. R. Green, *The British People*, 1874.
[2] J. B. McMaster, *History of the United States*.

the new republican ambassador to the United States, and by Fauchet, his successor. It was rumored too that the new state of Vermont, looking for new trouble to replace its old quarrel with New York, had suggested an invasion of Canada. Dorchester called for two thousand militiamen, a call answered by only nine hundred. The Governor's common sense told him that this meant not disloyalty but the disinclination of people grown accustomed to peace. A certain disaffection there was, but history should rather stress how little it amounted to than how much.

Take the case of the violent and treasonable pamphlet circulated in Montreal in 1794 under the title *Les Français Libres à leurs Frères Canadiens*. It emanated all too plainly from France. It rang false. Just as D'Estaing's proclamation of 1778 about Henry IV was too aristocratic, setting up a throne, this document was too republican, setting up a guillotine. Its contents, to most plain French Canadians of the day, whether seigneur or habitant, would seem abominable. It not only proposed Canada as a free state with equality for all, votes and offices for all, but it cut out all hereditary rights, titles, and claims, as also all the rights of the Roman Catholic Church, making all religious cults equal, with clergy elected by the people. This overshot its mark and effected nothing, except a sort of open invitation to rowdyism that broke out now and again when Dorchester's strong hand was gone (July 1796). There were many arrests and trials.

The assumption of power by Napoleon (1799) ended this form of Jacobin propaganda. It led instead to a sort of standing Napoleonic scare, rumor of invasion by a French fleet. There was also "secret" information that Jerome Bonaparte was going to lead an expedition against Montreal from the States. British agents in New York sent his description to Montreal, "twenty-one years of age, five feet six or seven inches high, slender make, sallow complexion, etc., etc." This was Napoleon's youngest brother Jerome, at that time in Baltimore, "marooned" in the States by the British Atlantic fleet. Later he was King of Westphalia and fought at Waterloo. From him descends the surviving Bonaparte family. If he actually came to Canada all record of it is lost. But, oddly enough, Napoleon did plan an invasion of Canada, of which these people never heard. It was not by way of Montreal. It was to be a roundabout attack from the rear, initiated from Louisiana and the Mississippi under the command of General Bernadotte, who told of it later when King of Sweden. The Louisiana Purchase of 1803 canceled it.

All this Napoleonic scare passed away with the Battle of Trafalgar. Here is how the news came to Montreal. On a December evening in 1805 a grand assembly and ball were being held at the Exchange Coffee House (St. Paul and St. Peter streets). The supper merriment was at its height when a messenger came in out of the snow with a great packet of English newspapers just arrived via New York. They contained Admiral Collingwood's dispatch recounting the victory of Trafalgar of October 21, 1805. In an instant the whole assembly was in a tumult of excitement. The very building, we are told, shook with the roaring hurrahs. But in the midst of the excitement many of the ladies suddenly broke into tears when it was announced that the victory had cost the life of Admiral Nelson. In this scene of emotion the chairman, Samuel Gerard, leaped up and proposed a subscription for a monument to Nelson's memory. All thronged to write their names. Enough money was subscribed in a few minutes. This is the Nelson Monument, completed in 1809, and now standing in Jacques Cartier Square.

These memories, alarms, and dangers, condensed into a page, look crowded. Spread over ten years they are too thin to attract attention. Life looked elsewhere. Above all it looked in Montreal to the rising commercial life, the new fur trade to the Northwest, the English settlement of the near-by "townships," the continued passage of immigrants bound for Upper Canada, and the new commerce of the river, now being revolutionized by steam.

In the eye of history the momentous event was the coming of steam navigation. Molson's riverside experiments took form. The *Accommodation* was launched as steam's first bride of the river, clumsy, bulky, but still a bride. She slid into the river sideways, down beside the brewery, in 1809. There are many pictures of this pioneer steamer, but none, we are told, that can be guaranteed, for photographs, even the fading daguerreotype in the silk case, were still unknown. But there is a picture, with every attempt at truth, in the charming little memorial volume, *Old Montreal*, a treasure of pictured history published—or may we say "brewed"—by the Molsons when the brewery was 150 years old (1936). We may put with the picture the contemporary account given by the Quebec *Gazette* of November 9, 1809, of the first trip of the *Accommodation* down to Quebec.

The Steam-Boat, which was built at Montreal last winter, arrived here on Saturday last, being her first trip. She was 66 hours on the passage, of which she was at anchor 30. So that 36 hours is the time which, in her present state, she takes to come down from Montreal to Quebec (over 160 statute miles). On Sunday last she went up against wind and tide from Brehault's wharf to Lymburner's; but her progress was very slow. It is obvious that her machinery at present has not sufficient force for this river. But there can be no doubt of the possibility of perfectioning it so that it will answer every purpose for which she was intended; and it would be a public loss should the proprietors be discouraged from persevering in their intention.

Little did the Quebec *Gazette* realize that the main "purpose for which she was intended," or which she intended herself, audible in every clank of her engine, was the overthrow of the Port of Quebec. That, of course, was a long way off. For two full generations yet, Quebec was the great overseas harbor, the great shipyard of Canada. Nor was Molson in any way discouraged from persevering. He lost no time. Within two years he had the *Swiftsure* in the water, in 1811. Here was a steamboat one hundred and twenty feet by twenty-four feet. She did the trip in twenty-four hours, laughing off a head wind as she came down. The innocent Quebec *Gazette* sang its own swan song in praise of the boat's "celerity" and "security" and "equality" to the best hotel.

The outbreak of the war with the States checked, but only halted for a time, the progress of the steamboat in the St.

Lawrence. From now on John Molson, among his other claims to eminence, was hailed by his French compatriots as the *"bourgeois des steamboats."*

The title carries a great meaning. It suggests the entire good will as between such leading British men of business as Molson, James McGill, Isaac Todd, and their French fellow townsmen. McGill, like many others, had married a French wife. It is true that many murmurs of discontent were already heard, presaging the Rebellion of the next generation. The new constitution granted just enough rights to give a taste for more. Money was still controlled and wrongly spent by the Executive. There were sinecure offices and favoritism, including the attempt to favor the Anglican Church. The Assembly at Quebec fomented controversy. The newspapers spread it abroad. But as yet it filled little place in the life of the community.

The War of 1812, while dislocating the course of trade and commerce, was only directly felt at Montreal for a smaller period. Recollection of it afterward must have been vivid and intense, but brief. The first main incident was the entry into Montreal (September 10, 1812) of the captive American, General William Hull, with his officers and men, which carries something of a comic-opera touch. Hull had been defeated by General Isaac Brock at Detroit, and he and his men were sent to Lower Canada for safekeeping. But their entry into Montreal appears in the record much like a civic reception. There were military bands, "escorts" of soldiers, the streets illuminated, with General Hull riding in an open carriage accompanied by Captain Gray. The procession headed for Government House, where General Hull was presented to His Excellency, Sir George Prevost, who invited him "to take up his residence in Government House during his stay in Montreal." The American officers were "guests" at the barracks and their men comfortably housed in town. . . . There is really much more than comic opera in this, namely, common sense and common decency. Acts such as this have helped to unite North America. The comic opera is that Hull, after a short stay, was exchanged for thirty British soldiers, went home, and was sentenced by a court-martial to be shot. President Madison canceled the sentence on two grounds: (1) that Hull had served well in the Revolutionary War, (2) that he was too old to shoot.

Here, then, we may pause, at the renewal of peace in 1815, and take a look around Montreal as it was in its happy, peaceful expansion between the peace and the Rebellion. An excellent guide is found in the map of Montreal, as issued in 1835 by order of the Mayor and Common Council, in the new pride of their life as a city which began in 1832. It shows at once the city limits as vastly greater, several times as great, as those of the old French town. The suburbs (*les faubourgs*) are now well occupied. The Recollet suburb and, west of it (the use of *west* instead of *south* now begins), the Ste. Anne, St. Joseph, and St. Antoine suburbs carry the inhabited city out to and past Guy Street to end at "Canning" Street (four streets on). Guy Street, as now, runs on up the hill as the Côte des Neiges Road. The largest suburb, St. Lawrence, runs all along between Craig Street, now named but not all developed, up to St. Catherine Street. This last runs east and west across St. Lawrence Main, reaching beyond Bleury Street on the east and about three times as far (to St. Helen Street) on the west. Dorchester Street cuts through the center of the St. Lawrence suburb, then takes a dive after the known fashion of Montreal streets and comes up west again. Lagauchetière Street, just below it, takes a similar dive east. The space between the St. Lawrence and the St. Antoine suburbs was relatively open. Here on the hillside stood Beaver Hall. In the life of a growing city early priority spells later poverty. The palace becomes the slums. The suburb presently houses the newer palace. This open space (from the Windsor Hotel to the Bell Telephone Building of today) was later to be the grandeur of Montreal. Above St. Catherine Street lie the beautiful farms and country houses extending to the foot of the mountain. Two very large ones, just beyond the west end of St. Catherine Street, are those of McGill, at this period under legal dispute, and the McTavish property reaching halfway to the Côte des Neiges Road. Cutting through the farms, from the McGill estate across to St. Denis Street, runs a beautiful country road called Sherbrooke Street, with already two or three houses on it. East, in the direction the French called north, lies the Quebec suburb greatly extended. The Bonsecours Church by the river still serves as a guide. This church, our Lady of Good Help, had indeed a special, a mystic meaning. It was first built, as already mentioned, in 1657, to carry above its roof an image of the Virgin Mary, brought from France by Marguerite Bourgeoys. The Virgin, looking down the river, watched over the safety of the sailors. Thank offerings were laid on the shrine. To her marvelous intercession was ascribed the great storm on the Lower St. Lawrence which broke up Admiral Walker's fleet, about to attack Quebec in 1711. The citadel, at the bottom end of the French town, has all been shoveled flat to make Dalhousie Square; the gates are gone and the city goes on and on for about a mile with Fulham Road as its last street downstream, and St. Marys Road (later part of Notre Dame Street) its main highway.

The new directions of east and west appear in the official parliamentary division of the two wards, for the Assembly set up in 1791. They are divided by the "main street of St. Lawrence," the East Ward being downstream and the West Ward upstream. They are all wrong with the compass; as explained above, the trouble rises in the Gulf of St. Lawrence, where the north shore *is* the north shore, and it comes all the way up. This makes Longueuil the south shore of the St. Lawrence which, at Montreal, it isn't. But if we call Longueuil south we must call Longue Pointe east.

In the lower town, of course, a great many of the old buildings public and private of the French Regime were still there. The Château de Ramezay was Government House. The Hotel Dieu was still on St. Paul Street. Old Notre Dame Church was still standing, but a new one, the present one, was begun in 1824. The old Bonsecours Church was still at the north end of the city, and the Recollet Church at the south. The Grey

Nunnery was still the Charron Building, the Hospital General of a century before. But the changes were more striking than the survivals: the wooden houses had mostly disappeared from the main part of the town. In their place were stone, rubblestone, and brick. There were now about 100 occupied streets and about 2500 houses, all numbered in the older city and partly so in the suburbs. The total population is put at 9000 in the year 1800, 22,000 in the year 1825. Montreal was as populous at night as now, for in those days all the merchants slept over their places of business and officials and professional men in their offices.

But the great change was that the old fortifications were gone, all knocked down except a few survivals on McGill Street and elsewhere. There are many lesser changes. The Jesuits being gone, their property has been built over with the Court House (1800), the gaol, the so-called "Old Gaol" of 1806–36, and the Champs de Mars, extended now to a space of 227 yards by 114, a parade ground and a fashionable promenade. In the new Jacques Cartier Square has been erected the Nelson Monument just mentioned. The Château de Vaudreuil, used for a time as a school and college, was burned. In its place is the new college, the Petit Séminaire, in the Recollet suburb. Large stone barracks have been built near where the Quebec gate stood. Spacious hotels stand on the Place d'Armes, and near the river, St. Paul Street, the main thoroughfare is crowded and busy all day. There is a new stone customs house (1836) built on the old French market square.

Between these days and the present time the whole aspect of Montreal, even of the lower town, has of course been altered, its river front, as it used to be, obliterated by the remaking of the harbor, the Craig Street hollow drained and built upon, St. Paul Street sunk to its present shabby appearance, Notre Dame Street altered from a dignified residential street to be the mere back annex of St. James Street, and the latter a narrow thoroughfare between tall buildings and skyscrapers, unrecognizable as the "Great St. James Street" of a hundred years ago, broad and half empty.

A sign of the movement of the times is the appearance and the multiplication of coffeehouses and hotels, things hardly needed under the Old Regime. In those days "hotel" meant a private mansion such as the Hotel Vaudreuil. A public inn was presently called a "hotel" as a sort of flattering compliment, like the word "funeral home" of today. But now with steamers up and down the river and the canal, ships from overseas, mail stages from Quebec and Kingston (for York) and to New York and, above all, with immigration on the move, the hotel came into its own. So we find now the Exchange Hotel and Coffee House, 170 guests; Orr's Hotel in Notre Dame; the Montreal Hotel, also called Dillon's, on the Place d'Armes, and half a dozen others. Most conspicuous was the spacious and beautiful Mansion House. This was a fine stone building, originally built by Sir John Johnson (of Mohawk fame) after he settled in Montreal. It stood near the Bonsecours Church, overlooking the river. John Molson bought it and added two big wings to it. It had a great terrace, 144 feet long and 30 feet wide, with an unimpeded view of all the stretch of river, islands, shore, and mountains that lay before it. Life in the Mansion House, with dinners and suppers and dances unending, with officers in uniform and beauty in the flowing dress of the day, with champagne at a few shillings a bottle, with the Beaver Club and the Bachelor Club to keep it moving, and the public library in the great room on the premises to keep it quiet, with the Théâtre Royal just over the way with French opera at five shillings a box, with boats for hire for a row on the river on a summer evening, with a military band in the distance and a tangle of fireflies in the foreground—perhaps the good old times were not so bad after all.

The old hotels are gone now. The Mansion was burned in 1812. Where Dillon's guests made merry is now the buried silence of a trust company. Where the guests gathered at the Exchange Coffee House once shouted the news of Trafalgar, the cable company and brokers' offices now click more vital news from Europe. All are gone except only the last of them, Rasco's Hotel, built just at the end of the epoch 1836 as its last word in grandeur. Rasco's is still standing today, ignominiously crowded out by a market, battered, dingy, its ornamentation gone, its garment divided, its very lettering fallen in part away, with nothing but the recollection of Charles Dickens' visit there in 1842 to keep a faint breath of survival stirring.

The Mansion House, we say, stood beside the water, and in front of it was the private wharf built by Molson for his steamers for Quebec and for La Prairie, from which town ran stages to St. Johns and thus to the States. This wharf was one of the first real attempts at improving the port and harbor facilities. The ships that came before the peace era were small, mostly about 150 tons, and very few. For example, in 1813 only nine ships in all came up to Montreal from the sea, a total of 1589 tons. These could lie almost alongside the riverbank, in places where the current had scooped the water deep, or so close that improvised stages were built out from the shore's edge to the deck. With this went the plan of running out horses and carts deep into the water to reach vessels hauled up, bow on. With the ships were the bateaux and the new and bigger type of Durham boat that came in after the American war. These were big flat-bottomed sailboats eighty or ninety feet long, with "center boards," which enabled them to beat to windward. In the harbor also floated the rafts, a conspicuous feature for more than half a century. There were firewood rafts bringing down cordwood for town use from farms up the river and big sections of rafts of square timber on the way to Quebec and England. These had come over the Lachine Rapids and were made up again in La Prairie Basin or below Montreal for Quebec.

But in the period after the war ended (1815), the port and harbor woke up. Wharves began to be built after 1819 alongside the riverbank. In 1824 a permanent town wharf 200 feet long was built. Steamboat navigation as between Montreal and Quebec greatly increased in the period between the peace of 1815 and the Rebellion of 1837. Molson had followed the *Swiftsure* with the *Lady Sherbrooke*, the *Car of Commerce*, and other vessels, which did service in the war and after it in general transport. The year 1821 saw the inception and the year 1825 the opening of the Lachine Canal. Limited at first to only four feet of depth it was little more than a barge canal, but it underwent a century of continuous deepening.

Steam, grown stronger, appears in Montreal, with the *Hercules* of 1823, in the tugging and towing service which was rapidly to revolutionize all the ports of the world. For Montreal overseas steam voyages were not yet. The *Savannah* had crossed the Atlantic in 1819, a clipper-built full-rigged ship, using auxiliary steam and very little of it at that. The *Royal William* built at Quebec crossed the Atlantic (Pictou to London) in 1833, an all-steam trip. Her engines (200 horsepower) were made in Montreal, and the *Royal William* was towed up from Quebec to receive them, at the foot of St. Marys current, tug power unable to haul her farther.

Sail and steam were to fight it out for fifty years, but for far-sighted people, Cunards and Allans, the end was in sight. A Mr. David Munk began building sailing ships in a yard at Montreal as early as 1806. He and his partners and others built various ships of about 200 to 300 tons, one even of 600 tons, before the War of 1812. After steam had got well started and the Lachine Canal opened, the building of steamers went on from 1829 to 1841 at a rapid rate on an increasing scale. The building firm of Shay and Merritt built for the shipping firm of John Torrance the *British America*, 170 feet long; the *Britannia*, 130 feet long; and for the Molsons, the *John Bull*, 182 feet long. All these were for the river trade, Montreal to Quebec. For overseas trade also were built sailing craft, the *Toronto* of 1834, a ship of 345 tons for the Liverpool trade; the *Brilliant* and the *Thalia*, 472 tons each, sailing to the Baltic, and various other ocean craft.

The number of vessels entering the port had greatly increased in this period. The year 1839 showed a total of 78 vessels from the sea, of which 16 were full-rigged ships, 26 barques, and 36 brigs. The following year the number reached 97 vessels. The tonnage for the two years was 29,760, showing an average for the vessels of 170 tons.

The newspaper sailing notices of the day carry us back more than a century to the passage of the seas, as it then was, from Montreal.

Here is the Montreal *Gazette* of November 11, 1830:

From Montreal the brig Canadian, Robert Hamilton, master, will take wheat flour or ashes. . . . Excellent accommodation for passengers Montreal Nov. 1830 James Millar.

Freight and Passage to London. The fine new fast regular trading Ship Arabian, Andrew Carr, master, now in port discharging her inland cargo, will be ready in a few days to receive Ashes, Wheat and flour. She can comfortably accommodate eight passengers in her cabin, it having been expressly fitted up for this number. She will leave this port about the 5th and Quebec the 10th of November. Montreal Oct. 28 1830.

We note the easygoing journalism of the day, the "notices" still inserted after the ships have left. The "ashes" carried as export were the dry hardwood ashes (potash) used for potassium, a great export of the day.

Under "FALL ARRIVALS" we read:

T. S. Brown is now receiving by the Niagara *from Liverpool a large additional supply of Hardware and cutlery which enables him to offer the most complete stock in town.*

This peaceful T. S. Brown of the hardware business had come to Montreal in 1818. His memoirs written some fifty years later (1870) are very interesting and often quoted, all the more so as Brown turned into a rebel "general" in the outbreak of 1837.

The most notable change was the installation in 1830 of a Montreal Harbour Commission with an appropriation of $4000 a year, which enabled them to begin building wharves along the shore. A mole was built to join to the mainland the little island, whose existence made a harbor first possible, the Ilot Normandin, Market Gate Island, Oyster Island. The wharf on the former island becomes from now on the principal wharf of Montreal.

There was also set up a branch of Trinity House, with the same commission as that of the famous Admiralty institution, to improve navigation by charts, buoys, and lights. There was much talk of deepening the insufficient natural channel. Preliminary surveys of Lake St. Peter were made in 1838, but the task was still too great. A further difficulty, not overcome till the present century, was found in the spring floods which lifted the river above all the structures along the foreshore.

Dotted along the years are those little features of town improvement and public works that mark a rising city; things that are tiresome to relate in detail but indicate in summary the milestones of civic progress. Waterworks began with the new century. Till then Montreal pumped water from domestic wells and hauled it in carts from the river. The town with 9000 people in 1800 had grown too crowded for that. A private company, the Proprietors of the Montreal Water-Works, undertook in 1801 to bring water from a mountainside pond in wooden pipes. The scheme failed. In dry weather there was too little water; in wet weather too much; in summer the pipes dried; in winter they burst. Some of these old pipes, banded with iron hoops and jammed together end to end, were found long after under Notre Dame Street. A second company laid down iron pipes in 1819 and pumped water from the river. The city bought the plant in 1845 and blasted out a reservoir below the mountain. The continuous concussions nearly blasted out of existence the feeble McGill College, just two years old as far as actual operation.

With water came better fire protection. Mention has been made above of the great fires of 1722 and 1734 in the old French days. A great fire (1765) just after the cession swept away 215 houses. With that began compulsory fire precaution, ladders, and buckets, etc., in every house. Then came a volunteer Fire Club, after that a Fire Society (cheerier still), created by statute; thirteen citizens were given by the justices of the peace the doubtful honor of membership, without pay. They organized volunteers and captains and bought engines. After the real city government began (1832) a fire department was part of it.

With fire went light. The old French town, apart from moonlight, was very dark. Yet there was little theft, all men being armed and the gallows ready. In the civic life of peace thieves bred fast. Hence the lighting of St. Paul Street, still the busy main street of Montreal, with whale-oil lamps set out by the merchants. People could now go shopping after dark. Other streets followed. Town lamps were supplied in 1818. Then came gas (1836), the latest European novelty, supplied by the Montreal Gas Light Company with the younger John Molson as its chairman.

A town with water, light, fire, and thieves needs police. In older days the justices of the peace kept order as best they could, with sheriffs and sheriffs' men and, if need be, soldiers. In 1818 appeared twenty-four "night watchmen," carrying long blue sticks and lanterns, with rattles and whistles to keep them awake. They cried "All well" at each half-hour, meaning "All awake," and they had a "station" at St. Peter and Notre Dame.

The influx of British Protestants after the conquest, and still more with the coming of the Loyalists, had long since made it necessary to supply places of Protestant worship. For this the Anglicans were permitted to use the Church of the Recollets (1764 to 1789) and later the Jesuit Church till they built their own Christ Church on St. James Street in 1814. After it was burned (1856) they moved up from the lower town and built, in 1859, the beautiful Christ Church Cathedral now standing on St. Catherine Street.

The Presbyterians also at first shared with the Anglicans the Recollet and Jesuit churches till they built a church of their own on St. Gabriel Street in 1792. A Protestant bishop, Rev. Jacob Mountain, was appointed at Quebec in 1793, and his son, Rev. George Mountain, became the titular Bishop of Montreal in 1837. The See of Montreal dates from 1850.

In a sense—the sense of lawyers—the greatest change of the time was in the institution in Montreal of city government. Hitherto Montreal, French or English, had been governed from above. Since the conquest, apart from the military authorities, there were, as said, the justices of the peace. The citizens, both French and English, had long agitated for city government. Nothing was done. Petitions and meetings multiplied. At length the Harbour Commission just spoken of was granted, in 1830, as a first installment. The year 1832 saw an act to incorporate the city of Montreal. It was of the usual type then running round the newly democratic world: eight wards, with sixteen councilors electing a mayor. The right to vote was given to all male citizens, at least 21 years old, qualified by property and residence. The Mayor received a salary of four hundred dollars. There is no need to give details. The act and the system lapsed in 1836, started again in 1843, and began that series of starts and stops which has represented for a hundred years the quest of Montreal for a new, clean, efficient government. A series of about a dozen new brooms, 1840, 1851, 1874, 1899, 1912, etc., etc., have attempted to sweep Montreal clean, and all have failed. There is a bill now under discussion to get clean government in 1943—or later. Municipal government has proved itself the blind alley of modern democracy, and if there is any duller subject to read about, most of us don't know of it.

With this period begins for Canada and for Montreal the incoming flood of immigration that made the country. The end of the great war in 1815 opened the new period of the "great peace," an era of progress and expansion as never before seen. Yet the first aftermath of war was the sudden slump of depression and unemployment, the hard times that still puzzle the economist. It was a thing that presently righted itself, "with no other aid than starvation and cholera." But at the outset the blow fell hard, especially on Montreal. From the first expansion of the epoch expressed itself in migration, indiscriminate, unlimited, and without control or care.

The British people were free to go. This was the new period of liberalism and liberty, glorious in its wider aspect, terrible in its unforeseen consequences. The new home of liberty, in which England became the workshop of the world, was a habitation bright with flowers in front, all darkness and filth behind. Behind the palace was the slum; behind the workshop was the workhouse. People were free to live or free to starve, to quit work and start starving any time they liked. Particularly they were free to go to any place, British or not—the glad good-riddance of the poor. Off they went, dirty and singing and triumphant, often in ships so foul and rotten that there was bubonic plague, the Asiatic cholera of the day, in every filthy plank in the dank, sunless steerage. Out they went to Quebec and on to Montreal, ever so many, dead or dying, the rest singing still, and plenty more to follow.

The policy of the day threw them on the colonies, as on Montreal, to live or die. In brisk times there would be bread and work for all, but in this opening era only for a few. Montreal had to look after the homeless and the sick as best it could. And here happened a strange thing, light coming out of darkness, good out of evil. There was in Montreal no English hospital. The little premises that humanity supplied, a four-room building on St. Joseph and Gabriel, called the House of Recovery, with a doctor in charge, and later the large house bought on Craig Street, with four attendant doctors (1818), turned into the Montreal General Hospital (1819). A lot was purchased on Dorchester Street, well out of town for the fresh air, and a building, the nucleus of the present hospital, opened in 1822. At that time there was no organized medical profession. This made one. Here began the Medical Institution of Montreal. There was as yet no teaching of medicine; this compelled it. And presently, when McGill University began actual work, this body became the Medical Faculty of McGill. All the glory of the General Hospital, of the Royal Victoria, and the Neurological, the Maternity, and the Children's Memorial, all the immortality of Osler and of—we know them—the McGill immortals of today, still mortal—all this was there under the humble roof of the House of Recovery. One can't get over it, so to speak. Those who watch in the present city the daily pilgrimage of the outdoor patients moving to the free clinics of the great hospitals of Montreal may see in fancy, hovering over them to direct their steps, the departed spirit of the stricken immigrant, from whose death came life.

Such was immigration into Montreal in its earlier days, and such the shadow of want and pestilence that darkened its coming. The better to understand this scene, in this shadow under which it lay, and in the sunlight that was later to illuminate it, we may recall the picture of Montreal as seen in 1830, the great

cholera year, by Mrs. Catherine Parr Traill, an English lady
arriving as an immigrant on her way to the bush settlements of
Upper Canada. Mrs. Traill was one of those distinguished Strickland sisters who showed what women could do fifty years before
other women did it. Her book, *The Backwoods of Canada*, and
the well-known book of her sister, Mrs. Susannah Moodie,
Roughing It in the Bush, are firsthand pictures of Canada of the
period of great interest. The fault of both writers lies in a
greater ability to see present hardships than to foresee future
happiness. Just as Charles Dickens could see nothing but swamps
and ague where now rise the great American cities of the Middle
West, so the Strickland sisters "roughed it in the bush" and
could not see that the "collection of log shanties" was going to
be the beautiful city of Peterborough. Mrs. Moodie concluded
her book with the statement that if it kept only one family
away from Canada it was worth the writing of it—an odd statement for those of us who remember her immediate descendants
as among the wealthiest and most respected people of Toronto—
the fate that migration to the "bush" brought them. So too one
must make similar reservations against Mrs. Traill's views.

We were struck [she writes] *by the dirty, narrow, ill-paved
or unpaved streets of the suburbs, and overpowered by the
noisome vapor arising from a deep open fosse that ran along the
street behind the wharf. This ditch seemed the receptacle for
every abomination, and sufficient in itself to infect a whole town
with malignant fevers.*

*The cholera had made awful ravages, and its devastating
effects were to be seen in the darkened dwellings and the mourn-
ing habiliments of all classes. An expression of dejection and
anxiety appeared in the faces of the few persons we encountered
in our walk to the hotel, which plainly indicated the state of
their minds.*

*In some situations whole streets had been nearly depopulated;
those that were able fled panic-stricken to the country villages,
while others remained to die in the bosom of their families.*

To no class, I am told, has the disease proved so fatal as to the poorer sort of emigrants. Many of these, debilitated by the privations and fatigue of a long voyage, on reaching Quebec or Montreal, indulged in every sort of excess, especially the dangerous one of intoxication; and, as if purposely paving the way to certain destruction, they fell immediate victims to the complaint.

In one house eleven persons died, in another seventeen; a little child of seven years old was the only creature left to tell the woeful tale. This poor desolate orphan was taken by the nuns to their benevolent institution, where every attention was paid that humanity could suggest.

Nor were sanitation and the prevention of disease the only things as yet defective at this period. Education also lagged behind. Under the French Regime what education there was was carried on by the Seminary and by the Congregation. The mass of the habitants got none. After the conquest the old Château de Vaudreuil was used, first for elementary teaching, then as a college. This building was burned in 1803. The Sulpicians built a college, the new college or Petit Séminaire, in what had been the Recollet suburb outside of the Recollet gate, that is to say, beyond McGill Street on a street that became College Street, now a continuation of St. Paul. This is "The College" mentioned in *Hochelaga Depicta* and books of the period. It had accommodation for 160 pupils, entering at eight to ten years old for a course of eight years.

Dorchester Street was, as said, only laid out in part. At this period all the ground beyond the angle of Dorchester Street and Côte des Neiges was called the Priests' Farm. It originally contained the old walled fort with the corner towers, and these premises (then called La Maison des Prêtres) were used as a week-end place of rest for professors and students of the seminary and the college. The Collège de Montréal (Grand Séminaire) was built later (1854–57).

The incoming of the Loyalists led to a demand for schools, for a school system. Elsewhere, as in New Brunswick, they succeeded at once; not in Lower Canada. A number of private schools struggled into existence. To aid them there was created by an act of the legislature in 1801 a shadowy body called the Royal Institution for the Advancement of Learning. This was supposed to act as a trustee, to receive funds and make grants.[3] But as the main purpose set forth in its creation was to teach English to French Canadians, it was born into the shadow of dislike. The French Canadian would rather know nothing in French than everything in English. Help was given to the British and Canadian (meaning French and English) school opened on Lagauchetière Street in 1826. But the French children dropped out when the political troubles began. It was to the Royal Institution that the aged James McGill, after much consultation with his young friend, the Rev. John Strachan, later the famous bishop, bequeathed, in 1811, £10,000 and his Burnside estate of forty-six acres and the manor house and buildings thereon. McGill died in 1813. Ill-omened fairies put the college asleep in its cradle for thirty years. McGill, as apart from the group of doctors mentioned above, never taught a student till 1843. But the Royal Institution still signs its name to the salary checks.

Thus not only college education but any general school system had to wait.

Yet while learning withered at the root finance grew apace. But the discussion of the epoch marked by the formation of the Bank of Montreal in 1817 is best deferred to the more spacious days that followed the union of the Canadas.

Montreal had no sooner started on its civic life than storms began to gather over it. What had been twenty years before little more than casual murmurs of discontent, the recollections of a lost cause, the memories that refused to die, now begin to ferment into a fierce quarrel—the "two nations warring in the bosom of a single state"—of which Lord Durham was to speak.

In Upper Canada the agitation that led to the Rebellion of 1837 was mere restive protest against the unfair privileges of a petty aristocracy and of a favored church. There was not enough to fight for, and in the sequel no one fought. In Lower Canada this grievance was there also but was lost in the deeper hostility of race against race. As agitation grew it centered

[3]Letter of the Anglican Bishop of Quebec, October 17, 1799.

mainly around Montreal rather than Quebec, for in and around Montreal was where the French and English were most mixed. Quebec was and remained quiet. The rebel agitators among the French were not really agitating for responsible government or even better government but for some method of voting the English off their backs. Louis Joseph Papineau and his associates presently (1834) put their grievances into the famous "ninety-two resolutions." They could have said it all in one.

What the English agitators of Lower Canada wanted was some way of voting monarchy off their backs. The basis of this was the call of the republic, so powerful in the springtime of democracy, and not weakened in Canada by contemplating across the water the morality of George IV or the intelligence of his honest brother. The racial call claimed Louis Joseph Papineau; republican freedom claimed such a man as Wolfred Nelson, and both called forth such generous youths as George Étienne Cartier, later a conservative Father of Confederation, and Dr. Chenier, whose statue stands in Montreal today, eager even in dead stone. With others, as with Dr. O'Callaghan, the sorrows of Ireland were added to the cup.

The agitation in the country was kindled in the legislature at Quebec, its flames fanned by the speeches of Louis Joseph Papineau. But the real seat of the trouble was in Montreal and in the district around Montreal Island and Isle Jésus and in the settlements on the Richelieu. Papineau lived in Montreal, his house being situated on St. Paul Street. He sat as one of the two members for the West Ward.

The year 1832 saw the first outbreak of violence. A by-election in the West Ward, involving after the old-time fashion several days of voting at the open poll, led to the gathering of a mob around the closing poll. In the scene of tumult which ensued the garrison soldiers (Colonel McIntosh with the Fifteenth Regiment) were called out. The Riot Act was read. The crowd refused to go. The soldiers advanced toward the mob in the Place d'Armes against a hail of stones which injured many, including the colonel. After ineffectual warnings McIntosh ordered a volley from the front platoon. Three of the crowd fell dead, two wounded. The rest vanished. Artillery was set to command the streets. McIntosh was arrested on a coroner's warrant but set free afterward. The French paper, *La Minerve*, shouted massacre. Five thousand people, among them Papineau, speaker of the House, walked in the funeral of the men killed.

It seems strange to think that it was just after this scene of disorder that there came to Montreal its first and most terrible visitation of the cholera, brought by the immigrant ships. In the middle of June of that year (1832) the deaths ran to 100 a day. In all there were some 3384 cases and 947 deaths in June.

After this first outbreak, meetings, organization, and agitation continued; the Papineau majority blocked all official business in the Assembly. The "ninety-two resolutions" were passed by the House in 1834. The British party formed Constitutional Associations in the same year. In Montreal many French Canadians adhered to the government side. But in the general election of 1835 the vote showed in Montreal 13,714 demanding reform against 6254 opposed. Circulars went from Montreal to the country, and to England, sent from both sides. Lord Gosford was sent out as Governor on August 23, 1835, specially commissioned to compose the quarrel. Sir John Colborne, ending his term as Lieutenant Governor of Upper Canada in 1836, was made Chief of the Forces in Canada. After a brief journey to England he took command at Montreal.

Even among these events the broken lights of history flicker between shadow and sunshine. Here in these mid-dangers we may forget a moment Louis Joseph Papineau and turn to a pretty midsummer scene, so often depicted and so full of sunlight (July 1836), the opening of the Champlain and St. Lawrence Railway Company, the first railway in Canada. The railway is to connect Montreal to New York by covering fifteen miles from La Prairie to St. Johns. The rest is just a matter of steamers, and a short rail journey in the state of New York. There is the scene under the trees—the train on its toy track of wood with strips of iron, its engine thirteen feet long, its two quaint cars like wooden playhouses, and all about it a sylvan scene of bright uniforms, gay crinolines, gentlemen in top hats, Lord Gosford, the Governor General, and off at fifteen miles an hour to St. Johns, and on arrival such a banquet and junketing, champagne and speeches, that we can for the moment quite forget Louis Joseph Papineau—or we could, except that Papineau was there, one of the top hats.

Thus began the railway, innocent as a summer day, gentle as a kitten, later an octopus, and then a "problem"—the machine age's first-born son, gone wrong.

At a meeting at St. Ours (above Sorel) Dr. Wolfred Nelson called for armed rebellion. "Sons of Liberty" were organized in Montreal. Papineau moved among the meetings. "The game which Mr. Papineau is playing cannot be mistaken," said Sir John Colborne, a veteran of Waterloo, smelling powder and ready to begin. Monsieur Latigue issued a mandament against revolt. A fierce riot took place in Montreal (November 6, 1837) between the Sons of Liberty and the Constitutional crowd, fighting up and above St. James Street and St. Lawrence Main. Thomas Storrow Brown was one of the injured. This was the Brown from whose peaceful memories of old age we have just quoted. He was one of the fierce young men of 1837, bitter against injustice. "A sense of justice," he wrote in his later memoirs, "that generous inheritance from a British ancestry, urged me on." Meetings and processions were forbidden. Warrants were out for Papineau, Dr. O'Callaghan, and T. S. Brown. Papineau left Montreal. Detachments of the military sent out to make arrests met resistance at St. Denis on the Richelieu. Thirteen rebels were killed and six soldiers. One of the British officers, Lieutenant Weir, was captured by rebels and hacked and shot to death. There came another fight next day (November 24, 1837) at St. Charles against troops better armed. Many rebels were killed, certainly nearly fifty, rumor said a hundred and fifty. Colborne led a column to St. Eustache. The rebels were trapped in the village church, in a scene of hideous slaughter. Dr. Chenier was shot attempting to escape by a window. Among those present was Captain Marryat, the famous veteran of the

Great War at sea who lived it over again in his sea stories. He was on an American tour and joined Colborne. He wrote:

I have been with Sir John Colborne, the Commander in Chief, and have just now returned from an expedition of five days against St. Eustache and Grand Brulé, which has ended in the total discomfiture of the rebels, and I may add, the putting down of the insurrection in both provinces. I little thought when I wrote last that I should have had the bullets whizzing about my ears again so soon. It has been a sad scene of sacrilege, murder, burning, and destroying. All the fights have been in the churches, and they are now burnt to the ground and strewed with the wasted bodies of the insurgents. War is bad enough, but civil war is dreadful. Thank God it is all over. The winter has set in; we have been fighting in deep snow, and crossing rivers with ice thick enough to bear the artillery; we have been always in extremes—at one time our ears and noses frost bitten by the extreme cold, at others amidst the flames of hundreds of houses.

Resistance ended for the time. Wolfred Nelson was captured. Papineau, Dr. O'Callaghan, and "General" Brown escaped. In Montreal there were many arrests including thirty or forty men of later prominence, two of them later on joint prime ministers, Louis H. Lafontaine (the associate of Robert Baldwin) and George Étienne Cartier (the associate of Sir John A. Macdonald).

Durham was all for leniency. He was an autocratic liberal, liberal enough to pardon even rebellion, autocratic enough to exceed his power in doing so. He made a general amnesty, sentenced to death the man he couldn't catch, and banished those already caught. This banished Dr. Wolfred Nelson into freedom. Durham was recalled. Rebellion broke out again in the autumn of 1838, fed by incursions from Vermont—Colborne stamped it fiercely down. At one place (Odelltown, November 9, 1838) fifty rebels were killed. Then came the trials held at Montreal. Twelve patriots were sentenced to death and hanged in successive groups (December 21, 1838, two; January 18, 1839, five; February 15, 1839, five). The last five—by a queer fashion of those rude times when highwaymen made speeches on the gallows—were given the privilege, or, shall we say, the "send-off" of a farewell supper, with aftersupper speeches. The place of execution was an open square in what is the east end of the city over which now passes the structure of the great Jacques Cartier Bridge. It has been christened the Patriot's Square (*Place des Patriotes*). The site of the scaffold is marked by a monument— a huge upright slab of stone which carries the twelve names of the men executed, six on one side, six on the other.

A tall stone column in the Côte des Neiges Cemetery also commemorates the "Patriotes." The historian Kingsford gives a full personal record of each. Six of them, he says, were sentenced not only for rebellion, but deservedly for murder. Even so, there are tears left for the others. Especial sorrow was felt for the young Chevalier de Lorimier who died last, a letter of farewell to his wife and children against his breast.

We may repeat again the words of Fox that rebels often save their country.

The more fortunate rebels had fled, or been banished, into safety. Later on an "Act of Forgetfulness" of 1843, called by the lawyers a "nolle sequi"—a "don't-follow-it-up"—allowed them to come back. Dr. Wolfred Nelson came back to practice his profession in Montreal. He was elected to the Assembly, was twice Mayor of Montreal, a Harbour Commissioner, and a father of the city. With him came T. S. Brown, no longer a general but returning to his hardware business like Cincinnatus to the plow. The return of Papineau, like that of William Lyon Mackenzie, was less fortunate. They found themselves forgiven and for- gotten—out of date as time moved on to other issues. Dr. O'Cal- laghan stayed in New York. Medieval warriors used to enter the cloister; O'Callaghan took to history, the "Documentary His- tory" of New York.

Such was the Rebellion of 1837–39, a sad chronicle, one stage in our slow method of groping toward freedom. After it, when the two Canadas were reunited by the Act of Union of 1840, there was done, on Durham's suggestion, what could have been done before. Canada received responsible government with the new Act, under which a colony could manage its own affairs. The system went round the world and preserved the British Empire. But in Canada it was connected with rejoining French and British Canada, and that was a different matter.

CHAPTER IX

Montreal
Capital of United Canada
1841–1849–1867

Montreal Burns Out Its Parliament. Hard Times.
Movement for Annexation. Public Works and Civic
Celebrations. The Railways. The Victoria Bridge.
Visit of the Prince of Wales. The American Civil
War. Confederation.

IN THE COMMERCIAL SENSE Montreal has been the
capital of Canada from the later period of the old French
Regime until today. Nor is it likely to lose this metropolitan pre-
eminence although it is quite possible that Vancouver may
presently surpass it in population. But in the political sense it
was the capital of Canada, of the United Province of Canada, for
only the brief years from 1843–49. It disgraced and disqualified
itself by burning down its own capital buildings in a riot and
doing its best to stone to death its Governor General, Lord
Elgin. The event had a peculiar historical bearing: it served as a
corroboration of the popular, democratic opinion that had
originated with the Reign of Terror in Paris, that the government (the political capital) should not be exposed to the dangers

of overthrow by a city mob. Hence the idea of a dream capital, all embowered in leaves, small and remote with no one near but shepherds, a notoriously angelic class. The idea wrote itself over the map of the United States; children and foreigners learn with surprise that the state capitals of the United States hardly ever seem where they ought to be; New York is not the capital of New York State, nor Chicago of Illinois, nor are San Francisco and New Orleans capitals, nor even, unkindest of all, Philadelphia, the city in which was signed the Declaration of 1776 that made it, in a sense, the capital of the world. At the same time the list of state capitals includes such names as Pierre, Boise, Cheyenne, and Salem. Some people, ignorant people, would hardly know where they belong. Now at the time when Montreal was burned this theory and practice were in mid-career, but still on trial. The sin of Montreal gave it new life. The four last capitals named above were made so later than 1849.

It is not necessary to explain in this book the details of the changes in Canada which thus made Montreal its capital. After the Rebellion of 1837–38 Lord Durham's Report recommended the union of Lower and Upper Canada into one province with a single capital city. He recommended the adoption of cabinet government, ministers responsible to the elected majority in Parliament. This was a great step, the turning point in the unity and pre-eminence of the British Empire. For this Durham's memory is part of our history. But his other recommendation was not so happy. This new freedom to vote as a majority was also to be used to outvote the French from control of the government. It was as simple as a conjurer's trick, taking a government rabbit out of a French hat. It was so simple that Durham's unhappy phrase, "their vain hopes of nationality," gave it all away. The French Canadians never forgave, have never forgiven, Lord Durham.

In the outcome Durham's plan failed. It was not possible, never has been, to get a large enough united majority of English to outvote the French. The converse happened. The only findable majority was one made up of a bloc of French and a bloc of English, and carrying on a dual government, with double prime ministers like twin stars, and legislation in one section, Canada East turned inside out to fit Canada West. Hence the peculiar double prime ministerships of Baldwin-Lafontaine (1842–49) and the later transient and unstable combinations that carried on in the United Province (1849–64) till they collapsed into a pile of wreckage, out of which was made the wider Confederation of 1867.

All of this is vital historical matter but its full depiction lies on a wider canvas. We are concerned here with the burning of the Parliament Building in Montreal. The new government of the Union was proclaimed at Montreal on February 10, 1841, by the first Governor General of the United Province, formerly Mr. Poullett Thompson but now raised to the peerage as Baron Sydenham of York and Toronto. The name of Montreal was already in the peerage, and still is, in the title of Baron Amherst of Montreal, conferred on General Amherst, the conqueror of Montreal, in 1788. His home in Kent was called Montreal. "On this day (of the proclamation) in Montreal," writes the historian Kingsford, "in the presence of all the dignitaries of the church and of civil life, of the Commander of the forces, of officers commanding regiments, and all who could be collected of the principal citizens, the oath was taken and the two provinces were established as the Province of Canada."

The first Parliament opened, as a temporary arrangement, at Kingston, Montreal sending its first two members there, Mr. Benjamin Holmes and the Hon. George Moffatt, on June 14, 1841. But it was as plain as it was reasonable that Montreal must be made the capital, Quebec being too French and too far east, Toronto too British and too far west. The choice was not finally made till 1843, nor the actual move till a Parliament House was provided in 1844. But immediately after the union the Governor and executive were much in Montreal, the Château de Ramezay was Government House, and a sort of sunshine of official importance broke out over the city, chasing away the retreating clouds of rebellion and repression.

It was precisely in this burst of sunshine that occurred the famous visit of Charles Dickens, himself in a burst of recovered sunshine in having escaped from the liberty of the United States back to the glory of allegiance.

All the world knows the story of his ill-starred visit to the United States in 1842, in the first flush of his phenomenal literary success. The roaring national welcome that he received ended in something not far from expulsion, on his part a glad escape—Dickens, like Mrs. Traill, had no eye to see. In what was the great epic of a nation on the march, of democracy enthroned by civilization claiming the Mississippi Valley, he saw nothing but chattel slavery, chewing tobacco, swamps, ague, and vulgarity. He had no eye for the Mississippi; he thought it mud. He could hear no music in the spring love song of the frogs in its marshes. Over and above all which, he was furious at what he thought the open theft of his books for lack of copyright. He came from the "Far West" into Upper Canada in a passion of loyalty, converted overnight from a young radical to an old Tory.

Hence to Dickens Montreal and all around it looked beautiful. He came down from Toronto and entered Montreal, as he himself said, "in grand style," driven down from Lachine. "Sir Richard Jackson sent his drag four-in-hand, with two other young fellows who are also his aides, and in we came in grand style." The titles roll off Dickens' happy pen: "Sir Richard's drag" . . . "Lord Musgrove wind-bound in his yacht . . . dined with Sir Charles Bagot . . . invited to play in theatricals with the officers of the Coldstream Guards" . . . Who wouldn't be delighted with that, after Sandusky, Ohio?

There followed the famous theatricals (1842) played with huge success in the old Théâtre Royal, to a "paper house" all invited by the Governor. No wonder that Dickens not only in the warmth of his private letters but in the cold print of his *American Notes* is enthusiastic over Montreal and the country round about. . . .

We traveled, he says, *by a stage coach for nearly four hours through a pleasant and well-cultivated country perfectly French in every respect; in the appearance of the cottages; the air, language, and dress of the peasantry; the sign-boards on the shops and taverns; and the Virgin's shrines, and crosses, by the wayside. Nearly every common labourer and boy, though he had no shoes to his feet, wore round his waist a sash of some bright colour; generally red; and the women, who working in the fields and gardens, and doing all kinds of husbandry, wore, one and all, great flat straw hats with most capacious brims. There were Catholic Priests and Sisters of Charity in the village streets; and images of the Saviour at the corners of cross-roads, and in other public places.*

Of the city itself he writes:

Montreal is pleasantly situated on the margin of the St. Lawrence, and is backed by some bold heights, about which there are charming rides and drives. The streets are generally narrow and irregular, as in most French towns of any age; but in the more modern parts of the city they are wide and airy. They display a great variety of very good shops; and both in the town and suburbs there are many excellent private dwellings. The granite quays are remarkable for their beauty, solidity, and extent.

There is a very large Catholic cathedral here, recently erected, with two tall spires, of which one is yet unfinished. In the open space in front of this edifice, stands a solitary, grim-looking, square, brick tower, which has a quaint and remarkable appearance, and which the wise-acres of the place have consequently determined to pull down immediately. The Government House is very superior to that at Kingston, and the town is full of life and bustle. In one of the suburbs is a plank road—not footpath—five or six miles long, and a famous road it is too. All the rides in the vicinity were made doubly interesting by the bursting out of spring, which is here so rapid, that it is but a day's leap from barren winter to the blooming youth of summer.

Dickens leaves also a picture of the arrival of immigrants, contrasting pleasantly with that of Mrs. Traill.

In the spring of the year, vast numbers of emigrants who have newly arrived from England or from Ireland pass between Quebec and Montreal on their way to the backwoods and new settlements of Canada. If it be an entertaining lounge (as I very often found it) to take a morning stroll upon the quay at Montreal, and see them grouped in hundreds on the public wharfs about their chests and boxes, it is matter of deep interest to be their fellow-passenger on one of these steamboats, and mingling with the concourse, see and hear them unobserved.

The vessel in which we returned from Quebec to Montreal was crowded with them, and at night they spread their beds between decks (those who had beds, at least), and slept so close and thick about our cabin door, that the passage to and fro was quite blocked up. They were nearly all English—from Gloucestershire the greater part—and had had a long winter-passage out; but it was wonderful to see how clean the children had been kept, and how untiring in their love and self-denial all the poor parents were.

But such sunshine as there was in the political sense in these opening forties was to prove too bright to last. It was easy enough for Lord Durham to recommend responsible government. It was another matter to know just how to put it into force, especially as between two such ill-assorted partners as Upper and Lower Canada, one British, one French, one nearly all Protestant, one nearly all Roman Catholic, one with seignorial land and one with individual ownership, one demanding municipal government, people's schools, and secular control, the other opposing all of them. In such an environment how much was the royal governor to do and how much not? Can a majority of the elected assembly have anything they cared to ask or only what is good for them? Is the Governor General only a rubber stamp, or does he work the handle? It was hard, in any case, for men hitherto expected to be men of iron to coagulate all at once into rubber. Sydenham died before the problem had quite risen. Sir Charles Bagot gave way and died. Lord Metcalfe refused to give way and died. Canada seemed to kill them as if a spell had come over the place.

After Metcalfe the question of responsible government was overshadowed and lost from sight in the war cloud that rose on

A View of the Water Front During the Intermediate Stage of the Port of New York

the horizon. Boundary disputes helped to keep active the chronic ill will that separated Canada and the United States in this era of rebellions, incursions, of sorrows and angers imported from Ireland, of unrestrained democracy and untaught monarchy. The Ashburton Treaty no sooner settled the Maine-New Brunswick dispute (1842) than the much fiercer conflict over Oregon, in a wide sense, over the control of the Pacific coast, brought war within sight. The little street in Montreal called Cathcart recalls the governorship of Lord Cathcart (1845), one of Wellington's veterans sent out to repel the coming American invasion. Responsible government slept. The danger past and Cathcart gone, it woke again.

Then came Lord Elgin, son-in-law of Lord Durham, to show what Durham had meant. Now it was just at this time that the political combination effected by Robert Baldwin in Canada West and Louis Hippolyte Lafontaine in Canada East made up an Assembly majority that gave them a constitutional right to be prime ministers and to bring in any legislation that they had, as such, any right to bring in. Among other things, they proposed to carry a bill called the Rebellion Losses Bill for paying compensation to anyone whose property had been destroyed or damaged in the rebellion. This meant especially the country property owners of the Richelieu and Montreal district.

The principle of compensation for damages done during the rebellion to the property of innocent and loyal citizens had been accepted on all sides immediately after the troubles. But time did not allow action before the union. After it the parliament awarded, with general consent, a certain compensation in what had been Upper Canada. But the claims in Lower Canada were far greater and more complicated. They hung fire, or rather boiled over a slow fire under the care of a commission. The report of the commission indicating 2276 claimants was followed by the introduction of Lafontaine's Rebellion Losses Bill proposing to expend £100,000 in compensation.

But the joke, or what we call in a pack of cards the joker, was that in Lower Canada many of the property holders were themselves rebels who had only suffered damages because they themselves rebelled and had done some of the damage. Yet as the Act defined a rebel as a person actually convicted as a rebel, and as the vast majority had been let off free, a rebel in actual fact was as likely to get compensation as a man of peace. One can easily see how the blood of the loyal Tories of Canada would boil at the thought of taking money out of their now united treasury to compensate a pack of French traitors who ought to have been hanged.

That was their side. But other blood boiled also.[1] It was notorious that Sir John Colborne had burned and destroyed, had at least let others destroy, beyond all military necessity. Surely the hundreds killed on the Richelieu and at St. Eustache, the fifty that lay dead around Odelltown were enough, and most of all those at the latter place who were shot down—men forced into rebellion, confused, unarmed, kneeling in the snow, their hands raised in prayer. Surely enough, without the furious burning of the barns and log cabins of owners who lay already dead, all debt paid. When we read such a phrase as "Colborne *sternly* stamped out rebellion" we must pause a moment to get the full meaning of "sternly."

Hence the angers, like evil spirits, that fought around the Rebellion Losses Bill in the Parliament of Canada. To the angered Tories it seemed like a fight against enthroned treason. To the "Liberals," the new name that was coming over the "reformers" of prerebellion days, it appeared as a glorious struggle for freedom, not as in this issue alone but as recognized for all time. Lord Elgin took it so.

The Parliament Building stood in what is now Youville Square, off McGill Street. It had been erected as St. Ann's Market but had been remodeled for its higher purpose. It was a plain but imposing two-story building, two main floors and a lesser one above, built of limestone, three hundred and fifty-two feet long and fifty feet broad. At the north end was the hall of the Legislative Council, at the south that of the Assembly; the rest of the space was made up of state chambers, offices, and the library. It

[1]A. Descelles, *The "Patriotes" of 1837.*

had been equipped without stint of money. The parliament mace alone, eight feet long, cost £600. There were portraits of Jacques Cartier, of Queen Victoria, George III and George IV, and lesser dignitaries. To help it burn there were in the library eleven hundred well-dried records and journals of the British House of Commons. As a further temptation, gas pipes, easily reached, ran through the building.

Fierce and angry were the speeches on the debate of the bill. The Tory leader, Sir Allan MacNab, denounced the French Canadians as "aliens and rebels." Hume Blake, M.P. for Toronto whose advancing career foreshadowed the future eminence of his family, speaking with Irish passion, called MacNab a rebel himself. MacNab in return called Blake a liar. Both rushed to fight. The gallery roared with shouts and seethed with hisses. The Sergeant-at-Arms hauled the two angry members into custody.

The bill duly passed its third reading. Lord Elgin, from what he held his duty, determined in spite of protests to give the royal assent. To do this he came from his residence at Monklands to sign the bill on the afternoon of Wednesday, April 25, 1849. As he left the House of Parliament "ironical cheers and shouts" (his own words) greeted him, and his carriage was pelted with missiles.

The town was in a tumult at the news of the assent. Handbills called a mass meeting that evening in the Champ de Mars. From there a riotous crowd descended on the House of Parliament, then sitting in evening session. A storm of sticks and stones broke the windows. The members fled. The mob invaded Assembly Hall, the very speaker's chair. They broke the furniture, the gas globes. Then, with the new devildom of the machine age, they tore out the gas pipes, and in a few moments the building was a sheet of flame, shaken with explosions. Nothing was saved except the portrait of the Queen, taken from its unwieldy frame and carried out by four patriotic men, of whom one was young Sanford Fleming, one of Canada's later "grand old men." The fire brigade let the fire alone. The soldiers, called to the spot, fired at the sky.

The city rocked for days with anger. Elgin, venturing in to reach the Château de Ramezay, was stoned out again. Lafontaine's house was burned. Oddly enough, the roles of the two main political parties were reversed. The Tories were now the rioters, the Rebels the men of order. Mixed with both were the impartial rabble willing to riot at any time. When the storm died down the name of Montreal was as black as the ruin of its Parliament.

As a result of the riots Montreal lost its place as the capital of Canada. A new arrangement was made whereby the capital alternated between Toronto and Quebec, three years in each, paradise alternately lost and regained. This pleased nobody. A new capital was selected (1858) at By-town, a lumber settlement laid out on the Ottawa by the engineer Colonel By, and connecting Montreal with a roundabout access to Lake Ontario by the Rideau Canal. Invading Americans would never find it. Goldwin Smith called it "the lumber village nearest the North Pole." It became the capital, as Ottawa, occupied by Parliament in 1865, and was chosen after Confederation for the dominion capital.

The closing years of the decade of the forties were indeed dark days for Montreal. There were sporadic riots for over a year after the burning of the Parliament. Fires swept the ill-protected city, still crowded with wooden buildings. The fires of 1850 burned out sections of Gabriel (now Ottawa) Street (June 15), destroyed two hundred buildings including St. Stephen's (Anglican Church), and destroyed (August 23) one hundred and fifty houses on Craig and St. Lawrence streets. Still greater fires of 1852 burned twelve hundred houses and left some nine thousand persons homeless. One of these burned out a great block of the old town (St. Peter to St. Francis Xavier —St. Sacrement to St. Paul). It was in this fire that Maisonneuve's house, later used as the first Seminary of St. Sulpice, was burned to its foundations. With difficulty the Hotel Dieu and Notre Dame Church were saved. Thirty great buildings were in flames all at once. The sick were carried out from the hospital by the garrison soldiers and volunteer helpers.

Nor was the fire all. Pestilence took an even larger toll. The crowding of immigrant ships, the lack of sanitation bred outbreaks of ship fever. Many died on shipboard. Hundreds, even thousands, arrived stricken with the disease and of these many never were destined to see anything more of Montreal than the great sheds hastily erected beside Point St. Charles to serve as hospitals. The historian, Sandham, says that six thousand died in 1847 alone. These were immigrants out of Ireland, of the dreadful days of the potato famine, fleeing from starvation in Ireland to find death in Canada. Many were buried in a plot of land near by the hospital sheds. Sandham unconsciously adds a touch of bitter irony to the story of their fate by saying that "As the city was rapidly extending in the direction of this spot," the place of burial would "probably have been lost sight of," except that ten years later workmen on the Victoria Bridge marked it with a great stone.

Even more terrible than ship fever was the bubonic plague, then called Asiatic cholera, which now renewed its ravages. Absent since the epidemics of 1832 and 1834, it reappeared in 1849; in two summer months one thousand one hundred and eighty-six people died of this loathsome disease.

We can hardly wonder that Montreal, with riots, racial anger, poverty, fire, and pestilence, began to seem like a doomed city. A Boston newspaper correspondent of the period wrote,

Montreal wears a dismal aspect; the population during the past few years has decreased some thousands and the removal of Government caused some four thousand more to leave. The streets look deserted . . . every third store seems to want an occupant and empty houses groan for tenants. The blackened walls of the Parliament House present an unseemly appearance and the fate of Sodom and Gomorrah appears to hang over the city. The citizens poke about in the dark.[2]

This, of course, was American journalism of the days of Jefferson Brick as seen by Dickens. The population was *not* decreas-

[2] A. Sandham, *Ville Marie*, 1870.

ing; the fate of Sodom was *not* approaching, and the citizens were *not* in the dark, except when the gas was out of order.

An old adage says: give a dog a bad name and then hang him. It might have added: he will probably hang himself. So it was with Montreal. The political turmoil, the lean years, the crowded, unfed immigrants, the contrast with American material progress, occasioned in these years of the closing forties a strange discouragement, a lack of faith that contrasted with the sturdy optimism of early days. The truth was that the community had now enough to make them want more, were sufficiently well off to be discontented. All that is needed for discontent is a window on the world; so with Montreal. It was rising fast in population, 9000 in 1800, 35,000 in 1837. Railways were reaching out but not yet getting there; opportunity of all sorts opening up but around the corner; a tomorrow that never seemed to come. Hence the sudden impulse that seized upon many of the leading people, descendants, some of them, from the Loyalists, and all stout patriots, the impulse to be done with it all, to commit hari-kari, to join the United States. This brought the famous Annexation Manifesto of 1849 that still disfigures our history, not with the shame of wanting to join the States but for the dullness of either not thinking of it sooner or never.

The Annexation Manifesto recited the hardships that Canada was suffering, spoke of possible remedies, protection to industry, renewal of the bygone British preference, and then proposed "A friendly and peaceful separation from British connection; a Union upon equal terms with the Great North American Confederation of Sovereign States." It sounds staggering; except for the one word "peaceful," it represents the ideal for which the patriots had been hanged eleven years before. Still more staggering is the list of the three hundred and twenty-five names attached, names widely representing the class that was ranked as best in the Montreal of the day, many families still with us. The names are such that it is kinder not even to whisper them. Why breathe on a mirror of reputation or rile the waters of benefaction? The curious many will find the principal names in Dr. Atherton's monumental and impartial book.

The Annexation Movement came to nothing. History has long since smoothed the grounds, explained it all away. "The outburst of a movement of petulance," said Sir John Abbott (Prime Minister, 1891–92), speaking in 1889 to the Canadian Senate. Abbott had himself signed the Manifesto. Boys will be boys.

The movement in a sense came to nothing; but in another sense it came to a lot. It stimulated the British government and Lord Elgin to readjust relations with the States by the famous Reciprocity Treaty of 1854, after which Canada blossomed like a rose and Montreal was as busy as a beehive. But in reality the basis was all three. The half-finished transport, the half-built structures only called for completion. A railroad gives no return till the trains run. A bridge, even a Victoria Bridge, connects nothing until a Prince of Wales drives the last silver rivet at its center. In reality Montreal was having its darkest hour just before the dawn.

One pauses to gather together the economic factors that contributed to the forward movement of Montreal that presently ensued. We may take, as a sort of text, the recital of the following odd circumstance. In 1855 William Dawson, the newly arrived principal of McGill,[3] was dispatched by the Governors, already proud of him, to spend his vacation at Toronto, the seat of government and the source of benefaction. The Grand Trunk Railway still lacked a year of completion. River steamers were laid off for the winter. Dawson started out in a canoe, the only way to cross the broken ice and water of the St. Lawrence River. A train took him to St. Johns, and from there by land, water, train, and sleigh he went to Albany, Niagara, Hamilton, and Toronto. The journey took five days. A year later trains ran daily to Toronto and Chicago and, four years after that, thundered over the Victoria Tubular Bridge bound for the Eastern Townships Portland, Boston, and New York.

This development was all based on the rise of the Port of Montreal under the influence of the steam tug, the river steamer, the ocean sailing steamer, and the ocean liner. The movement was already started in the year of depression just described. The

[3] C. Macmillan, *McGill and Its Story, 1821–1921*, 1921.

Harbour Commissioners were authorized in 1850 to raise money to deepen the river channel. Commerce already justified the expense. In that season two hundred and twenty-two vessels came in from overseas, a total tonnage of forty-six thousand. Immigrants were arriving in Montreal at the rate of about thirty thousand a year. Hitherto the immigrants had been almost entirely settlers in transit going up to the farms and towns of Upper Canada. But after 1850 a great many stayed in Montreal. The building of the Grand Trunk Railway, now going on under the control of British contractors, brought, as it did everywhere, a flock of Irish "Navvies," meaning originally and as a joke "Navigators," fellows who travel. The Irish built the first railways in England, in France, and even in India, where Asiatic labor ate less but loafed more. With these and other Irish and British settlers came our "Griffintown," the nickname given to the area west of McGill Street, between the new railway and the new canal. This wretched area, whose tumbled, shabby houses mock at the wealth of Montreal, was the first of our industrial "slums," the gift of the machine age to replace the bush farm of the settler. It was and remained mainly Irish, a new breaking of the solid French area of Montreal. Others followed. The railway shops and works and the building of the great bridge made Point St. Charles. Factory industries began in Montreal on a real scale after 1850 with the factories rendered possible by the creation of rail and canal transport side by side. There came the rapid settlement of the riverbank beyond Point St. Charles, where used to run, still runs in part, the famous old Lachine Road, along the waterside. This made Verdun a separate town, now a separate city, crowded and almost metropolitan now with sixty thousand people, but still open ground at the time of which we speak. Yet between the buildings, the huge "plants" that outclass the factory as the factory once outclassed the shop and that border the Lachine Canal, and the close-built area of Verdun, and such, beside the river, there still lies an unoccupied space, along the line of the new aqueduct wide and open yet so screened on both sides by bush never cleared that the road through it is lonely to the verge of uncanniness. Montreal Island

and its environs have many of those strangely isolated and lonely spots—the islands that divide the Lachine Rapids (Heron and Goat Island) and the north end of Isle Perrot where till a year or so back the express trains for Toronto and Chicago plunged through two miles of tangled bush, unchanged since the days of the Iroquois.

The port, we say, fed the industrial development. Tonnage increased each year; it reached fifty-eight thousand tons in 1851, a great total as compared with the ten thousand tons twenty years before, not so great as beside the nine million of 1938–39. Now begin the transatlantic steamers, ships combining sail and steam, which ran for the next forty years and which, almost till the end of the century, were the outstanding feature of the port. First to come was the *Geneva*, a boat built of iron, seven hundred tons and one hundred and sixty horsepower, and arriving in 1853. The same year saw the arrival of the *Lady Eglington* and the *Sarah Sands* (twelve hundred tons). With these boats began steamship mails. They took from two to three weeks to come out from Liverpool, but with the prevailing westerly winds were two days better in going home.

The Crimean War broke up traffic for the season of 1855, the steamships being commandeered as transports, but after it ocean steamers moved ahead with the formation of the Montreal Ocean Steamship Company, for which Hugh Allan acted as agent in making a contract for a fortnightly mail service from Montreal to Liverpool. The service almost at once (1858) became weekly, and the company after 1860 became the "H. and A. Allan Co.," whose Allan Line passenger freight and mail became the outstanding name in the annals of Montreal known all over the world. All in all the Allan Line covered nearly a century, for it began in the sailing-ship day when Captain Alexander Allan sailed his brig from Glasgow to Quebec. The captain and his five sons followed up the trade. They built and owned ships, some of them clippers trading into Quebec. Hugh Allan sailed as a boy from the Clyde to enter a ship agent's office in Montreal that became the scene of his life and achievement. His brother Andrew joined him. They were first agents, then owners. The first mail steamers (those named above) had, like Molson's first *Accommodation*, too little power. The Allans boldly offered to put on ships with three hundred and fifty horsepower, to make (as they succeeded in making) the passage out from Liverpool in thirteen days and back in eleven.

The years that followed are a record of maritime progress like the rush of steam itself. The Allans saw that the days of wood were over and so they built in iron. They installed more and more power. Larger and faster was the word of the day. The *Anglo-Saxon* made the Quebec–Liverpool voyage in nine days. There were twenty vessels in the Allan Fleet in 1861. Success in those days reaped a huge reward when the freight on wheat was thirty cents a bushel, the days being still unknown when standardized competition and mechanized transport were to cut it to four or five cents, or even less, or even the vanishing point, grain going practically as ballast. If the profits were great so were the risks. The lighting and buoying of the river, the training of pilots, all such things were in their infancy. There were terrible disasters on the route, eight great ships wrecked in eight years (1857–64). Nor were the losses only on ocean traffic. Appalling disasters happened when steam was new. The explosion of a boiler on a Montreal–Longueuil ferry (1856) killed thirty-five people, scalded and injured many others. Even worse was the tragedy of the river steamer *Montreal* that caught fire in the St. Lawrence when carrying five hundred Scottish immigrants bound from Quebec to Montreal. The boat grounded in an attempt to reach the shore; flames swept its wooden structures. There was a panic rush that swamped the boats. The scene of horror that ensued was saved from its full effect by the bravery of the crew of another steamer which brought boats alongside of the burning vessel and rescued many of the passengers and crew. It is not known how many lives were lost. Many had leaped into the water. It is thought that two hundred and fifty perished. Fifteen charred bodies, twelve of them children, gathered from the wreck were brought to Montreal for burial. They lie in two graves in the cemetery on Mount Royal.

Such was the price of progress, new dangers for old, as later with the navigation of the air. Yet navigation went on apace. The deepening of the river showed sixteen and a half feet in 1854, eighteen in 1857. The government of the province of Canada took over the dredging of the river in 1860; by the time it handed it over to the new government of the Dominion in 1867 the channel was twenty feet deep. In the last year of the old province (1866) five hundred and sixteen ocean vessels entered the Port of Montreal, their total tonnage 205,775, an average of nearly four hundred tons.

With the development of steam transport by water, parallel to it but a little behind it, went the development of railways. Water routes by lake and river were so widespread throughout Canada that, but for the Canadian winter, the railway might have waited as long as it did in New Zealand for Auckland to be joined to Wellington, or in seagirt Australia where the railways to a great extent are waiting still. But in Canada winter held the trump card. Even at that railways came slowly. There was a lapse of twenty years between the scene of 1836 described in the previous chapter and when the Champlain and St. Lawrence was opened at the opening of the Montreal–Toronto (Grand Trunk) in 1856. Railways, as in the United States, were built in bits and later joined into trunk lines. The first road was followed by the Atlantic and St. Lawrence, chartered in 1845, which nibbled its way, Longueuil to Richmond, in 1851. Later, as part of the Grand Trunk (1860), it connected Montreal to Portland. The Grand Trunk itself was chartered in 1852, building in sections toward Chicago on the west and Rivière du Loup on the east. It connected Montreal with Brockville in 1855, with Toronto in 1856. Its special meaning to the town lay in its extensive yards at Point St. Charles. It established railway building shops and there constructed as its masterpiece the Royal Train, including a locomotive with a funnel shaped exactly like a funnel, which carried the Prince of Wales during his visit of 1860.

Along this path of alternative stagnation and progress, of difficulty and achievement, moved Montreal in the days of the province of Canada.

Peculiar features of the life of the city at this stage of its growth were the recurrent "civic jubilifications," held to mark each happy milestone of progress. For this the city was now the proper size (35,000 in 1839, 57,000 in 1852, 91,000 in 1861), big enough and not too big, for public rejoicing by all the people, for everybody to be happy over everything all at once. Such good fortune belongs only to the past. The people are too many today. Nothing short of a royal visit or an armistice can lift them all up together. The opening of a new fire hall lights up only the firemen; waterworks leave brewers cold and the public dry; a new wing added to a college fails to enthuse the stock exchange; a motor show is nothing to the ski club. But in the 1850s everybody was willing to be glad over everything, or at least to stop work, to drink its health, and follow in a torchlight procession. Paid amusement no doubt has also helped to displace these simpler rejoicings.

They had begun even in the bad times of the riots and fires and cholera. Montreal celebrated the London (Crystal Palace) Exhibition of 1851 by having a local exhibition of things going to the London Exhibition. "Immense throngs," we are told, "visited the city during the week in which it was held." "A regatta on the river . . . A dinner given by the Mayor and corporation, at which," says the chronicle, "some excellent speeches were made . . ." Why not, indeed, since the history of Hochelaga began with Indian oratory? There was a great ball in which eight hundred "joined in the gay scene" and a torchlight procession under the management of the fire brigade. The brigade, as just shown, knew all about torches. The celebration ended with fireworks on the island wharf. But such an occasion was as nothing to what was done when good times began to join forces with glad hearts.

The same year witnessed the celebration of the St. Lawrence and Atlantic Railway mentioned above, with a "grand procession, ball and dinner and triumphal arches." The decorations were hardly faded when there came the celebration of the Grand Trunk Portland Railway (in 1853); the dinner and demonstration for the arrival in port of the *Geneva* (as above); the celebration of the laying of Pier No. 1 of Victoria Bridge; the exhibition for five days (1855) of exhibits going to the Paris Exhibition, with "an immense number of strangers thronging the city," with the Governor General, Sir Edmund Head, as the guest of the city; grand civic reception to French Commander De Belvège whose French ship of war was the first at Montreal since the conquest. But all this rejoicing sounds faint as beside the terrific reception accorded to the officers and men of the Thirty-ninth Regiment, Crimean veterans arriving in Montreal at the close of the war. Two special steamers brought them from Quebec, the guests of Montreal. "The citizens thronged the quays, parapet walls, the windows and roofs of the stores" . . . "The Montreal Artillery" . . . "roar of cannon" . . . "Cheer upon cheer" . . . "Address by the Mayor and corporation" . . . "a great procession" . . . "Banquet at the city concert hall" (Bonsecours Market Building still there) . . . all free . . . "One thousand two hundred guests," all the regiment, the volunteers, Mayor, city council, and a flow of oratory that would have made Donnaconda seem silent.

"Continued excitement," says the chronicle. Hardly was it over when there came the opening of the new McGill Buildings (Arts), the old Burnside Buildings having been burned down with or without the fire brigade in 1856. Right after that came the opening of the new waterworks with water thrown a hundred and ten feet high against the Notre Dame Church (October 10). Still breathless from that, the citizens rallied to the big celebration, November 12 and 13, 1856, of the opening of the Grand Trunk (Toronto–Montreal) Railway, which beat them all. Three thousand sterling was subscribed for "a procession, a banquet, an excursion and a ball." As the day approached, says the record, "It was evident that the city was going to be a bumper" (a Victorian word now almost forgotten, meaning a huge drink) . . . "Immense trains of cars . . . crowds of strangers . . . the streets like Cheapside . . . a huge procession . . . a great banquet on the railway ground at Point St. Charles . . ." "The crowd was immense" . . . "Four thousand present" . . . "A sea of heads" . . . Speeches by the Governor

General and other Indians, a torchlight procession, and that was only the first day . . . Next day a military review at Logan's Farm, but why go further? Incidentally, it may be explained that Logan's Farm was one of the most easterly and one of the largest of the great farms that lay above the city as marked on the map of 1856. A part of it is now the Parc Lafontaine. At this period it was the chosen ground for military reviews.

From such fabric can we build up the past life of our city as no document or statistics can show it, and with it, the great change in the outlook of human life and fortune in the century, almost a century that separates us from it.

We can realize that when the Prince of Wales arrived in the city in 1860 the city was all ready for him. A main feature of his visit was to be the official opening of the new Victoria Bridge. The project and enterprise of a bridge over the St. Lawrence was initiated by the Hon. John Young, a member of the Hincks cabinet (1854) and a Harbour Commissioner of Montreal, 1853–76. "Through his foresight," so his monument of 1908 on the water front bears witness, "Montreal has become the national port of Canada." A long, hard fight was needed to carry the idea of throwing a bridge over a mile and a half of water, with a flood level twenty-five feet above its normal surface, and a torrent of ice and snow bearing down on it every spring with all the flood of water gathered from Lake Superior and hurled at it by Lachine. The thing seemed madness, but in the end it was done.

The Victoria Tubular Bridge, tubular no longer since 1898, was one of the triumphs of the world's engineering at a time when engineering was young. It was a first great lesson in that "ice engineering" which has become, under such men as Howard Barnes of McGill, one of the great specialized achievements of practical science.

Engineering in 1850 was limited, structural steel in its infancy. It was not possible to pass across the stream with the huge strides, the towering height, and vast steel structures of the stupendous Jacques Cartier Harbour Bridge of 1930, two miles downstream. Nor was it possible to span the river by a suspension bridge thrown across from cliff to cliff, as at Niagara, a kite first, with a string, the string pulling a wire, and then more till the gathering wires swung like cobwebs in the sky. In this instance there were no cliffs to suspend from. In any case the distance is too great. Even with present materials suspension ends, the engineers say, at about seven thousand feet.

So the bridge had to get across the river, pier by pier. The problem was how to set the piers to resist the ice. It was at first proposed by the engineers to make the piers of cribs so big, so solid, so close together, and so heavy and so foursquare that nothing could budge them. The irresistible force was to meet an immovable object. Local wisdom knew better. Immovable objects won't do for ice. The bigger the crib, the harder the shove. Ice, like all the forces of nature, cannot be conquered; it must be led aside, fooled into doing something else. Such is the wind, glancing off a windmill, and the water "escaping" as it throbs through a Niagara turbine, or the radio wave, off into eternal space forever, but fooled into imitating a human voice in leaving. So with the ice. Each pier of the bridge on its upstream side thrusts out against the current a long stone foot, a cutwater, that is ninety-two feet long at its base with a cutting edge of smooth stone. Against this the ice may rip and tear, hurling itself sheet upon sheet, piling up only to fall again, but powerless, once thus divided to exercise its power of expansion by which it overthrows anything that shuts it in. Along the abutments of the bridge, two hundred and ninety feet on each side as first built, and chiefly on the St. Lambert side, the south side, which catches the full swing of the river, the ice smashes and piles thirty feet high. Let it pile. There's lots of room in the air.

Such is the Victoria Bridge. As first constructed, it carried above its piers a great iron tube, or, rather, a series of twenty-five tubes fitted together to make one. These tubes were made of wrought iron, boiler plate, one quarter to three quarters of an inch thick.They were not round but rectangular, sixteen feet wide, and in height they began at each side of the river at eighteen feet, six inches, each tube coupled about the last one with a rise of six inches, making the center twenty-two feet high. Inside the tube ran a single track for a train. The tube had

windows, its sides covered with boards, and over it a board and
tin roof with a footwalk (not for the public) along the flattened
peak. From the summer water level to the bottom side of the
tube the distance was sixty feet. The purpose of the tube was
to protect the track against the accumulating snow and ice of a
Canadian winter. This was an engineering error in oversafety,
corrected later. . . . But the main feature of the engineering
plan, the piers against the ice, succeeded.

Thus was built the Victoria Bridge crossing a mile and a half
of water, and with its abutments 9,184 feet long. Hon. John
Young supplied the driving power. The great railway engineer
Robert Stephenson designed the structure; with him was A. M.
Ross. The famous London contractors, Jackson, Peto, Brassey,
and Betts, built it, with James Hodges as builder in charge. The
first stone was turned in 1857. Three thousand men were working on it in 1858. The first passenger train passed over on
December 17, 1859. The bridge cost $7,000,000. The Grand
Trunk Railway paid the bill and owned the bridge. It remained
for the Prince of Wales to declare it open.

The young Prince Albert Edward, released from the over-
control and overeducation of his German father and his everlasting German tutor, was now having a good time on his own,
visiting Canada and the United States. He was at a time of life,
and lived in a time of history, when it was still fun to be a
prince—a poor trade now. Albert Edward was prepared to attend
everything, open anything, shut anything, dedicate anything,
review soldiers all day and pretty girls all evening, pray and be
prayed at, dine for two hours and dance it off in eight. His
visit of 1860 was as happy as that of his grandson the Prince of
Wales of 1919.

There is no need to recount in detail all that was done by the
Prince of Wales and for the Prince's entertainment on his visit
of 1860. As soon as the merchants learned of the coming visit
they decided to build a Crystal Palace, commenced forthwith
on Peel Street in the open fields above St. Catherine.

The Prince spent his first day in Montreal, a prisoner on shipboard in a deluge of rain. Next day Sir John Rose's house (later

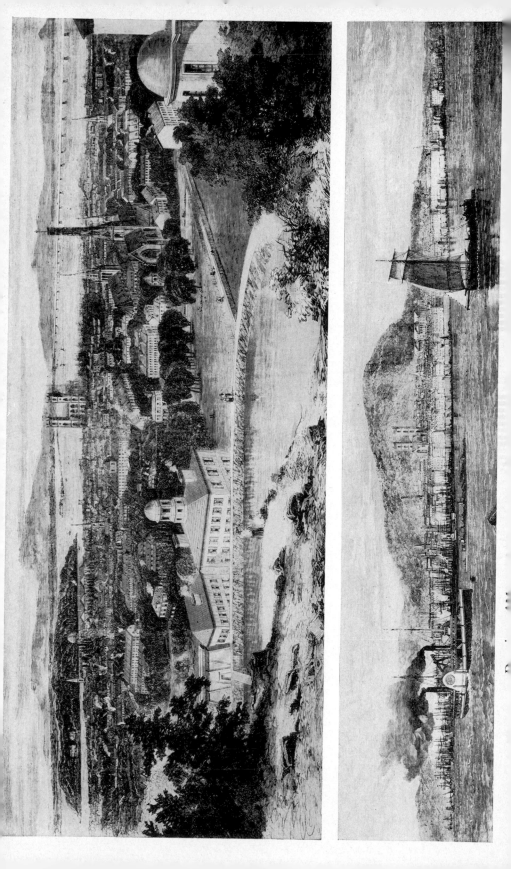

the Ogilvie family's house) was placed at his disposal during his visit. The Prince began his good works on Saturday, August 25, 1860. He opened the Crystal Palace; he then opened the Victoria Bridge; on crossing it, received from the Grand Trunk Railway a gold medal; attended a monster civic lunch; rode in procession; witnessed fireworks in the harbor in the evening. On Sunday he attended the new Christ Church Cathedral; gave it a Bible; listened to a cantata of four hundred voices in which sang, unknown, Marie Lajeunesse, a girl of fifteen, the later Madame Albani. That week there followed a great ball in the Crystal Palace, a review on Logan's Farm, a torchlight procession with the inevitable firemen, a People's Ball in the Crystal Palace—and the Prince off for Ottawa.

A memento of his visit is the Prince of Wales Terrace on Sherbrooke Street, then and long afterward the last word in genteel residence, now leaving much to be said. Another is the rechristening of Victoria Square, previously Commissioners Square and commonly called the Haymarket. The stimulus of the visit helped no doubt to create the Art Association, born in that year.

The Prince's happy visit came just in time, for the sunshine was soon to be eclipsed. The outbreak of the American Civil War brought in the autumn of 1861 the unhappy "Trent Affair" —the seizure by a U.S. ship of two Confederate envoys taken out of a British Royal Mail Steamer. War seemed certain. There was just time before winter, with steam navigation, to pour heavy reinforcements into Montreal. The barracks overflowed. Stores newly built where the Hotel Dieu had stood, and the old college buildings of the lower town were improvised as soldiers' quarters. The streets were loud with the bagpipes and the fife and drum and gay with the scarlet coats and tossing plumes that were the uniform of the day. The young men of the city drilled in the closing evenings in companies of volunteers, eager to learn and ready to fight. To the old people going out with the ebb tide, it seemed as if the tide was turned back fifty years, to the Montreal of 1812, the soldiers in the streets, and the Battle of Châteauguay.

Wiser counsels prevailed. Much was owed to Queen Victoria's husband. The Prince Consort was soon to die. In the full career of his active life an advancing shadow fell across his path and in that darkening light he saw more clearly than those in angry quarrel in the sunshine. Much also was due to Abraham Lincoln, who had left his Springfield home never to see it again and who had already had the first of those prophetic visions which made him henceforth like a man who walks alone with God. To such wisdom do we owe it that England and America were not torn asunder. We can see now what would have been the meaning of such a disaster.

So the diplomatists, as we now say, "found a formula," that is, a way of admitting that both sides are right. War was averted. The bagpipes of the defenders of Canada turned from a pibroch to a Highland reel, the drum and fife to a polka, and as the winter waxed and waned the Montreal garrison remembered the girls and were merry. Then came the spring and the river opened, calling the reinforcements away. The hospitable town staged a "Crystal Palace public entertainment"—not a banquet over in one day, but a feed in relays, fifteen hundred soldiers at a time, day after day till all had eaten. There was "nothing to drink," in the soldierly sense of drinking, for a new shadow was falling on old-time gaiety. But in return the soldiers ate a ton and a half of sandwiches, a ton and a half of cake, two and a half tons of tarts, topped off with fifty barrels of fruit. Then the bagpipes wailed farewell and the ships dropped down the river.

Yet a large garrison stayed, from then until Confederation and long after. For the Civil War brought new dangers. Southern refugees and Southerners organized to raid Vermont, kept apprehension alive. But in spite of the anxieties of the Civil War years Montreal was a lively city. There was lots of money. Southern refugees, British contractors, garrison officers spent it like water. A lot of it changed hands in the old St. Lawrence Hall, the fine old hostelry that had now arisen on St. James Street, still going strong at the turn of the twentieth century, lingering on as a coffeehouse on Craig Street when built out of

existence on St. James Street, and with still many a regret for its
memory. As elsewhere in the British Empire, "society" favored
the South; the plain people, doing enough hard work to understand chattel slavery, favored the North.

Later on the issues got mixed when the close of the war
brought the Fenian Raids across the border. They were easily
repelled by the garrison and volunteers of Montreal but remained
as a bitter and unhappy episode of our Canadian history, fortunately no part of the story of this book.

Yet the Civil War turned aside hard times from Canada. The
conflict in the States, with the open frontier of the reciprocity
treaty, brought markets such as never were. There were bread
and work for all now, and for the adventurous a three-hundred-
dollar bounty to be had by stepping across the line into a blue
coat. Five hundred and fifty-two new houses were built in Montreal in 1862, and in 1863 a record building of 736 houses. The
next year went beyond that again with 1019 houses, while
the Civil War years are marked also with the building of Trinity
Church on the Place Viger, the Church of Gesu (Bleury Street),
the American Presbyterian and Knox Church on Dorchester.
With these evidences of spiritual faith went also the tangible
evidence of temporal welfare expressed in the building of the
Molsons Bank on St. James Street.

The overseas tonnage entering the port in 1866 was 205,775
tons, of which 69,000 tons represented steam vessels, the latter
of course still carrying sails. The shipping was nearly all, about
96 per cent, British.

One pauses a moment before letting the curtain fall on the
Montreal of the province of Canada henceforth (1867) to rise
on the metropolis of the Dominion. How greatly it has changed
in the hundred years since the conquest. The fortifications are
all gone. In their place appear the masts and yards of the close-
packed ships of the harbor. Hardly any of the large spaces, the
open gardens, are left—little but the open space that once was
the Jesuits, the garden of the Château de Ramezay, the garden
secluded from sight behind the Séminaire. Large sections, blocks
of the city, have been burned out and rebuilt. Stone stores and

shops and country houses replace cloisters and the churches. The greatest difference of all perhaps is that what were the "faubourgs" of the old French town, the "suburbs" of the early English days, are now grown as to be part of the town itself. Craig Street and St. Lawrence Main and the side streets off them are all built up; beside them to the west the open space that became the Haymarket is now Victoria Square.

St. Ann's suburb has turned into Griffintown, an ill-built crowded area, rendered still more wretched by the great spring floods, which at times, as notably in 1857 and 1861, laid it under water.

Not the most conspicuous but the most subtle of the changes is that from romance to finance, from church to counting house, that marks the rise of commercial Montreal. Maisonneuve still stands guard over the parish church of Notre Dame, holding the Place d'Armes against the Iroquois, but the Bank of Montreal watches over them both. The streets of the Saints are now the addresses of the stockbrokers whose opportunity to live arose out of the organization of share companies and whose growing transactions enabled them to organize as an exchange in 1863. Thus as romance has flown out of the door finance has come in at the window. With romance has fled also in great measure religion, or at least its earthly tabernacles. The churches are moved, as they always aspire to do, upward. The labors of the Montreal Fire Brigade have assisted at the change; Christ Church, burned in 1856, has gone to St. Catherine Street. St. Stephen's was burned out in 1850. Still left are the parish church of Notre Dame and the earliest of all, the Bonsecours Church beside the river. The Virgin on the roof of the latter still watches over sailors, but her intercession is supplemented by the hydrographic charts of Trinity House and the navigation marks of the government of the province of Canada.

The banks had begun early in this century with the Bank of Montreal, at first a partnership body which dates its business existence from 1817 and its corporate life from 1822. It was followed by the short-lived Bank of Canada, incorporated in the same year, and in 1836 by the Bank of British North America, operating under British charter in all the provinces. The Molsons dates from 1855; the Merchants from 1861.

Most notable to the casual visitor is the change in the currency from the old pounds, shillings, and pence to the dollars and cents, a change necessitated by the growing trade across the border. Here began the quaint method of reckoning foreign exchange between Montreal and London which lasted till the Great War. From now on a bank teller had beside him, hung on a nail, a little table which showed him that 9½ was par, at which resting place a hundred pounds' sterling was worth $4.86⅔ in Canadian money. No teller ever knew why 9½ was par. The secret was closely kept. It really meant that if you added 9½ per cent to the old-gold value of the American dollar, viz., $4.40 equal to one sovereign, then you got the new value of the American dollar after the coinage alteration of 1834 had taken some of the gold out of it, viz., $4.86⅔ cents equal to one sovereign. The table form ran up and down the full swing possible for the exchange pendulum with a gold standard and free shipment. But why the table did not give $4.86⅔ as par is a secret carried by the bankers of the 1850s to their graves— and then on. In 1914 the Great War moved exchange clean out of the table (£1=$6.00) and it never came back to it.

We know, of course, and need not ask, what they did in Montreal when the British North America Act was duly passed, and it was known that the Dominion would be proclaimed on the first of July 1867.

"Early in the month of June the attention of the citizens was called to a public meeting"—we can guess it—"to be held for the purpose of considering the most appropriate measure in which to celebrate the inauguration of the New Dominion."

The reader can easily reconstruct the rest, "city decorated with flags," "Sunrise heralded by the roar of cannon," "a grand review of regulars and volunteers on Logan's Farm" . . . "fireworks" ($1,000 worth) on the mountain side . . .

And in the echo of the cannon and the reverberation of the speeches, Montreal passed into the Dominion.

CHAPTER X

Montreal
Seaport of the New Dominion

*Montreal in the Wider Life of Canada. Its In-
creasing Commercial Predominance. The Red River
Rebellion. Fenian Raiders from Vermont. Montreal
and Home Rule. Hard Times and Public Charities.
National Policy, Manufactures, and Industrial
Montreal. Growth of the Port. Sail and Steam.
The Allan Liners. The Timber Rafts. The Flood
of 1886. The Ice Palaces. End of the Century.*

A S THE ST. LAWRENCE RIVER moves toward the sea,
the current slackens as it goes. The river has become so
wide and deep that its movement is hardly felt although its volume
is far greater than that of the waters foaming at Lachine. So it is
with the history of Montreal, indeed to some degree with the
history of any city as it grows from early settlement to metropolitan life. Its history merges more and more into the wider
history of the nation; for Montreal into the wider field of the
growth of the Dominion of Canada. The panorama of events

after the Confederation of 1867—the acquisition of the Northwest, the Red River Rebellion, the extension of Canada by a Pacific Railway to the Pacific Ocean, the settlement of the Northwest, the Rebellion of 1885, the rise of great manufactures, the growth of wealth, the warning episode of war in South Africa, the era of bounding prosperity that opened the century and fell into fragments with the first World War—all of this is not Montreal, but Canada. Yet Montreal shared in each phase of it, gathering out of it the central metropolitan position which it grew to occupy.

The general effect of the great changes that followed the Confederation of the Dominion was to shift Montreal to what is somewhat pedantically called a new "orientation." In its commercial life it expands from a merely provincial status to take on a continental character. As the successive additions of new territory and provinces, the Northwest (1869), the province of Manitoba (1870), British Columbia (1871), and Prince Edward Island (1873), carry the Dominion from sea to sea, Montreal is carried with it as the center of finance and commerce for all. We can realize this change when we reflect on the limited meaning of the name Canada before 1867. To the Maritime Provinces, to the Northwest, and to British Columbia, it meant an entirely separate area from their own, a community of a different aspect with whom they had little in common and little sympathy. The older people in the Maritimes thus used the term "Canada" for a full generation after Confederation.

But in proportion as Canada grew to mean a national area with interests in common Montreal rose to be the chief city of the Dominion, quite distinct from any of the others. Halifax retained a peculiar aspect in its imperial character as an outpost of defense, keeping its British naval establishment till 1903, in other words for a generation after the inland imperial garrisons had left in 1870 and 1871. Victoria with the naval Esquimalt alongside of it kept something of the same character. A little later the ready-made seaport of Vancouver (1885) began its existence as a Pacific and national port. Quebec, as the sailing ship and the timber trade passed away, sank more and more into a purely

historic position on the map of Canada, exalted or at least animated by whatever new life grew from its position as the provincial capital, and from the fact that it remained a French-speaking
city. But from the new Canada of the plains and the Pacific
coast, Quebec was quite unknown, was little more than a city
in a schoolbook. All the inland towns of necessity carried and
still carry a provincial aspect. Even Toronto was in many ways
little more than the endless multiplication of a town. Ottawa,
tamely accepting the social control of the province of Ontario
over its manners and morals, was the most provincial of the lot.
It was merely a place in Ontario where outsiders came.

But Montreal under the influence of Confederation rose to
a metropolitan position all its own, giving it in the general policy
of the Dominion an extraordinary, if not an overgreat, influence.
Although technically Montreal had no other representation at
Ottawa than three elected members of the House of Commons,
raised in 1896 to five (now standing at sixteen for Montreal
Island), there soon grew up a very direct and active connection
between Montreal and the government, the Cabinet, of Canada.
It is true that there is nothing of this in the law, written or un-
written, of the Dominion. For the rest of Canada, the great size
of the country and its varied areas and interests dictate, for its
form of cabinet, a "sectionalism" not known in Great Britain.
All the sections, both the races, both chief religions, and cross
combinations of each, must be fitted into the peculiar mosaic
of a Dominion cabinet. The system has been denounced ever
since Mr. Christopher Dunkin's famous denunciation of Confederation itself, as mere sectionalism, but no other working
system has yet been found. Granted the appointment of all the
members of a Canadian cabinet except one, Mr. Sherlock Holmes
could tell Watson at once that the remaining member must, let
us say, come from Quebec province, from the British part of it
called the "Eastern Townships," must be an Irish Roman Catholic, have a strong sense of humor, and, if possible, a wooden leg.
If Watson demurred to the wooden leg, Holmes would answer,
"Veteran of the Great War, Watson, veteran of the Great
War."

But the representation of Montreal in the Ottawa cabinet contrives itself without contrivance. The size and wealth of the city naturally offer a choice of leading men, native sons of the city, such as the prime minister Sir John Abbott. Moreover, people seldom grow poor in Canadian politics—with conspicuous and honorable exceptions—and rich and successful politicians float into the city on the tide of their success. We may add to this the fact that Montreal contains a large share of the great industrial leaders and financiers, representing the tariff interest, the export interest, and the shipping and transportation interest all the way from Great Britain to Japan and Australia. Hence the danger is not of representing Montreal too little, but too much: hence the accusation from various radical and agricultural quarters of the control of Canada by a clique of Montreal politicians and Montreal businessmen, the kind now christened "interests" lumped together under the fatal term "St. James Street."

This idea of Montreal dominance, no matter how true or false, undoubtedly aggravates the economic dislocation of western from eastern Canada, which nature itself creates and policy fails to alleviate. Prejudice replaces reason. Many, perhaps most, western farmers would prefer to spend, even to waste, any quantity of money on railroads in the west owned by the government, than on a railway, no matter how efficient, paying dividends from Montreal to shareholders in St. James Street, Wall Street, and Lombard Street. This is not adduced as what the farmers ought to think but what they do think.

Montreal, as said, had its full share of interest and participation, here more, there less, in the events which made the national history of Canada in the later period of the outgoing century. Very close was its interest in the renewed danger of Fenian invasion which appeared in the opening years of Confederation. The Fenian movement, as it affected Canada, was organized across the border by Irish Americans and friends of Ireland who proposed to show their affection for Ireland by taking it out on Canada—a process quite logical to the Irish mind. Fenianism from first to last met with no sympathy in Montreal, nor in

British North America at large. Even in Great Britain it was little more than criminality, or at best the counsel of desperation of men embittered by long tyranny, by unrequited wrongs, and by the coercion of armed force. Something may be said for the "Manchester Martyrs" of 1867, nothing at all for Fenian raiders into Canada. The seal of public condemnation on Fenianism had already been set in Montreal by the great public funeral that moved in solemn procession on its downtown streets in honor of Thomas D'Arcy McGee, first member for Montreal West in the new Canadian Parliament, a former Irish patriot, assassinated in Ottawa (April 7, 1868) as an act of vengeance against such treachery to Ireland as serving the Queen in Canada. The photographs taken at the time of the event show the streets a vast flood of crowded and silent humanity through which moved the tall black catafalque that bore the dead.

Yet the repulse of the previous border raids of 1866 did not deter the Fenians from planning a new enterprise for 1870, this time to be based on a raid into the Eastern Townships which would sever the connections with Montreal to Portland, Boston, and New York. The invasion was organized under a self-appointed "General" O'Neil, whose followers differed from the ordinary rabble of malcontents in that they were dangerous men in the military sense, many of them trained to arms in the American Civil War. Information of the approaching raid was received in advance from the British Legation at Washington. Montreal was at once filled with indignation at the proposed invasion of Canadian soil and with military ardor to repel it. The city was turned to a tumult of excitement and parade, the days of Châteauguay come back again. Fortunately there were still imperial troops in Montreal, awaiting the final departure of the garrison. Among these were the regiment (seven hundred strong) of the Prince Consort's Own Rifles, in which served, as a new arrival in Montreal (August 1869), the young and popular Prince Arthur of Connaught, much lionized by society and by the fair sex and representing royalty at the opening of rinks, schools, and art exhibitions. Forty-five years later Montreal recalls the Prince, changed to be the "old Duke," but military and erect as ever, inspecting troops on the McGill Campus as Governor General during the Great War.[1]

To the Prince's regiment were joined other troops of cavalry and infantry and a large body of volunteers recruited for the occasion in Montreal. The assembled forces, Prince and all, moved toward the frontier. But the Fenians had had enough of it before it began. After a brief and bloodless clash at Cook's Corners they made off across the border and Fenianism came to an end in Canada. The decorated veterans of the raid, as proud of their exploit as Waterloo pensioners, were with us in Montreal, it seemed, till yesterday.

For Fenianism Montreal had no sympathy but for the Irish cause, in the better sense, very much, both then and always. It was just at this moment in history that the underground criminal movement of Fenianism was altered into the open and aboveboard movement of Home Rule, which began with the annual academic motions of Mr. Isaac Butt and presently grew into the organized crusade of Charles Stewart Parnell and his associates. This, as a constitutional movement, claiming rights similar to those enjoyed everywhere by British and Americans, drew sympathy from all over the world. Especially it drew from the Dominion of Canada whose status it proposed to imitate and to adopt; most of all in Montreal where a large percentage of the British people were Irish by race, and practically all the people, French, Scotch, and everything, sympathetic to the "cause of Ireland" as long as consistent with British sovereignty and free from methods of criminality and despair. Not so Toronto, which exhibited always the defects of its own merits, the reverse of its medal of loyalty, by containing an element more loyal than the Queen, more Orange than William III, and more Protestant than the Archbishop of Canterbury.

Hence the pro-Ireland attitude of Montreal in a world (1870–1914) still so little troubled by wars and tyrants of its own that the disputes of landlords and tenants in Ulster and Tipperary could echo around the globe; hence the St. Patrick's Day parades which through two generations have been a feature of the city

[1] Ob. 1941.

life of Montreal. For these each year, by the courtesy and custom of the town, everyone turns Irishman and wears green. St. George, St. Andrew, and St. David feast alone; St. Patrick invites all Montreal, the saint's great church on Dorchester Street the center of the faith. This custom of annual honor to St. Patrick is in part a consequence of the peculiar Montreal climate. St. Patrick's seventeenth of March falls just right to encourage those false hopes of an early spring which find new life each year—the bright sun, the streets all adrip and aglisten with a March thaw, the snow partly gone (in reality shoveled away), the talk of old-timers of having seen dust blowing in the streets of Montreal on St. Patrick's Day—all this lends color and character. A day or two later a March blizzard buries the city in snow again, but St. Patrick has had his day.

Hence one can understand the wide sympathy and support given to the Home Rule movement in Montreal from its inception to its eclipse in the Great War. St. Patrick's Society of Montreal, dating from 1834, as an all-Irish society, with the Irish Protestant Benevolent Society branching from it in 1856, took Irish Home Rule under its especial tutelage, telegraphing its congratulations to Mr. Gladstone on the Bill of 1893 and inviting Irish-American orators to Montreal. The older generation can still recall such large and enthusiastic Home Rule meetings as the one held to meet Mr. John Redmond early in this century. Home Rule has gone. Eire reigns where Erin wept. St. Patrick's Day in Montreal drifts into the veiled shadow of the future.

Less concerned was Montreal, and French Canada at large, with what was really a far more momentous episode for the Dominion than the abortive Fenian raids—the transfer of the Northwest Territory to Canada and the rising which ensued in Assiniboia, in and around Fort Garry. As far as French Canada knew or cared about the "Red River" troubles, sympathy was all with the métis or French half-breeds who had risen at Fort Garry in armed protest under Louis Riel against what they understood to be the loss of their customary rights, their peculiar system of land tenure, threatened by the new surveys, and the supposed danger to their language and religion. Ignorance and neglect alone created the trouble. Canada had no intention of destroying rights and disturbing language and religion. The Manitoba Act of 1870 presently made this clear. The rising itself, after a winter of rebel rule, 1869–70, still under the Crown, at Fort Garry, faded away and dispersed on the approach of an expeditionary force under Colonel Wolseley and under the promise of amnesty and redress. But meantime Louis Riel had clouded the issue by his brutal murder at Fort Garry of Thomas Scott, an Orangeman of Ontario. This deed threw Ontario, especially its Orange element, into a fury of anger; hence by reaction it helped to line up the French Canadians on the side of the rebel métis, who were, after all, their own kinsmen. With the collapse of the rebellion the fires of anger died down but left the ashes ready to fan to flame in Montreal with the Northwest Rebellion of fifteen years later.

Meantime Montreal was only directly concerned with the Red River troubles of 1870 to the extent that a battalion of 362 volunteers from the province of Quebec shared in the expedition. But of these only seventy-seven were French Canadians. The Imperial Royal Artillery and Riflemen who served in the expedition left Canada on their return east in 1871—the last of the garrisons.

As the decade of the seventies drew on, hard times fell like a moving shadow across Canada, and where they fell economic life wilted at the root. Confederation, it seemed, had failed. The obliteration of American trade when reciprocity ran out and the Civil War purchases stopped came like paralysis on the Maritimes. Ships swung idle at their anchors; grass grew in the streets. The root crops rotted, worthless, in the field. For the newly created Ontario the collapse of grain prices in Great Britain spelled ruin to a community dependent on export sale—the weak limb, then and always, of our Canadian structure. Mortgages fell like snowflakes, alike on the finished homesteads with brick houses created by a generation of work and of late enriched by the Crimean War and on the bush farms, the half-made clearings, with the new frame houses standing half finished and abandoned, the snow drifting into the doorways. In French Canada the habitant suffered least, snug in his self-sufficient holding, as old as Frontenac.

Montreal suffered most. The collapse of outside trade and inside business left the city stranded, crowded with workless people and tradeless shops. Its factories were as yet too limited to keep it going. Railway building had been checked, its first era over. The collapse of business brought down two banks, the Mechanics and the Jacques Cartier, in 1875. Population had risen by 1870 to over one hundred thousand but the increase only meant more people with nothing to do and nowhere to go. Immigrants still crowded in looking for work among the workless. In the first year of Confederation thirteen thousand immigrants came to Canada; in 1871 there were twenty-three thousand; in 1873 fifty thousand. There was then no dole, no public relief, nor any legal right to it. The poor were still God's children. There were institutions of charity and many of them, for after all Montreal was itself a work of piety, founded as the Mission of Ville Marie. Even the earliest foundations were still there. There was the Hotel Dieu of 1642, originally giving aid to all in distress, moved since 1861 from its original location in the old town to occupy its present site on Pine Avenue, but limited now to the medical sphere alone. There were still the Grey Nuns of Madame Youville, though no longer housed in the "Old Grey Nunnery" on McGill Street that arose out of the General Hospital of Charron beside the Little River. They occupied then, as now, the Grey Nunnery on Dorchester Street.

In addition to these earlier institutions was also at the time of which we speak the Montreal Ladies' Benevolent Society, a Protestant organization, which had arisen (1841) out of the suffering of the cholera years and had found that suffering did not end with cholera. Its care was for aged women and destitute children. There were the Sisters of Providence (Roman Catholic) founded by Madame Gaulin in Montreal in 1828, a charity that took the form of houses of refuge for the destitute old age and for orphaned infancy. These houses spread wide, in Montreal at first, then over North America. With them were the Asile de Montréal, an institution that arose also out of a cholera year, 1832, its work being the shelter of Roman Catholic children left orphans. Of similar origin and work was the St. Patrick's Orphanage, a product of the Irish immigration. It had built St. Bridget's Refuge on Lagauchetière Street, where Lord Dufferin came as a visitor in 1873. Its present home is on St. Catherine Road, Outremont. The Harvey Institute (Protestant), first offering a shelter to those ill of ship fever (1847), undertook presently general relief and education of the children of the poor. At this time it was just moving (1875) from a humble house on St. Antoine Street to better premises on Mountain Street. Later on (1908) it moved out to the purer atmosphere of Westmount. An offshoot of the Institute, the Protestant Infants' Home, had just been founded in 1870.

These good works were supplemented by the Protestant House of Industry that arose out of a private bequest of houses and buildings on St. Mary Street in 1808 and was even longer in its cradle than McGill University, and perhaps for the same reason, since it did not get into organization until 1863. The St. Vincent de Paul Society had begun work in Montreal as early as 1848.

It is to be noted that the best-known and the most widespread of our present institutions only began after the destitution and suffering of the period here discussed. Indeed they largely arose out of it, for it was this new industrial poverty, the outcome of machine industry itself, this failure of bread and work for all in the very heart of nature's bounty, that first quickened the public realization that poverty was not a crime, that self-help is helpless for those idle in the market place, and that it is not enough to assign to the poor as their portion the kingdom of heaven. They can't wait. The earlier Victorian creed, bred in the complacency of British commercial success, began to seem hard and brutal—the creed that assigned poverty to the workhouse, left low wages to the survival of the fittest, and left the workless man to sleep on a bench, the child to die in the slums. Tears of pity that arose from earlier springs, from older soils, began to fall anew on the stones of this new pavement.

For look how limited in its scope in the Montreal of the 1870s and in other cities was the public relief of distress. Here were homes for the orphan children of the fatherless with no thought of keeping the father alive. Here were shelters where destitute men might sleep, but none where they might wake; public soup kitchens like those that appeared in Montreal in 1873, where a free meal would stand off starvation, for a day, with no further thought of tomorrow. And as the final stage in life's cavalcade of poverty, homes where indigent old age might ponder as it faded out on what had made it so.

It was this sense of insufficiency which presently brought to Montreal, to the world, the wider work of the Salvation Army, of the Charity Organization Society, the Victorian Nurses, and such other institutions and efforts. They stand halfway between the old grudging charity, that gave with a sob and spoiled the gift with a reprimand, and the new legislative code that began a generation later to take over all social relief of poverty, illness, and idleness as a function of the state itself. Such things (belonging to the Australasia of 1890 and the Great Britain of 1910) were still a long way from the thought of Montreal of 1875. Further on still from all of them is the new world dawning, or dying as it dawns; we cannot yet tell which.

The oncoming of the hard times had brought down the government (of Sir John A. Macdonald and Sir George Étienne Cartier) in 1873. Its fall is commonly associated with the Pacific Scandal that arose out of Sir John A. Macdonald accepting money gifts for the party purse from one of the rival companies bidding for the Pacific Railway charter. The offending company belonged in Montreal, and its wickedness dropped another blot on the map of St. James Street. But it is a little hard for elementary students to see the difference between this subscription to party funds and those later gifts that ranked as patriotism itself and earned knighthoods, except that they were larger. But the inquiry does not concern us here. In any case the government was falling. The impossibility of fulfilling its pledges in hard times made its fall inevitable. The Pacific Scandal was just the last push given to Humpty Dumpty. In place of Sir John ruled Alexander Mackenzie (1873–79).

The new Liberal Government adopted as its policy of what to do the grand old Liberal policy of doing nothing. This was to be combined with rigid economy, absolute honesty, and unflagging industry. All these things proved out of date. Industry must flag if want of opportunity flags it, and mere honesty and economy by themselves, with nothing else, are as useful as half a pair of scissors. The government dragged on. They knew that things would come right in the end: all things do; death sees to it. They waited for the hard times to blow over; they did, but they blew the government over first.

The change to the vigorous National (Tariff) Policy of 1878, the creation of the Canadian Pacific Railway Company,[2] the opening of the West, the Manitoba Boom, the revival of the European market—these things quickened the life of Montreal and cleared the sky as does the autumn wind off the Laurentians.

There is no doubt that Sir John A. Macdonald's policy of tariff protection in industry (1879), since maintained by all Canadian administrations, however sinful in the eyes of the Cobdenites and whatever the burden it placed on the farmer, served as a great stimulus to the manufacturing cities and especially to Montreal. It is true that Montreal had made a certain start in manufacture without it, indeed even before the moderate protection granted by the old province of Canada in 1859. Sugar refining had been established as far back as 1854. The American Civil War stimulated all and every kind of manufacturing possible at the day. But the plants did not yet exist for metal work, iron, and steel on any large scale, nor for any great extension of the rudimentary textile industry. The cotton industry began in a small mill in Hochelaga in 1874, but after the adoption of National Policy it grew with every year, a number of mills joining into an amalgamated company.

The manufacture of bridgework and structural steel at Montreal begins with the opening of the twentieth century. The opening of the Canadian Pacific brought the Angus railway shops. At the same time the manufacture of tobacco was expanded into a leading industry. With the next decade appeared

[2] J. Murray Gibbon, *Steel of Empire*.

the manufacture of electrical apparatus. The manufacture of railway cars, rolling stocks, steam engines, leather, cement, and a large variety of minor goods converted the Montreal of the closing century from a purely maritime aspect to its later appearance as a great manufacturing center attached to a seaport. There is no need in the present record to recapitulate other than in general terms the facts and figures expressed with greater feeling and detail in the statistics of the Dominion government.

Indeed a new town arose as an addition to the old one. What had been the flatlands and meadows and broken, straggling woods, along the valley of the Little River, the ground which had offered the natural terrain for the Lachine Canal, now with each succeeding decade reared its clumsy factories and shabby plants, its lifting cranes and iron runways, obliterating and disfiguring nature but offering a new beauty to the eye of the shareholder. Nor were they presently without a beauty, or at least an imposing majesty of their own, such as Brangwyn has loved to convey—red-litten windows all aglow at night, long streamers of lurid smoke and flame pouring into the darkness, or even in the daylight, the beating of the hammer, the whistles of the boats in the canal, and the peculiar attraction that goes with things in a straight line, the rectilinear canal, the power wires straight as perspective itself, the long rows of casks piled high and all of a piece, acres of boxes neat as a garden—the new symmetry of arrangement which necessity imposes on engineering, converting man's latest efforts back to nature's oldest forms. Such is the new Montreal that sprang up in these later decades of the nineteenth century between the city and Lachine, duplicated presently by the downstream manufacturers below the original port.

Thus strangely has changed the character of Montreal—a mission, a fort of the fur trade in the wilderness, a French colonial military town, a British port of trade, a Canadian metropolis of shipping and manufacture with arts and letters on the hill behind it.

Most notable and visible, of course, was the development, the progress, of the harbor and Port of Montreal. It is true that the

port and its facilities and equipment as now existing are the
product of the present century. But under the first generations
of operations by the Dominion after 1867 it moved a long way
forward from the "granite quays" of Charles Dickens' visit, and
even from the day when the Prince of Wales opened the Victoria Bridge.

The port and with it the care of the ship channel and the
navigation guides of the river below and above it now passed
under the care and enjoyed the aid of the government of the
Dominion of Canada. It remained under the administration of
a body of Harbour Commissioners appointed by the government, an arrangement which lasted until 1935, when the control
of the Montreal Harbour, along with those of other Canadian
seaports, was given over to a centralized body at Ottawa. To
the Commissioners was added, some years later, a Harbour Corporation (1894) in which were vested the port area, docks, and
properties.

At the time of Confederation the ship channel down the river
had been dredged from its original eleven feet in the shallow
stretches to a depth of twenty feet; constant dredging guaranteed a deeper and deeper channel, rendered necessary by the
increasing draft of the steamships of the period. By 1882 the
depth was twenty-five feet; by 1887 it was twenty-seven and
one half. The docks themselves were as constantly improved as
the channel. The wharfage of Montreal in 1870 already covered
three miles (it is now ten). Most of these were low-level wharves
that have disappeared today in favor of the high-level piers of
the present harbor, a change that began just at the end of the
century. The Victoria Pier stands in the harbor plan of 1877 the
same as today.

The greatest evidence of the progress of the port is the increase of its tonnage from the 205,000 tons of 1866 to the
1,000,000 tons of 1892 and its reach beyond 1,500,000 at the
close of the century. (It stood in 1938 at 9,000,000 tons.) Pro-
gressive changes came over the character of the shipping with
the change from sail to steam, from smaller ships to large. The
tonnage of 205,000 in 1866 represented 516 overseas ships, an

average of about 400 tons. The 735 ships that totaled 1,036,000 in 1892 show an average of 1400 tons, and the 868 overseas ships totaling 1,584,000 in 1898 give an average of over 1800 tons.

For years after Confederation sail predominated over steam along the water front in the ocean shipping at Montreal, as distinguished from the steamers of the trade of the upper river and the Great Lakes. Thomas S. Brown, the retired "rebel" general of 1837, mentioned earlier, speaks in his old-age memoirs of the crowd of sail in the harbor of 1872. There were "20 ships, 22 barques, 3 brigs, 4 brigantines and schooners," in all forty-nine vessels under sail. Sailors will recognize the types as corresponding to the old pictures of the harbor: the brig two-masted and square-rigged; the brigantine with a fore-and-aft sail on the mainmast; the barque, a three-master with a fore-and-aft on the mizzen. But what the pictures, seemingly authentic, show as "old-time schooners" at anchor in the lower harbor do not correspond to the true fore-and-aft schooner of the New England coast, having three masts with only the mizzenmast rigged fore and aft. But the point is one of interest only to sailors, mostly dead. The ocean ships under sail, however, greatly exceeded in the Port of Montreal of the seventies the ships under steam. The sailing vessels named above are set against twenty-one ocean steamers.

But indeed, in a sense, all the ocean vessels in and out of Montreal, with steam or without, were still sailing vessels and remained so till the end of the century. For those were the days of the old-time passenger liners, such as those of the famous Allan Line, driven principally by steam, but carrying also in a fair breeze a great press of sail on three tall masts that retained all the old-time glory of the sea. Such good old ships, the *Sarmatian,* the *Sardinian,* the *Polynesian* (otherwise the *Rolling Polly* and later the unrolling *Laurentian*), and the last and latest queen of the river under sail, the *Parisian,* back and forward on the Liverpool voyage, carry a wealth of memory as a chronicle of the times. Their outcoming voyages filled with the new settlers from Britain, the "quality" dining in the saloon, the quantity

The *Sarmatian*, Which Carried the Writer of This Book in 1876 as a Child of Six on His Way to Canada. The Picture from the Allan Line Records Is Supplied by the Courtesy of the Canadian Pacific Railway Company.

feeding in the steerage, are a part of our British history. Some people think that all the fast duchesses and windless empresses ever built cannot remake the romance of the St. Lawrence voyage as it was.

For in those old days of the Allan Line the Atlantic voyage, Liverpool to Montreal, in the seventies and the eighties had a far different, far deeper meaning than what the voyage had come to signify fifty years later. The Atlantic service, even in the years just before the Great War, had become an Atlantic ferry —fast, efficient, luxurious for those who could pay for luxuries, comfortable for all. Most of the people traveling had crossed the ocean before, many of them several times. All expected to cross the ocean again. There was nothing left of the farewells to England of the departing emigrant, no falling tears as the green shores of Ireland, soft with rain and dotted with the sunlight on the yellow gorse, faded out of sight.

In the days of which we speak it was far otherwise. Most of the outcoming people on the Allan liner had never crossed before, hardly expected to cross again, were saying "good-by" in a sense lost in our present world of radio and aerial flight. The writer of this book can recall such a voyage, of 1876, coming out as a child of six, in the Allan liner *Sarmatian* (built in 1871), a grand ship with a tower of canvas on its square yards— a ship, the real thing, its masts reaching upward in a network of ropes and rigging, men calling from aloft, a great brass notice on the mizzenmast: "Do not speak to the Man at the Wheel"—and the speechless and unspeakable helmsman there in sight, his hands on the wheel, his eye on the compass and the clouds. The Liverpool–Montreal boats of those days lay at anchor in the Mersey. There was no floating dock. The people came on board in a tender, and when all was ready the word was given and the anchor hauled up from a capstan by the crew, with the passengers and even the children tailed on to the capstan ropes. All sang—it was the custom of the line,

> "*Cheer, boys, cheer, no more of idle sorrow,*
> *Courage, true hearts, will bear us on our way*"—

a song that ended with the assertion that the *"Star of the Empire glitters in the West."* As beside such a ship, clearing the Irish Channel in a steady breeze under a cloud of sail, the sun on the canvas, the wind in the rigging, a great liner of today is just a floating apartment house to play cards in.

Thus went out the British people, singing, into exile, with hope ahead and behind them a memory of home that time could not obliterate, nor adversity tarnish, nor even fortune lull into forgetfulness. It is strange that we do not learn that the greatest British asset is the British people, the chief import of the Dominion, more and ever more of them; empty-handed, it doesn't matter; empty hands made Canada.

To be exact, the *Sarmatian* was a vessel of four thousand tons, with a single screw and large single funnel and three masts. Her lines resembled the beauty of a clipper ship, with the clean run of a single deck, the boats swung on davits at the side, with nothing of those superstructures which later on rose on the decks of the liners when masts and sails disappeared. She was square-rigged but carried also as the lowest course of sail on each mast a large fore-and-aft sail, the "cro' jack" of nautical parlance, used either in place of the mainsail or in addition to it. The mizzenmast carried no square yards. She had no bowsprit but carried headsails before the foremast and thus could present, if need be, a great press of canvas to a favoring wind. Under steam she easily made fourteen knots. "The *Sarmatian*," said the London *Graphic* of 1878, "is one of the finest passenger vessels in the world." She had served as a troopship in the Ashanti War of 1873–74, carrying the Black Watch to West Africa. In 1878 she had the honor of carrying the Marquis of Lorne (the Governor General) and the Princess Louise to Canada. She was in and out of the Port of Montreal till the opening of the present century.

As tonnage increased, it was found that mast, sails, and rigging were just dead weight, nor likely to be of any use once the Gulf of St. Lawrence was passed. As steam power increased with the larger-sized boats it was plain that sails were not worth-while.

Each new queen of the river surpassed the last in size and luxury but with less and less sail. The *Parisian* of 1881, reconstructed in 1897, the last word of the day as a "floating palace," practically abandoned her sails. The later boats, of the opening years of this century, such as the *Tunisian* and the much larger *Victorian* and the *Virginian*, carried no sail at all. The masts shrunk to derricks or returned, as ghosts, to carry wireless.

If we shed tears over the departed glory of the sailing steamer, we may spare a few also for its contemporary, vanished also, the St. Lawrence timber raft. This, too, arriving in sections down the Lachine Rapids and remade at leisure above or below the harbor, was a familiar feature of the Port of Montreal for two generations and more.

Nor was there ever a more unique feature of Montreal Harbour and the St. Lawrence above it than the bygone timber rafts that played so picturesque a part in our Canadian commerce of last century. They are all gone now. The last of the rafts came down the river and over the Lachine Rapids to Montreal in 1911. The movement of lumber and pulpwood is still a vast trade; but sawn lumber and pulp sticks travel much like other freight or cargo. Anyone who ever saw a raft of square timber a quarter of a mile long floating down the St. Lawrence was looking at one of the strangest sights in the history of navigation.

The basis of the industry was the vast forests of red and white pine found all over the St. Lawrence watershed. Pine not only floats but floats so buoyantly that it can help to support the hardwoods, elm, oak, etc., which float either not at all or with difficulty. The ultimate market was in England, where square timber was the raw material of all the carpentry and building trade. With this went to the same market the beautiful straight sticks of pine of special length and a quality that were used for the masts of sailing ships and specially culled and selected for the Royal Navy. The seaport of the trade was Quebec, where a fleet of timber ships gathered every year. These were an odd assemblage. Any old ship would do to carry square timber; leak as it would, it couldn't sink. Hence we are told that the harbor of

Quebec, when sail was on the decline the world over, "was filled with the queerest collection of shipping, old barques and brigantines, ships 'swifted' with chains passed round their hulls to hold them together, full-rigged ships that perhaps had once been East Indiamen, even the occasional old man-of-war, much degraded and disguised, turned into a sort of cart-horse of the sea."

Montreal had only the lesser share in this glory. It was only a midway point of the trade where the rafts, after coming down the Lachine Rapids in sections, were reassembled for their final journey to Quebec. Indeed Montreal helped in the end to kill the trade when the lumber ship, after about 1880, filled with sawn lumber that came to Montreal by rail, replaced the timber ship of Quebec. Nor did Montreal have any share in the square-timber trade that came from the Ottawa and passed down behind Montreal Island by the Rivière des Prairies and the Mille Isles. The Ottawa system was different. Small "cribs" of lumber passed the rapids in specially constructed chutes, the last in 1908.

For both the Ottawa and the St. Lawrence the trade came to an end when British lumber merchants were at last persuaded to buy their lumber already cut. Squaring timber in the bush wasted one third of it. The British buyer would take no stick unless sound to the heart. Hence many trees were felled and left unused. Vast quantities of what are now slabs, edgings, battens, strips, and moldings, went up in flames in the Canadian forests. So the timber raft ultimately went the way of such picturesque, non-economic things as the stagecoach, and the sedan chair.

But the timber raft while it lasted was curious and unique. And it lasted a long time. It had its infant origins in the old French Regime, was boosted by the Napoleonic Wars, reached its height between 1850 and 1880, declined and died in 1911 a painless death in the arms of newer industries.

The timber industry was evidently well established at the time of Charles Dickens' visit to Canada in 1842 for he writes of seeing a huge timber raft on his steamer trip from Toronto to Montreal. "Going on deck after breakfast," he writes, "I was amazed to see floating down with the stream, a most gigantic raft, with some thirty or forty wooden houses upon it, and at least as many flag-masts, so that it looked like a nautical street. I saw many of these rafts afterwards, but never one so large. All the timber, or 'lumber,' as it is called in America, which is brought down the St. Lawrence, is floated down in this manner."

Indeed the origins of the industry go a long way back before Dickens' time. French settlers cut and floated pine logs, for masts or lumber, to any near-by market. It was a help-to-live industry like the pulpwood of the back-north settler of today. After the conquest the British turned this into a regular trade and then, about 1800, into a sea-borne trade (masts and square timber). Napoleon, when his decrees shut the Baltic, made himself the godfather of the Canadian timber trade. The steam tug arrived in time to be its wet nurse. The preferential duties till 1843 acted as its guardian. After that the raft was grown up and floated on its own, a quarter of a mile long, did we say?—let us make it half —down Lake St. Louis in the mists of the morning.

The lumber—chiefly pine with elm and oak—was first cut round the shores of Lake Ontario and gathered behind booms in river mouths and bays. As the pine was cleared the cutting moved further back; the lumber shanty crawled north away from civilization like the movement of the American frontier toward the West. At first Lake Ontario had the whole trade; the logs were unable to negotiate Niagara.[3] The Welland Canal opened Lake Erie, and then on and on—that is, backward and backward—moved the timber trade. The logs gathered in Lake Ontario were at first floated as rafts; the lake proved too big, too rough. Hence as the trade was organized they were sent in timber schooners to the foot of the lake among the islands near Kingston. Here special timber firms who had no necessary connection with cutting the lumber or shipping it beyond Quebec made it up into rafts and ran it down.

A St. Lawrence raft was built in six or eight sections called "drams." To make a dram they built first a frame of hewn timbers (6" × 7" square), a parallelogram, an oblong floating in the water, the logs just over forty feet long end to end and pinned together. The oblong was about 60 feet wide and was con-

[3]A. M. Lower, *The Trade in Square Timber*, 1933.

nected crosswise with "traverses" (crossties about four inches in diameter). When the frame was set floating logs were pushed under it (by men standing on them), the logs all being set side by side to fill the frame. They were bound to the traverse not with chains or ropes but with "withes," sapling trees pounded, as it were, into shredded cable and with a wonderful power of yielding to strain without breaking. The logs thus pushed under were the first tier. They had to be pine to make the upper tiers float. Above them, laid crosswise, was a second tier and, if the raft was all pine, a third tier lengthwise; if there was oak in it the third tier was perhaps not filled up, or only in part.

A completed pine dram averaged 600 pieces, or 25,000 cubic feet, or 300,000 board feet of lumber. A raft of eight drams would mean 2,400,000 board feet.

When the raft was complete a cabin was built on the leading dram, the foreman's cabin with two bunks, a table, a stove, to serve the office for supplies, etc.; on the dram behind this was a bigger cabin with bunks for the men (about eight bunks). The whole regular crew was eight or ten with extra men taken on for each big rapid and dropped off at the foot of it.

Poles were set up to act as masts for big square sails. A mass of "kit" also was carried along and brought back upriver from Quebec again—anchors, windlass, cables, pike poles, cant hooks, oars, crowbars, lanterns—an endless list. A raft carried a big boat (fifteen men) and a smaller one.

When all the drams were pinned together the raft was ready to start. Mr. D. D. Calvin, whose family were connected with the trade for generations, has given us a picture of a raft "leaving port" that has much of the charm of an old-time sea story. "Given a fine summer day—in retrospect a raft inevitably left on a fine afternoon—it will be understood that the last hours of preparation were a delight to youngsters. The ordered confusion of getting all the gear aboard, the half-guessed secrets of the boxes and bags of grub, the characteristic scents of clean pine timber in the sun, of the raw wood of the cabins, of the fresh straw of the mattresses, combine to make a delightful memory, in which the sounds are the shouts in French, the signal gong in the towing steamer's engine room and the wash from her paddle wheels as she backed to stop along side the raft."[4]

The description is that of the closing days, of a towing steamer hauling the raft all the way. Such a journey took the raft from Kingston to Montreal, barring heavy bad winds or other delays, in three days. But in early days there was no motive power but the sails and the current. It took weeks to get to Quebec. The river current on a still day would give a "speed" of three miles an hour, the broad flood of Lake St. Francis or Lake St. Louis scarcely any. From the earliest days to the last passengers took trips on the St. Lawrence rafts for the sheer strangeness of it, to loaf and read and dream. Many of us even now might dream of such a passage, floating on a windless summer day on Lake St. Francis, reading, let us say, Egyptian history.

But when the rapids came, the loaf and the dream were suspended. The first rapids come below Prescott. The rafts went down the Galop Rapids and the Rapide Plat (Morrisburg) all in one piece, heaving and lifting and quivering to the swells. But just above the Long Sault (Aultsville) the raft was stopped; a special crew of about fifty men came on board; the raft was disjointed into its six drams, and away they floated in the fast water, faster and faster, the crew strung out in a row across each end, with every man at a long oar, ready to row *sideways*— a sight to make the Royal Navy laugh. But they could do it. As the dram splashed and heaved, pounding even a rapid white, they could just swing the raft enough to make the difference between stranding and going clear, till down she floated into the quiet water below. Off got the special crew, on went the raft, past Cornwall and down Lake St. Francis with a new crew for the Coteau Rapids, then on down Lake St. Louis. They came to the final descent in the maelstrom of Lachine. The raft was stopped well above, broken into drams, and away they went down the foam, too late now for salvation if anything went wrong. They took it all. Canoes used to take to the sides of the rapids. Steamers pick the channels; but the timber-raft drams took the whole rapid. At the foot of it the drams floated into

[4] D. D. Calvin, *In a Quiet Corner*, 1941.

the La Prairie basin, to be remade there, or go through Montreal Harbour and be remade below. From Montreal to Quebec the raft went in peace.

Anyone who has looked at a picture of the Montreal Harbour of earlier days, anywhere from 1830 to 1880, will notice that the artist has put into it what seems to be the tragic spectacle of a few unhappy survivors on a small but very heavy raft, the kind people die on in the Indian Ocean, with some kind of canvas or wood shelter rudely erected on it and their few poor belongings lying beside them. What makes the picture all the more harrowing is the apparent utter disregard of their distress on the part of the officers and crew (for there must be such) on board the huge frigates and various other craft in the harbor. What we are looking at here is the artist's symbolic imagination of a timber raft.

Photography came to the world just in time.

But in justice to the artist of such drawings we have to say that he may be trying to depict a "firewood" raft such as used to be brought down to Montreal Harbour by farmers from Châteauguay and such places immediately upstream. These, however, were not square timber, but logs waiting to be cut up into cordwood, commonly sold at $2.00 a cord. They used to be anchored alongside the shore. Unhappily such pictures seem to depict something which is neither the one thing nor the other and is wrong either way.

Midway in this period came to the Port of Montreal the record flood of 1886 which helped its progress along, as a swift kick accelerates movement. The flood, that is to say, helped to initiate the subsequent bold and comprehensive effort that led presently to what seems the final conquest of the St. Lawrence.

The rise and fall of water in a tidal harbor is a thing that can be measured, predicted, and circumvented from day to day, from tide to tide. But the spring flood of a great river, a Mississippi or a St. Lawrence, which carries down the waters liberated from the winter's ice, is another matter. It no sooner makes a record than it breaks it with a new one. Flooding waters had always been a feature and a factor in the development of Montreal, the more so because of the ill-adjusted nature of the river-bank. It no sooner rises to an all-the-year dry altitude (Notre Dame Street) than it falls off again (to Craig Street) far below the spring level and sideways to what was once the sunken bed of the Little River. Floodtime has been part of its history. Champlain with his peculiar prophetic vision tried out the prospect of flood by setting up a sample piece of wall in the plan of his Place Royale to see what the river would do. He was not there the following season to see what it did, but we can guess. Near this spot was Maisonneuve's first cemetery, grimly desecrated each spring by the river. All the land in that area (now at the foot of McGill Street and along the Harbour Front) has been raised since. In the Old Regime the town moved up to high ground, its skirts withdrawn from the water. But the spring flood washed round it and below it. When the British town spread later on into Griffintown on lower ground the waters followed it.

It is quite impossible for steamship visitors to Montreal, looking down from the heights of the deck and the dock on the river far below, to realize the extent to which the spring flood of the St. Lawrence, just before navigation begins, can lift the water of the river. When they see, inside the railway tracks that run along the docks, the sturdy revetment wall of solid stone they can hardly realize that this wall, rising above docks, tracks, and all, is intended to keep out the St. Lawrence.

Yet the river flood takes us back to the earliest history and down to the latest.

The unhappy settlement of Griffintown, as said, built on lowland for the working class, who must take what they can get, was subject to annual high water that in seasons turned to submergence under a flood. The flood of 1857 saw the lower stones of the houses flooded, the people coming and going as best they could in boats.

The spring flood of 1861 was long remembered. The river, with appalling suddenness, invaded the city in the evening of Sunday, April 14; so fast it rose that it poured into the churches of the lower town. St. Stephens in Dalhousie Street and the Methodist Church, Ottawa Street, extinguished all lights and left the congregations marooned in the dark with six feet of water over the pews. Boats rescued some. Others "roosted" all night. Bitter cold set in, and in the days following there came a fierce blizzard. Traffic was impossible. The new Grand Trunk Railway was all flooded out as far as Lachine. One quarter of Montreal was under water. Boats carried the people from the islands that had been the wharves and buildings on the water front and landed them up on St. Paul Street. Other boats carried them to Beaver Hall Hill to get to the upper suburbs. Such was the ferocity of the river, nature's protest against man's contrivance.

Then came the great flood of 1886, destined to hold the record, a steady-rising inundation that put the water five feet deep over the feeble wooden wall, the revetment wall of the river slope. It filled all Craig Street with an inland lake, reaching high up on Beaver Hall Hill. It lasted a week.

But times had changed in the twenty-five years since the Methodist ministers waded in four feet of water in the dark to bring help to their roosting congregations. The ingenuity of commerce here stepped in to replace prayer by a five-cent ferry from St. James Street to Beaver Hall Hill.

But it was felt that the river had gone too far. The aid of Ottawa was invoked; a heavier and higher revetment held back the river until later, but not till the new century was there built (1901) the present all-stone wall, braced wide and squat, gated like a fortress, and thus far the last word against the St. Lawrence.

An odd departure of the Port of Montreal, which proved, however, a blind alley, was the attempt to facilitate transriver traffic by running trains over the ice.

An attempt to use the Montreal ice was also made in a quite different way, to make of it not a railway track but a palace. Here begins with the year 1883 the first building of the Ice Palace of Montreal, for which the city acquired such a name, and which ended from the fear that the name was the wrong one.

Montreal, of course, had always had its winter sports. From the old French days had come snowshoeing, in its real purpose a means of locomotion, and heavy and tiresome at that, but a thing which can in proper company and for lack of anything better pass as a sport. Skating similarly had always been a necessary feature of winter life beside Canadian rivers and lakes and lent itself naturally to winter amusement. Curling, with its proper accompaniments, had been imported early from Scotland. As a consequence there had been in Montreal various kinds of winter celebrations long before the Ice Palace of 1883; indeed, it had become the custom to hold a yearly winter carnival as a regular event, with lesser and children's carnivals at odd intervals.

The Ice Palace was a new departure as proposing to let in outsiders on the Montreal winter. This was a delicate point and on this the Ice Palace was in the long run shipwrecked, or melted. There has always been a great misunderstanding and a great sensitiveness about the climate of Canada in general and of Montreal in particular. The truth about the climate of Montreal is that it is not a cold climate in any brutal sense. The winter has its "spells" of cold, lasting three or four days or even longer, with the thermometer well below zero at night and struggling to get above it by day. But each spell is succeeded by a sort of meteorological repentance, bright sun on pure snow, blue skies with just a fleck of cloud, and a kiss of soft wind on the cheek to heighten beauty and encourage audacity; a climate when it is delightful to be out of doors and glorious to come in again.

There is indeed no comparison as between Montreal and really cold places such as will be found in the Far West. These are inland places on exposed prairies, many miles further to the north than Montreal. Those of us who love Canada and admire the West maintain in this matter a conspiracy of silence. But we know—and say it to one another and in whispers—that such places are not really fit to live in. It has been truthfully said that on the day of a blizzard in—let's leave the name unsaid—a man walking with his back to the wind has no difficulty in knowing which side of him is which.

But only recently have Montreal people thrown off all misunderstanding and false shame about the climate. In the past the very praise they gave it was apologetic, as if to explain that it wouldn't really hurt anybody. Here before us lies a little booklet of 1883 to advertise the great Winter Carnival and the Ice Palace that began its life that year. How ancient it looks already, this little booklet *Over the Snow*, with its faint type, its mild advertisements, its moderation! How little they knew how to shout in 1883. "We cannot," says the little book, "put up samples of our dry, cold, clear and healthy winter . . . but when on the spot you can see what absurd opinions have been held of our climate." There are four pages of this, including a statement that the London *Times* is mistaken in saying that our thermometers in winter have to be brought into the houses at night to be thawed. The author almost gets hysterical about it, stating that the Montreal snow is "like feathers" and that he can roll in it and come out dry "almost any day in winter."

This attitude of Montreal toward its winter, midway between apology and praise and at best something like the defense of an old friend gone wrong, is well illustrated by the history of the Ice Palace. This famous structure first appeared in 1883. The palace, like those that followed it in successive years, was built on Dominion Square, out in front of the New Windsor Hotel. In aspect it was made to look, and was officially declared to look, like a medieval castle, with a tall central tower and corner turrets, with battlements and crenelated walls. It measured one hundred and sixty-five feet in length and sixty-five feet in depth; its central tower stood one hundred feet high. Each block of its ice was forty-two by twenty-four inches and weighed five hundred pounds; the whole Palace contained forty thousand cubic feet of ice and fifty men at a time worked to build it. The last item of information about the Palace, given out to stagger the public, was that it cost no less than $3900. This item has lost its direct power to stagger but gets it in reverse gear. It now means that you can have, or could have, a first-rate ice palace for

Winter Sports in Montreal in 1884, with a Picture of One of the Ice Palaces

less than $4000. People who, in the mad winters before the depression, spent as much as that, and ten times as much, for a single party at the "coming out" of a daughter might think of having one now "come out" of an ice palace as a snow princess.

The Ice Palace was the scene of terrific doings, "*fêtes de nuit*" with thousands of snowshoers in line, all with torches, with fireworks, with a "bombardment" of rockets and an assault and defense, and after that the rounds of "scotch" well deserved after such a fete. Of all this nothing is left today except the last item. A single girl and a pair of skis supplies the rest of the fete. Our grandfathers went a long way to get a little.

For the Ice Palace fell on evil times. Business decided that it was "a bad ad," that it looked too much like winter, and cut it out, just as business decided that the beautiful big elm trees in Phillip Square looked too much like summer and cut them down, as bad for business. Those of us not in business often wonder why it can't just be natural.

Later attempts were made to revive the Palace. One in particular will be recalled when it was put on Fletcher's Field, just under the mountain. But somehow it wouldn't work. Perhaps the mountain overshadowed it; at any rate it looked small. It was no use telling us that it measured this or that. It couldn't have. Then the thaw and the rain came all wrong and the Ice Palace began to drip like a wet hen. They made a brutal attempt to freeze it with ice water from hoses, but it didn't work; cracks opened in it; the sun came through; it began to tilt over, and when somebody said it looked just like the Middle Ages that ended it. They let it thaw.

A beautiful monument stands in Dominion Square to commemorate the South African War which rounded out the century for Montreal as for the Empire. The huge stone block graven with the Dutch names of British victories surmounted by a spirited figure-group of trooper and charger is admirable as sculptured art. Montreal specially connects with the war through the name of Baron Strathcona, at that time in the intervals of his London service as High Commissioner, a resident of Montreal in a beautiful stone house on Dorchester Street, which frequently served, through his generosity, as Government House for the visits of the Governor General, like the Hotel de Vaudreuil in the old French days. At Strathcona's cost was raised and equipped the famous troop of Strathcona's Horse. Of the value of the gift and of the war itself time alone can judge. South Africa must be united; it cannot now, it could not then, exist in security and prosperity as two antagonized communities of Boer and Briton. But whether it would have been better united in the long run with the South African War or without is a question which history has not yet answered, and may be answering now.

CHAPTER XI

Montreal
in the Twentieth Century

*Montreal Moves Uphill. The Electrical Age Spreads
the Town. The Tunnel. The Search for Clean Government. Growth of Finance and Fortune. The
Plutocrats of Plutoria. Annexation and the Lion's
Den. Westmount in the Woods. The Great War
and Its Aftermath.*

RIP VAN WINKLE fell asleep, but, after all, when he woke
up again he reappeared in his own village. Not so, if he'd
fallen asleep in Montreal. Let us say that he fell asleep in what
he understood, fifty years ago, to be Montreal and to be the
premises of the well-known house of Henry Morgan and Company. When he woke up he would find himself still in the arms
of Henry Morgan and Company, bigger arms than ever, but
apparently no longer in Montreal, but transported somewhere
away uphill, among leaves and lanes, clear away to the country,
to a pleasant road called St. Catherine's. Near by he would find,
as he walked about, other familiar names and would realize that
Montreal had moved uphill—had moved or was on the move. A
few old Rips like himself still lingered on in the old town below,

leaning over empty counters and fumbling at empty tills. The old place was gone, the grand old shopping district of Great St. James Street, once gay with bright dresses and loud with the sleigh bells of society on the shop.

The change which Rip observed, and which probably killed him, was well under way as a feature of the opening twentieth century, the removal of the shopping district uptown. St. James Street, too great for shops, now shelters only banks, brokers, finance, shipping and communications, and the metropolitan press. Such little shops as remain are tucked in edgeways, as neat and bright as ever, selling cigars to the brokers, neckties to bankers, expensive silverware and diamonds to anyone whose stocks have suddenly risen, and umbrellas for those out of luck. You couldn't buy a corset, let alone a pair of them, within half a mile.

The foresight of Henry Morgan and Company, the pioneer explorers of St. Catherine Street, was fittingly rewarded by the success and celebrity of their colossal store. Their example was widely followed in the whole orbit of retail and domestic trade. A few firms, even department stores, lacked faith to look upward and died a lingering death below. A famous fish firm moved halfway up and couldn't bear to go further from the water. An enterprising Scottish house, too well-known to name, moved too far: the town hasn't caught it yet; being Scottish, they're waiting for it.

This move of Montreal uptown came along with, indeed arose out of, the new electric age. Fast urban transport spreads a city out; telephones put the suburbs within talking distance; lighted streets and comfortable streetcars invite movement abroad; and on the heels of all that the motorcar puts anybody anywhere. People are forgetting now the limitations of earlier days. Consider this. On the slope we now call Westmount, an occupant of any of the few but pleasant houses there situated sixty years ago, if sudden illness came to his house at night, must needs go out to the stable (every house had a stable), hitch up a horse, and drive to Montreal at full speed (eight miles an hour) to fetch a doctor. Such an expedition attended the coming into the world of some of the present elderly barristers and businessmen of today whose people moved out into Westmount in its St. Antoine days. On this scene broke the telephone in 1880 with four hundred subscribers. As elsewhere, and as with the telegraph before it, the telephone suffered from its first reception as an amusing toy. It was, as we now see it, slow in coming into its own. The Montreal streetcar had gone tinkling along the streets ever since the "Montreal Passenger Railway Company" of 1861 put their horsecar on Notre Dame Street. With its extension to the upper part of the city began the long agonies of the streetcar horse, hauling a cluster of human beings clinging like bees to the rush-hour car up a cruel slope, exactly equal to the utmost power of the animal. Then came electric cars in 1893, and the streetcar horse found its first rest in death.

These new facilities, and the rapid suburban trains now put on by the railways, made it possible for Montreal to spread out, to get rid of the congestion of its close-packed streets, its solid rows of houses; a still greater opportunity came with the boring of the tunnel under the mountain, a work undertaken by the phenomenal but ill-starred Canadian Northern Railway that was spreading at this time like a web all over Canada, built up of odd bits and odd benefits. At least it had enterprise. It needed a direct route from Ottawa to Montreal. Mount Royal was in the way. So the railway dived clean under it. The making of the tunnel through the solid core of rock that is the remaining base of a volcano was a marvelous piece of engineering work. The tunnel was begun from both ends at once, on Dorchester Street and behind the mountain, and duly met in the middle with absolute precision.

The opening of the tunnel meant that any Montrealer who liked could now live in the pleasant open country behind the mountain and be whirled into town through the tunnel in ten minutes. Convenient car or bus lines could connect, fan shape, with the suburban tunnel station. Wise people saw at once that this meant a wholesale migration to the back of the mountain. Hence came into being the new suburban town of Mount Royal. But the wise people were wrong. Montreal wouldn't move. It still clings to its tenements and its rows and its clustering nests of piled-up apartments.

The reason is simple. It's the cold. One has only to look at the wide expansion of Toronto, a city smaller in population, under the influence of the electric age. Toronto now reaches so far that where it ends it is called Aurora, or something else.

For we must remember that there is all the difference in the world between waiting for a suburban bus on a summer night in California, or even Toronto, and waiting for a suburban bus on a winter night in Montreal.

The scene is California. The night is soft and still, the air heavy with the scent of the peonies, their drooping heads fallen asleep upon their stems. Around us and about us, as we stand, the leaves of the magnolia stir faintly in the night air. Above us the velvet sky is soft with a myriad of stars, and from somewhere in the distance—so still is the night—we can hear the murmur of the sea. On such a night Young Love stands hand in hand together, waiting for the bus, talking of the stars and whether people love one another there also and hoping the bus will never come. . . . Even Middle Age stands silent in something that feels almost like religious contemplation but which is really digestion.

Now change the scene to Montreal, in the heart of a winter night, with a blizzard blowing. "A rough night," the Joneses said as they put us out of their suburban apartment after the game of bridge, as you put a cat out in the snow. A rough night, indeed! As we stand on the corner, waiting, the blizzard drives the hard-frozen snow against our faces . . . it blurs the electric light . . . we can hardly see the few scattered houses around us . . . nor the few frozen people huddled for shelter. The sidewalks are drifting fast with snow that piles in ridges and wedges, and all the sky is one great smother of gray. "Is that damn bus never coming?"—and at the burst of profanity nature rebukes us by lashing the snow in our faces. . . . Even Young Love stands speechless in the lee of a lamppost, its temperature down to what science calls "absolute zero." "Didn't they say one every twenty minutes?" "Ah, here it comes!" The headlights show, blurred but powerful, through the driving snow . . . the bus crunches to the sidewalk. "In we get"—"What! This one going east?" Going and gone . . . Jones may keep his suburban rock garden and his asparagus bed. We don't care if he grew more lettuce than he could eat: let him eat less. We are going to some place, 25×50, out of the cold.

We turn back again for a moment to the uptown movement which has utterly transformed Upper Montreal—St. Catherine Street West and its side streets—within easy living memory. When the move began the street was hardly to be called a street at all, a pleasant country road bordered with houses. It had nothing of the aristocracy and grandeur of Sherbrooke Street, just above it and parallel to it. The houses were modest buildings of two stories and an attic, with a little bit of garden in front or a big bit of garden behind. The side streets were built up to a good extent with stone houses in rows, but with much open space of gardens and orchards. Ten years later St. Catherine was still a street of houses but with many stores jostled in among them and square buildings going up on the best corners. Ten years after that it was a street of continuous shops but with many of the houses still showing, plastered over with false fronts, re-vamped, the lower stories gutted into bigger floor space. On the chief corner where Windsor Street, in crossing, changes its name to Peel, in true Montreal fashion, there stood a church. Presently the church was refaced, boarded, and bricked into a department store but with plenty of church showing. Then the church gave place to a real building, and later on the whole wide block was demolished and shoveled up to make room for the vast modern building that now stands there, the Dominion Square Building, perhaps the most symmetrically beautiful of the commercial buildings of Montreal.

This last, of course, was after the Great War. For it was not till then that building on a scale proportionate for the oppor-tunity began. Within a few years a long stretch of the street was crowded with tall buildings, department stores, business build-ings, and the side streets rapidly invaded with all sorts of mongrel halfway transformations of dignified old stone houses into un-dignified "cafés," "night clubs," and the mushroom growth which precedes the real reconstruction of a modern city quarter.

Sojourners in the Mount Royal Hotel, one of these vast new structures, might be interested to know that not so long ago the hotel was chiefly garden and orchard, then a large high school and playground. The streets around were residential, quiet and filled with trees. Hard by there lived a Montreal poet, John Logan, whose friends still treasure his memory, and who wrote a poem on the singing of the birds that sang to wake him in the early morning. It began:

> *I have no garden, but a quiet street,*
> *Meeting another makes a cool retreat . . .*

The hotel stands on one of the quiet streets where the birds sang. Other birds sing there now, and even earlier in the morning.

The pity is that the rebuilding has been all wrong from the start and condemns the great shopping street of St. Catherine to the narrow width and hopeless congestion that has been the fate of New York. It is too late to alter now; it was so easy then. They had only to slice all the houses on one side of the street into two halves and throw away one half. It seems that the only wide streets ever laid out are in towns that never grow.

This new age of expansion threw upon the city a larger and larger need for public works and a greater and greater oppor-tunity for public theft. Hence the period witnessed, as culmi-nating in the year 1910, the greatest and most resolute struggle for clean government that had yet marked the history of Montreal. This struggle for clean government had been going on ever since the city had been a city; but so had the struggle for dirty gov-ernment. The struggle for clean government took the form of trying to find some method of election, of tenure of office, of area of representation, which would mean honest administration. The struggle for dirty government took the form of providing increasing temptations which would mean dishonest administra-tion. It was like Milton's battles in the sky: at times the citizens looked up and watched it; mostly they didn't. The final result after a hundred and ten years is to leave the city of Montreal burdened with so huge a debt at so high an interest that in many areas the annual taxes for property eat up its entire rental value.

It will be recalled that under the original incorporation of 1832, proclaimed in force June 5, 1833, the city government was based on a universal vote of men over twenty-one (there were no women then) resident in the city twelve months and possessing real estate. These elected two councilors from each of eight wards, the original wards being East, West, St. Joseph, St. Ann, St. Lawrence, St. Louis, and St. Mary. These sixteen men chose one of themselves as Mayor. The Mayor was to receive a salary of four hundred dollars, the councilors nothing. It looks as simple and honest as early Massachusetts. The Council sat modestly in a rented house (of Madame de Beaujeu) on Notre Dame Street. When we add that the Mayor and Council selected as the figures on the coat of arms of the city a beaver, a rose, a shamrock, and a thistle (meaning something for everybody), and their motto, *Concordia salus*, the thing seems complete. The corporation took over the old local administrative duties of the justice of the peace; the act gave it power to buy and sell property and to borrow money. That was the thorn in the rose.

This government was authorized to last till May 1, 1836. They let it lapse, unwept, and went back to justices of the peace. Then came Lord Durham, horrified at the lack of municipal liberty. His report started a clean government movement that created, by Act of the Province of Canada, a new city government under Mayor and councilors, with six aldermen, to keep their eye on the councilors, chosen from the Council. This time they had only six wards. In 1845 they tried five wards. In 1851 they found it didn't do to let the Council choose the Mayor, so the people elected him. In 1874 the distinction of aldermen and councilors was abolished. All were elected as councilors.

Under this city government Montreal staggered along as best it could until 1909. It was never satisfactory. In the earlier years the English element "ran" the city Council. But English-speaking people, honest and dishonest alike, are not keen about the emoluments and casual profits of small office. They want something bigger. Hence the men elected presently brought the Council into disrepute. "To be quite frank," writes a local chronicler, "there was a long period during which the English-speaking people seemed to think that almost anybody was good enough to make an alderman."[1]

On the other hand, the French thought that the job of alderman was good enough for almost anybody, and so, says the same authority, "they had the good sense to elect their ablest men." It is indeed characteristic of the French, both here and in what was France, that they are far more keen on securing the certain tenure and the assured living of a government office than the English ever are. One may count it in a sense to their credit. Life, in its sordid sense of livelihood, being thus assured, they may turn to the real things of life—the garden, the library, the picture gallery, the game of chess, or the diversion of love. Not so the English; they want to take risks, go after big things, put in years of sustained effort up the hill of life to gain the eminence, the wealth, the wide horizon of the hilltop. Often they gain it, to find it empty and windswept.

Such in miniature was the course of our city government. The bulk of the English people, those not interested in franchises and contracts, lost interest in the city government. They have never regained it, except in a sort of feverish make-believe as in 1909 and in 1939, when people tell them that the city government is rotten and the fault is with the citizens.

Hence the French element took over the city government and have held a majority control ever since. The annexation of outlying French-speaking suburbs, such as Hochelaga in 1883, St. Henri and St. Cunégonde in 1905, and the steady refusal of British Westmount to join Montreal (which surrounds it) helped to maintain French dominance.

Meanwhile, after 1890, the electric age had put a new face, or at least a much bigger face, on the city government. Huge sums had to be spent on lighting and tramways and telephones, on repaving streets and remaking sewers, and that, too, in connec-

[1]Henry Dalby, Montreal *Herald,* 1913.

tion with technical engineering services of light and power on which the intelligent citizen could have no proper judgment at all, and which the honest alderman couldn't understand and which crooked aldermen didn't need to.

The result was a new cry for clean government, a movement in 1898 to recast the whole city charter. A commission was appointed to prepare the legislation to submit to the Provincial Government. There was much genuine enthusiasm, much repentance for past sins. Here was prominent the work of young Mr. Herbert Ames, a rising businessman who both practiced and preached the doctrine of civic interest in civic affairs, lecturing and writing on the government of Montreal. He began here the career that later carried him to well-deserved eminence at Ottawa and Geneva.[2]

The new statute called for a longer term—two years; for a Mayor possessing $10,000 worth of real estate in the city; for a Mayor's salary up to $4000; for aldermen with property worth $2000 and salaries, called an indemnity, of $600. A salary means pay for what you do; an indemnity means compensation for what you don't. It is felt in civic circles to be the more complimentary word.

The new act contained various gadgets for "special committees" and "special meetings" on casting votes—everybody to watch everybody like cats and rats. But all to no avail. Within ten years it had all gone to pieces. The new broom swept as dirty as the old one. "Towards its close," writes Dr. Atherton, too kindly a critic to convey an untrue accusation, "corruption and inefficiency were rampant under the monopoly of a few who became stigmatized in the mouths of the citizens as the 'twenty-three.' " The indifferent citizen was as indifferent as ever, bankers as willing as ever to lend at high interest, contractors as willing as ever to pave anything, light anything, or tear down anything. In those days it seems that, after all, the city must be good for it. There had as yet been no war, no depression, no repudiation of Western debts, no shadow of Mr. Aberhart lengthening out in the sunset to shadow the East.

[2](Sir) H. B. Ames, *The City Below the Hill*, 1897.

Hence the rope was woven for the neck of the property holder of today, who at times perhaps looks enviously at repudiated debts, the severed ropes of Western communities.

Montreal had thus got into the position of little Jim of the nursery rhyme, who never washed:

> *His friends were much hurt to see so much dirt,*
> *And often they made him quite clean,*
> *But all was in vain; he got dirty again*
> *And never looked fit to be seen.*

Meantime the year 1908–09 witnessed a great civic revival as earnest as an old-time camp meeting. All classes in Montreal, except the criminal class, had become utterly disgusted and seriously alarmed at the flagrant dishonesty of the alderman. A "Citizens Association" began agitation for reform in 1908. Powerful influence obtained from the province the appointment of a Royal Commission (which means a nonpolitical body) under Justice Cannon, which made its report on December 12, 1909. It declared that since 1892 the administration of Montreal had been "saturated with corruption"; that "the majority of the aldermen have administered the committees and Council in such a manner as to favour the private interests of the relatives and friends, to whom contracts and positions were distributed to the detriment of the general interests of the city and of the tax payers"; that "25% of the annual revenue of $5,000,000 had been spent in bribes and malversations of all kinds," and of the balance "the greater part in works of which the permanence has very often been ephemeral."[3]

The storm of anger drove twenty-two of the twenty-three aldermen out of office. The eager approval of all the best citizens accompanied Judge Cannon's recommendation to the Provincial Government in the advocating of scrapping the whole system as it existed and setting up a "commission government."

This, it will be remembered, was democracy's latest remedy for its own ailments in the early part of the twentieth century.

[3]*Report of the Cannon Commission,* 1909.

The prevailing method of election of councils too numerous for individual responsibility, bribable one by one, with too little power for honest control and plenty for stealing, had led all over North America to a desire for something else. What was really wanted was a new heart, or rather an old one renewed: the fault was not in the form but in the spirit. A crooked alderman is no worse than a crooked commissioner.

But they asked for commission government—a government of strong men with large power, longer terms, and great responsibility, men too well off, or at least too well paid, to need to steal—government, in a word, on a business basis of efficiency.

Much was made of the experience of the city of Galveston, flooded out for its sins by the angered Gulf of Mexico and reborn under a commission of businessmen. This was a part of the apotheosis of the "businessman," as the man who knows everything and can do everything, which lasted till he fell like Humpty Dumpty from the wall of Wall Street in 1929. "Oh yeah!" said the world.

But the current ran strong in Montreal. A plebiscite endorsed the request for commission government. Hence a new city government was created by a provincial statute of 1910, in which the Council surrendered its financial powers to a Board of Control.

There is no doubt that the institution of government by a Board of Control marked a real determination "to be good," a real intention on the part of the citizens to keep their eyes on the city government, a genuine rebirth of public spirit. "This government," wrote a local authority at the time, "is now on trial." Then came the Great War and put all else in the shadow. The best men had better things to do than keeping their eyes on aldermen. And so somehow government by commission in Montreal, a new broom that swept very clean at first, was presently discarded again and a statute of 1921 restored aldermanic government. This time the city Council consisted of a Mayor and thirty-five aldermen of whom five were selected by the whole body to act as an Executive Commission. This arrangement merely added the new problem of too great a division of authority. Things were soon as bad as ever. "City administration in the dark thirties," says a current witness, "called desperately for action."[4] Hence another wave of clean government enthusiasm led to the adoption of an entirely new system in 1940. This time reliance was placed on the patriotic citizen, not a professional politician, serving without pay for service's sake. Under this system Montreal is administered by a Council composed of a Mayor and ninety-nine councilors. The Mayor is elected by a general vote of the ratepayers. Of the councilors, sixty-six are elected, six from each of eleven divisions of the city; of each six, three are elected by property holders, three by all the voters. The other thirty-three are appointed by various business and educational bodies, such as the Board of Trade, the Chamber of Commerce, McGill University, the University of Montreal.

But the system has already worn thin. Unrequited service is easy to enlist but hard to keep at drill; and at times it is hard to distinguish between patriotic citizens and busybodies. A new provincial statute will set up something else.

The truth is that the theory of government by commission is a fallacy, or at best a half-truth. It is no good without the proper spirit in those who operate it. A crook with a long term of office is just as crooked as a crook with a short and is crooked longer. A crooked man with large responsibility can steal more than a crook with less. A crooked rich man is not as good as an honest poor one. Plebiscites of all the citizens are admirable if the citizens know what they are plebisciting about; but in technological questions of power and light and transport how can they?

There is a deeper trouble still, an unsolved problem for Montreal and other cities. There is no doubt that municipal government is the dead end, the blind alley of democracy. In early days, in little towns, it could enlist the same devoted interest and unselfish service as can national government in a decent nation. In national politics, the function of government involves the real issues, life-and-death issues, of a nation and not just the dollars and cents spent in making a city sewer. A quite different set of

[4] J. I. Cooper, *Montreal*, 1942.

motives enter in. Some, perhaps many politicians, in the national sphere, steal or get rich by happy accident. But others don't; for them there is in public life a tremendous temptation to be honest, not only honest but ostentatiously honest, conspicuously poor. One thinks of the conspicuous poverty of Daniel Webster, living in majestic debt; of our own Joe Howe of Nova Scotia whose friends had to pay his fare across the Atlantic; of such men as Sir John Macdonald, of Laurier, of Fielding, who "never had a cent." Incidentally, the politician who "never has a cent" seems to have just about everything else in the world except a cent, but that's another matter.

There is no remedy for these things in Montreal or elsewhere that can be marked out with a rule and compass, framed in the four corners of a statute, or even achieved by the threat of the penitentiary. Civic interest won't do. In the complicated technique of city services today, full civic interest would leave no time for anything else. You will find in Montreal, no doubt elsewhere, many doctors, lawyers, professors, and professional men, leading citizens, who in thirty years have taken no interest in the City Hall except to swear at it. Quite rightly. Their work lies elsewhere. All they can do is to ask some honest men of special knowledge whether a light, heat, and power, or a tramways contract is fair and honest and vote accordingly. There is, in short, no remedy but in righteousness, no virtue in democracy of any sort unless it carries with it the spirit of righteousness. All government comes to that.

The position of dominance of Montreal in the economic life of the Dominion during this era was accentuated by the fact that it was not only a great shipping and manufacturing center, but also had become the center of finance. It was at once Liverpool and Lombard Street, Pittsburgh and Wall Street. This had come about as the natural and deserved result of the institution in the old days of Lower Canada of the sound banking system based on Scottish tradition that came with the foundation of the Bank of Montreal. The banking system set up in the province of Canada developed into the system of chartered banks with branches organized under the Dominion of Canada and a conspicuous success. The branch system naturally meant centralized finance as the head offices of banks in the chief cities, such as the Bank of Montreal and the Molsons Bank in Montreal, added to metropolitan dominance but made for security and mutual support.

With banking had arisen the Montreal Stock Exchange. Even before Confederation shares in the Bank of Montreal and the other banks of the period, together with shares in the new railway companies, etc., were traded back and forth and offered by newspaper advertisement. This led to the formation of a (unincorporated) group of traders, first associated as the Board of Brokers in 1863.[5] The traders met daily, at first in a private office, then in a rented room in the old Board of Trade Building. They were incorporated by a provincial act as the Montreal Stock Exchange in 1874. At that time they were dealing in sixty-three different issues, including the shares of twenty-one banks, in nine government and municipal issues, in the stock of four railways, ten industrial stocks, and minor securities. It is notable that in those days mining shares only represented three issues out of a total sixty-three. There was a daily average turnover of eight hundred shares.

Business grew rapidly. In 1901 sales ran to seven thousand a day. There were forty-five members: the value of a seat had risen from $2500 in 1876 to $12,000. The exchange in 1904 built its own building on St. François Xavier Street on land that changed hands for the first time since the Sulpicians received their fief in 1663. When the Great War broke out membership in the exchange had reached seventy-five and the turnover ran to ten thousand.

The fortunes of the stock exchange after that point belong rather to technical monetary history than to the present work. Its eclipse during the Great War was followed by a spectacular revival in the decade of the 1920s. The press of extramural trading led to the formation of the Montreal Curb Exchange in 1926. The activities of the two culminated in the trading mania of 1929 when in a single day (October 29) the combined turn-

[5]Carl Bergithon, *The Stock Exchange*, 1942.

over reached 730,195 shares. The price of seats had risen with the volume of business; it stood at $27,000 in 1921 and increased about ten times to its high mark of $225,000 in 1929. Then followed the slump, the spasmodic recoveries and falls, and then the new eclipse of the present war. Trading, though under the Foreign Exchange Control and a multitude of regulations, is not suspended by law, but merely by fact. The Stock Exchange sits in the ashes. Later, like the phoenix, it will rise from there: indeed, many of its younger adherents and offspring are in the air already.

There was once upon a time, namely about thirty years ago, a McGill professor who was called away to another chair and who shook the dust of Montreal off his cap and gown with the bitter denunciation, "an oppressive and plutocratic atmosphere." There was something in it. The accumulation and concentration of wealth in Montreal had been made all the more evident and conspicuous by the fact that most of the superrich lived in one and the same residential quarter. It was an area of unsurpassed beauty, undisturbed, from the very nature of its situation, by the noise of traffic or by the passage of the passer-by. This is the district that we recall as lying just at the foot of the mountain, unoccupied under the French Regime and comprising in early British days the beautiful farms and the stone manor houses of the McGills, the McTavishes, and such that reached all the way from what is now Fletcher's Field to the Côte des Neiges Road, covering all the river face of the mountain slope.

For this area McGill University presently formed one boundary. The rest was laid out into spacious side streets running up the hill from Sherbrooke Street till they could run no further. Each street was thus blind with that happy blindness that spells peace. Nature aided man. The elms that grow so easily on Montreal Island, thus left in secluded growth, fashioned each street to a Gothic cathedral. Here in generous grounds arose the mansions of the rich. Where nature's utmost effort ended art took up the task with lawns and shrubberies and flower beds gay from the earliest glowing of the crocus till the last drooping beauty of the aster. Great glass conservatories turned even winter into a vision of tropical beauty. Nor did art stop here: for the private picture galleries collected in Montreal and housed in this happy area became known throughout the world. Every social group acquires its particular habits and hobbies. People in villages keep bees; people at the seaside collect shells. The super-rich in the Montreal of forty years ago collected pictures. It is the easiest and simplest of all collecting hobbies: the price tells you exactly what you are getting; you have only to look on the back of the picture to appreciate it.

These circumstances gave to society in Montreal, in the pre-war days that are never likely to come again, the peculiar, the distinctive complexion described by the professor. We are speaking here of society at what is called its top end, not at its bottom end, the base of the pyramid, the long rows of tawdry houses and the tumbled slums of Griffintown, among people who wouldn't know a Correggio from a Colorado Claro. The rich in Montreal had too much. They got in the way. They annexed the art of the painter and they stole the history of the professor; for a man who buys a whole room full of early Canadiana, with signatures of Montcalm and Wolfe, must surely know more history than one who merely talks about them; and the man who can buy Japanese mezzotints must have a finer sense of art than the man who wishes he had the money to spend on something else. The rich annexed these things, it is true, rather as patrons than as partners. It is true, also, that the love of art in some of its rich patrons was very genuine, and genuine in proportion as it talked least. It is true also that many of the superrich men who "made Montreal" as heads of banks and railways and captains of industry were very fine men, and that some of them asked nothing better than to enjoy their own society undisturbed, paying out generously right and left to colleges, churches, and charities with never a thought of interference. Those of us who remember the era can think of one such, richest of all perhaps, whose simple evenings were spent alone, reading the evening newspaper under a droplight, smokeless, for he knew too much about it, drinkless for he didn't care for it, and speechless for he seldom had much to say, except "yes" for another million.

Yet the fact remains that the rich in Montreal enjoyed a prestige in that era that not even the rich deserve.

In any case the "oppressive and plutocratic society" is all gone now. The war swept over it and set up newer and better values in soldiers and patriots. Then came the depression and cast down the mighty from their seats, mingled the old rich with the new poor, and left the fairyland of this Plutoria under the elms, a wreckage of mortgages, a placard of "sales," with many of its mansions empty and others gone and vanished under "demolition." There are many rich in Montreal now, but not gathered and focused as they were.

"They say," says Omar Khayyám, "the lion and the leopard keep their court where Jansed gloried and drank deep." Call the lion and the leopard the income-tax inspector and the property-tax assessor, and Persepolis has nothing on Montreal.

Montreal shared in the movement for expansion and the annexation of outside municipalities which came as a general tendency all over the United States and Canada in connection with the electrical age. The development of rapid transport and the introduction of the motorcar brought with them the "commuter" of the new suburban district.

The cities all expected larger population, one and one making three, and an expanded retail market. The movement ran apace, even more so in the "advanced" province of Ontario than in conservative Quebec. Cities annexed towns, towns annexed villages, and villages annexed the back street. No one foresaw the future. Repentance, for the smaller areas absorbed, came later. It then appeared that annexation meant taxes. Country properties that had known no higher burden than those imposed in a township rate and a school-section school tax now rose to the full honor of participation, at high rates, in urban facilities that reached them only in name. But there was no way out. The footsteps of annexation led into the metropolitan lion's den. None out.

Montreal shared in this. As between the beginning of the movement, with the annexation of Hochelaga (down the river from the main port) in 1883, until the outbreak of the Great

War it annexed twenty-seven municipalities, a total area of 22,000 acres and a population at the time of union of 124,000. Inside what may be called the city itself there was the annexation of St. Henri with 21,000 and St. Cunégonde with 11,000 in 1905. The annexation of St. Louis brought in 35,000 in 1910. The same year saw the rich prize of Notre Dame de Grace, its population only 4000 but a favored district, clean and bright as the morning, with nothing to live down, like Verdun, nothing to unmake like Griffintown, destined for obvious growth. Just at the back of the mountain Montreal took over in its sleep the little village of Côte des Neiges, hitherto only explored by snowshoe clubs and a point of pilgrimage to Lumkin's Tavern. The city reached out across the island, picking up the old settlement of St. Laurent on the way and reached the back river with Bordeaux and Sault au Recollet as part of the city of Montreal. Nor did the process stop with the war. Maisonneuve and other towns came in. But the process slackened and then halted. Not all the municipalities wanted to come in, and after the exposure in 1909 of the corruption of city government in Montreal the shadow of the twenty-three aldermen fell cold on the threatened areas. Hence it is that the topography of Montreal shows a number of municipalities not forming part of it but included in its borders and entirely surrounded by it—what they call "enclaves" in European diplomacy. Here belong the town of Mount Royal, the tunnel town mentioned above, the city of Verdun (with sixty thousand people), the cities of Outremont and Westmount, and the greatest of these is Westmount.

Just to the west of Mount Royal, to the left of it as you see it from downtown, is a smaller mountain, separated from it by the miniature mountain pass called the Côte des Neiges Road. The slope of the West Mountain, the Little Mountain, is the site of Westmount, which descends its sides till it meets Montreal at the bottom of the slope, just below the Canadian Pacific Railway. Montreal thus entirely surrounds Westmount.

Westmount has a place all its own in the make-up of Greater Montreal. Its history is, in a sense, older than that of Montreal. Excavation shows that the site of Westmount was an ancient

Indian burial ground, so old that the remains are not recognizable, from the method of burial, as those of Hurons but are those of antecedent dwellers, possibly the Flatheads of the Lower Mississippi Valley. But there is a gap in the history of Westmount as between the Flatheads and its present population. It had no share in the sorrows and the glory of New France and practically none in British Montreal till yesterday. On the country road, the Côte St. Antoine, that runs on a westward slant out of Montreal, rising as it goes, certain of the fur traders of the Beaver Hall days—Holliwell and Clarke and others—built substantial country houses. Other Montrealers—the Honorable John Young was one—bought near-by farms and set up country seats. The locality was originally part of the Parish of St. Henri. But it was sufficiently settled to be incorporated in 1874 as the village of St. Antoine. Then in 1890 the village, still in deep seclusion but with a population of 1850, became the town of Côte St. Antoine. Then the age of expansion reached out for it. The main thoroughfare of Sherbrooke Street was extended to meet the Côte St. Antoine. The electric cars found it in 1894 and electrified it into rapid settlement and into the farseeing town-planning that has made it the charming place it is; neither urban nor rural, neither straight nor crooked, embowered in trees, shopless (except for the lower area, too far gone to save) and saloonless, too rich for the poor but too poor for the superrich, and throughout clean and beautiful.

As such it needed no saint to look after it. It took to the plain title of the town of Westmount in 1895. Its population passed ten thousand with the outgoing century and the year 1908 saw it made the city of Westmount. Since then it has lived and flourished, multiplying its good works in its schools (the "Westmount High" is second to nothing in Canada), in its public parks, playgrounds, and conservatories, its public library, its Victoria Hall, and the sheltering arm of its public welfare. The population of the city is at present twenty-five thousand; it is 88 per cent English speaking, over 70 per cent of British origin. It is small enough for civic pride and devoted civic service in office; too young to steal, too wise to be led into the lion's den of Montreal

—except to get a drink. For Westmount doesn't tolerate intemperance. It voted heavily for prohibition. It has no licenses, no bars, no "bogus night clubs." You can get anything you want in Westmount, except a drink: if you sink to that you must go down into Montreal. There is no doubt on all sides that Westmount, thus included in Montreal, is an oasis of something in something else: people differ only on the question of what in what. On the other hand, Toronto visitors pay the high compliment to Westmount of saying that it is just like a piece of Toronto.

At least Westmount is clean and honest in its government. To realize that, you need only open the annual report that the Secretary-Treasurer lays at the feet of the Mayor and aldermen of Westmount every thirty-first of December, a report in print as neat and symmetrical as a Westmount garden, bound in an orange cover fit for Belfast. There you may see it all, every figure, nothing concealed, money from taxes so much, from licenses so much —not liquor licenses, of course, but licenses for dogs, bicycles, bakers, knife grinders, and musicians—all the revenue and expenditure set down in a plain, understandable way, and every addition correct.

In the days before the Great War, the days of the great fortunes and of the great snobbishness that went with what the McGill professor, mentioned above, called the "oppressive and plutocratic atmosphere" that surrounded the richer class in Montreal, in those days the idea of Westmount carried something of a touch of second rate, something that could almost be pushed to the comic point of a standard joke. The old burlesque companies on circuit always carried as part of their stock in trade the name of a "dud" suburb to go with each theater town, Chelsea for Boston, Parkdale for Toronto, and so on. Westmount was saved from this by the existence of Verdun with an asylum in it. But even at that it seemed to lack class. Those days are long gone by. Westmount grew beautiful as Montreal grew shabby. The Prince of Wales Terrace is a dingy place beside the Upper Boulevard, and Westmount ladies get their hair dressed and their beauty renewed on Sherbrooke Street, Montreal. The millionaires' houses are being demolished, rushing in piles of brick and dust down the contractors' chutes. The Westmount houses climb higher and higher to the sky.

It is no part of the present work to discuss the story of the Great War as it affected Montreal. Such a chronicle belongs elsewhere. But in a sense Montreal was perhaps more profoundly affected by the reaction of the Great War and of the collapse and depression which followed it than any city in Canada. The war brought a great shift of personal and social values. The leaders of finance, explaining in their clubs that the war would only last six months because big business wouldn't allow it to go further, soon gave place, disregarded, to other leaders and other thoughts: to the volunteers drilling on the McGill campus, men who are the generals of today humbly learning to form fours; Professor Auckland Geddes as the man of the hour, the man who knew and had known; with him the little old Duke, the Governor General, back on a soldier's job, up and down the campus beside Auckland Geddes, which in front, which behind, no one knew; the departure of the overseas regiments of 1915 marching to the ships, their women clinging in their ranks, then later, as wisdom intervened, the port closed as now, troopships that moved silently down the river in the early morning, with never a farewell except from hands that waved good-by from the windows of factories where work never stopped. All this needs no recital. It is back again.

After the war followed the brief aftermath of high prices, the momentum of the war machine mistaken for the new impetus of peace. Then followed the collapse of prices that struck down agriculture, nature taking a hand in with dust thrown in the western farmer's eyes; with this the wreck of factory industry, with nothing to make and no one to buy; and as the consequence, not the cause, the reflection, not the light, the mirror, not the picture, the collapse of the Montreal Stock Exchange values that demolished, part of it forever, the world that was. It is claimed by some people that the financial dominance enjoyed in Canada by Montreal may not survive. Finance was struggling back to life as best it could between the depression and the present war, but certain large and new interests had sprung up, notably the northern mining interest, which Montreal was either slow in seizing or unfortunate in not getting. It is said, or at least whispered, that Toronto now seriously threatens the financial priority so long held by Montreal. Yet for this no one need worry. When peace comes and with it, under a wise extravagance instead of a foolish parsimony, the new development of Canada begins on a scale never before known, there will be plenty of finance and money for both cities. After all, there are two classes that we have always with us, the poor and the rich.

CHAPTER XII

The Port of Montreal

The Magic of the Sea. Geographical Advantages of Montreal. Twentieth-Century Improvement of the Ports. The Jacques Cartier Bridge. The Barrier of the Ice. The Shipping List. Many Cargoes. River Steamers and Lake Freighters. The St. Lawrence Seaway.

FOR ALL PEOPLE of British and kindred descent there is an abiding attraction in a seaport. The shipping that comes and goes connects the harbor with the seven seas and the faraway peoples of the outer world. The poet who wrote a hundred years ago of "the mystery and beauty of the ships and the magic of the sea" found words to express the common thought of all the people whose national heritage has been the sea.

Montreal has a rare and picturesque scenic beauty; mountain and river and its far horizon give it an unsurpassed interest for the eye. It carries all the romantic charm of its varied history. But for many people its most appealing aspect is that of a great port, one of the greatest in the world and in many senses unique among all the ports of the globe.

Many a simple dweller in the city whose life and livelihood are quite unconnected with the operations of the harbor, who perhaps rarely visits it, unconsciously feels it a part of himself, bringing him a touch of maritime life, a whiff of the open sea. Such people follow in their morning newspaper the annual fortunes of the harbor as a part of their own existence. They live in an unending sea story. They feel a new awakening each year at the news that the Gulf is all clear below Anticosti, news of heavy northwest winds at Fame Point, no ice in sight from the Seven Islands, and light breezes to dead calm reported off Rimouski. There is a charm in the names of these queer places, strung into a thousand miles along river and gulf, with no other meaning or history than points of navigation, places for range lights, fog bells and weather reports, ending at the Strait of Belle Isle where the last ice goes out to let in the first ship. Such people feel a personal pride in the annual spring victory of the great icebreakers pounding against the ice jams below Lake St. Peter and follow the award of the harbor's annual gold-headed cane for the first ocean ship in port as inland people follow the ball games of their league.

Such a reader in the heyday of the summertime, with dog days of heat and tourists, finds his delight each day in looking down the long and varied shipping list that covers a page or more of print, the calendar of the great liners ready months ahead and arrivals and departures from all over the world. Then comes the autumn and with it the rush of the grain ships that warns of the annual passing of navigation, the winter sleep of the port. The great passenger liners drop out in wary prudence, while the grain carriers fight on to the last, fed by the lake boats from a thousand miles up, making their last trip out of Fort William in blinding snowstorms and bitter cold. Presently the last is gone, the buoys and marks removed; Fame Point is silent; the river steamers are packed tight in their harbors, fast asleep until spring—and the ice rules again. If it were not for the barrier of ice Montreal might easily be the greatest port in all the world. But the "if" is as large as the St. Lawrence and the Gulf below, both of which are utterly unconquerable.

But for the ice! For consider what an extraordinary geographical position is occupied by the Port of Montreal. It is the farthest inland seaport of any importance in all the world, one thousand miles from the sea. Yet by the good fortune of geography it is closer to Liverpool than any seaport in the United States. Montreal shows a distance from Liverpool of 2760 miles, Portland 2783, Boston 2861, New York 3043, and Philadelphia 3179. Yet conversely, apart from the Hudson Bay route, Montreal is the nearest ocean port to Central Canada and to the Middle West of the States. The great technical development of the Port of Montreal, in relation to engineering facilities for unloading, loading, and storage of freight, its extent of berths and wharfage and its ability to meet the great expansion of the passenger trade, did not, as already said, take place until the present century. The change came because it had to. The increasing size of modern steamships involved not only deeper and deeper dredging but facilities for mechanical loading, fueling, and repair. The reference is here not to the increasing size of freak ships, such as the *Great Eastern*, or record ships, blue-ribbon ships needed for national prestige, but the increasing size of what is called the "economical" ship, giving the maximum returns for a minimum of proportional cost. The increase of economical size comes from increased efficiency in building, new methods of carrying and using fuel, and the increasing opportunity to secure large cargoes without delay. Such economical ships of first-class commerce runs now represent a tonnage that runs up to twenty thousand tons. A port unable to gather freight rapidly enough, load and unload fast enough, and offer water deep enough to float these ships could not survive as a world port. Montreal has never been concerned with "big ships" in the world's top class. The top ocean tonnage before the present war was represented by the *Queen Elizabeth* (85,000 registered tons), the *Normandie* (82,435), a group of a dozen ships of more than 35,000 tons. These ships fill a large place in the world's eye, a small place in the world's trade. Montreal's 20,000-ton Duchesses represent the main fleet of the world's commerce.

The *Empress of Britain*, whose tragic fate was a disastrous episode of the present war, was the largest boat ever on the St. Lawrence (42,000 tons), but only ran as far as the port of Quebec. The ocean cargo tonnage entering the Port of Montreal in the years just before the war ran to an average of about 5,000,000, the cargo tonnage outward about 4,000,000.

The ship channels of the St. Lawrence cover a distance of 210 statute miles from Montreal to South Traverse which is fifty miles below Quebec. Between Montreal and Quebec the channel offers a minimum draft of thirty feet at autumn low water; in the lower part of it high tide makes a lift of five feet more.

For over three years now the harbor of Montreal has been secluded and surrounded by all the grim secrecy and mystery of wartime. No one may enter its precincts except upon his lawful occasions. Sentries guard the approaches. There are no reports or arrivals or departures of ships, no sailing dates. Silent vessels slip away to unknown ports.

Even such general and vague statistics of shipping, incoming and outgoing tonnage, etc., as are made public are only given in a retrospect that makes them harmless. Information of any sort is forbidden, its disseminator liable to be called to account. Nor would any detailed account of shipping and of operations in the harbor serve any good purpose just now although it might aid a bad one. The war has so entirely altered the nature of the import and export trade that present figures would be meaningless as an account of the national life of the port. For that reason it is better to drop back a few years and view the Port of Montreal at the high point of development it had reached toward the closing years of the 1930s.

The present century has witnessed an extraordinary progress in this development of the Port of Montreal. As the first of the harbor improvements to be noted is the building in 1901 of the present heavy stone revetment wall, already spoken of, designed to hold back floodwater. At the same time the old Common and Commissioners streets were further widened: these originally represented, it will be remembered, the open space between the old fortification wall and the foreshore of the river. Now began, with the construction of Elevator No. 1, the building of the great grain elevators that are the most obvious feature of Montreal Harbour. Their towering height, the shapeless size, with no proportion to the site or scene they occupy, make them, to the eye of art, a blot upon the landscape, a disfigurement of nature's work. But they have a beauty all their own to a milling company. In any case they mean so much to the life and industry of Canada, to the life line of imperial safety, that the eye that looks on them becomes trained to a new adjustment. The four now standing on the harbor front represent a capacity of 15,260,000 bushels.

Any prejudice against the appearance of the elevators is greatly lessened for anyone who has enjoyed the privilege of seeing the inside detail of their operations. One is lost in admiration at the ingenuity of contrivance which they represent. The movement of the grain along the carriers, its downpour through the chutes, its passage out along the aerial carriers running above the dock sheds to carry it to any needed point—these things represent the last word in the mechanical economic carriage of grain.

The building of the great modern piers or docks that now line the harbor front began at the same period, with the Alexandra and King Edward piers, and Elevator No. 1. What was left of the little Islet Normandin (Market Island), the original shelter that made such a natural harbor as there was beside Champlain's Place Royale and Maisonneuve's Ville Marie, was now shoveled away (1903). The island is gone. The ocean liners pass over it. The addition of more railway tracks, a total present length of nearly sixty miles, new sheds, and the building of the Hochelaga high-level wharf, 575 feet long, marked a continuous progress. The harbor was itself extended by Act of Parliament in 1909, from its old boundary just below St. Marys current, and declared to occupy sixteen miles on each side of the river. Its boundary upstream is a line crossing the St. Lawrence 3760 feet above the Victoria Bridge, and its lower boundary is placed at Bout de l'Isle eight and three quarter miles below Longue Pointe Church. The original little harbor had no natural advantages, other than that it was better than anything else available, being just a casual shelter for a few odd vessels. But on the new scale Montreal Harbour has the outstanding natural advantage that it can expand to any extent. Nature placed obstacles upstream, none down. The harbor can go on forever. Whether Montreal stands in the wrong place and whether Maisonneuve should have put it below St. Marys current at the start, is a matter it is now too late to discuss. But for the movement of freight for the erection of plants, works, docks, the lower downstream the easier. The mountain is just in the way.

All these things were done through and by the Harbour Commissioners whose efficiency had been greatly increased by reducing their number to three and multiplying their actual power and responsibility. Montreal owes much to their energy and foresight and in particular to the devoted service of the Chairman, the late George Washington Stephens. It came with a shock of surprise, or worse, to many people, when the Harbour Commissioners lost their posts because the government in power at Ottawa changed in 1911 from the long and fortunate Liberal regime of Sir Wilfred Laurier (1895–1911) to a Conservative administration. It was thought proper to invite the Harbour Commissioners to resign. There was no exact precedent to follow, and so the office was treated as what is called a "political" one. Under British practice a political officer—there are only a hundred or so in the army of officials—is in charge of general policy in the relations between the department and the government. He is not a departmental worker nor a departmental expert. The First Lord of the Admiralty never goes to sea and wouldn't know the lea-scuppers from the main chains. These people resign as a body on a change of government. Quite different are "permanent" officers trained to work in the department as a lifework. These never resign. The storms of politics, mostly summer lightning, go over their heads. They go on working.

One may judge to which class should have been assigned the Montreal Harbour Commissioners, especially the chairman, who had taken their work as their life and their cause, hoping some day to stand in stone on the Harbour Front beside the Honorable John Young whose statue they set up in 1908. It was not to be. Out they went. This is not to say that the men who followed them in office did not do excellent service. Improvement and expansion went right on. Nor did they terminate when the commission itself was abolished in 1935 in favor of the present centralized system by which all the chief Canadian seaports are under the single control of a National Harbors Board at Ottawa. Each port has its local port master and staff. The change occasioned surprise in outside circles at Montreal, with a certain sense of being degraded in rank. But it was taken on the high authority of Sir Alexander Gibb, whose aid had been solicited for a National Port Survey of the Dominion (1931).

The further deepening of the channel continued till it reached its present thirty-five feet maximum. Elevator No. 3 dates from 1910. The floating dry dock, one of the notable facilities of the harbor, dates from 1912. The Great War brought special labors and for the time checked capital development. But further improvement and construction were carried on more vigorously than ever after the war. The substitution of electric engines for steam (1919) proved a mistake and was abandoned but the construction of the cold storage plant (1919), the purchase of (grain) Elevator B (Windmill Point) from the Canadian National Railway (1923) and the construction in the same year of Elevator No. 3 (Maisonneuve) are marks of the active progress made.

The first of the 20,000-ton Duchess vessels arrived in port in 1928. The close of this epoch saw Montreal by the middle of the 1930s, four hundred years after Jacques Cartier first landed on the island, as the second greatest seaport in North America in the value of its imports and its exports. By the present time the completed wharfage of the port covers ten miles. Its average export of grain before the war was 146,000,000 bushels a year. Ships could load at the rate of 1,000,000 bushels a day.

But the most striking of all the changes, though with nothing to do with the harbor as such, was the construction and completion of the vast Harbour Bridge that now spans the river clear over the top of all the shipping, just at St. Marys current. In order to get the necessary height (162 feet above high water) to clear the highest masts or superstructures of ships coming to Montreal, the bridge had to start far back from the bank of the river (at Lafontaine Street), rising above the houses and over the streets. The monument of the "Patriotes," executed in 1838, in the Place des Patriotes is almost directly under it. It lifts across the river to piers beside Île Ronde and St. Helens Island in one vast cantilever span of structural steel. From there it runs along a succession of deck trusses on stone piers across the shallow water to the South Shore between St. Lambert and Longueuil. It has a total length of two and one eighth miles. It was officially opened as the Harbour Bridge on May 24, 1930. But the fatal arrival in 1935 of the four hundredth anniversary of Jacques Cartier's discovery proved too much for Montreal. The bridge was rechristened the Jacques Cartier Bridge.

The bridge is not a railway bridge but only for vehicles and pedestrians. It has a roadway of thirty-seven feet to carry four lines of vehicles, room for a tramway on each side of the road, and outside all a sidewalk five feet wide on each side of the bridge. The bridge came as a consequence of the hopeless crowding and congestion of the Victoria Bridge after the advent of the motorcar. This latter bridge had been remodeled in 1898, the tube structure removed, and a new deck constructed for trains and vehicles on the original piers. It proved hopelessly inadequate. A further relief for transriver traffic was given by the Honoré Mercier Bridge at the west end of the island from Ville LaSalle (near Lachine) to Caughnewaga.

No feature of progress has meant more to the Port of Montreal than the unremitting fight against the ice which has successfully lengthened the season of navigation. The port is now open for seven and a half months each year, a gain of nearly a month on the conditions existing half a century ago.

But in spite of all that has been done the closing in of winter is inexorable. More than that: we have to accept as a permanent condition of the activity of the Port of Montreal the fact that we have now reached the limits imposed by nature on the lengthening of navigation. Two myths, always present in the popular mind, prevent the acceptance of this unwelcome truth. One is that the increasing mildness of the Montreal winter will render it more and more easy to keep the river open. The other is that the further progress of ice breaking and the treatment of ice with thermit explosives and similar methods may enable the channel to be kept open no matter what the winter is like.

Each of these popular ideas is an utter fallacy which it is important to explode. Let us take first the climate of Montreal, and put it down on paper with the pen point of impartial truth. We have already spoken of it in certain regards. Let us follow now the round of the seasons. The climate of Montreal is for many of us the best in all the world. Beside it London is dark and California garish, Winnipeg cold, New Orleans hot, Philadelphia neutral, and New York impossible. But we don't call it a mild climate. In Montreal the approach of winter is gradual, its departure rapid. September is clear and cool with blue skies and nearly always snowless. October is sharp but still bright, and bright with the glorious autumn color of the Canadian trees, with now and then a driving flurry of snow, a mimic snowstorm, and later, as if in repentance, the still and mellow Indian summer. November is, as it is everywhere, November—with wind and rain and mud, snowfalls of wet snow that at times bring the permanent winter snow to the city by the last week of the month. The temperature of November averages 33.4; the lowest record in forty years is zero, the highest 68 above. December sees winter, the real winter always threatening and never quite there, Christmas always risking to be "green" and vindicating itself with a Christmas snowstorm, the temperature averaging 19.8 above zero. January opens, at least by tradition, with a January thaw, the streets all aslop with wet snow that is turning to slush; then after this piece of fooling it turns to real cold with but little break or letup till February is over; by real cold we mean an average of 13, with spells below zero, snow that keeps falling and lying in the streets, and, where not shoveled away, great piles of it accumulating beside the sidewalks. In March the temperature falls but the winter stays.[1] Montrealers, as already said, debate each year the prospect of "dust on St. Patrick's Day," but few have seen it since St. Patrick. April, we pretend, is spring, with an average temperature of 41 degrees, but winter keeps coming back, with snowstorms, with ragged snow on the mountainsides, the port still frozen up but with news of the icebreakers bringing relief from below Sorel. Gradually, with a new annual surprise, the icebreakers reach the port, the port opens, a deep-sea captain gets a gold-headed cane, and first thing we know it is Maytime, all tulips and willow buds and soft airs, and after one week, no longer spring—midsummer.

CLIMATE OF MONTREAL—FORTY-YEAR AVERAGE

Average Temperature	Record High	Record Low
Jan. 13.3	53	−27
Feb. 13.9	47	−27
Mar. 25.8	68	−15
Apr. 41.6	83	2
May 55.3	89	23
June 64.7	92	38
July 69.6	95	46
Aug. 66.5	96	43
Sept. 58.4	90	32
Oct. 46.6	80	22
Nov. 33.4	68	0
Dec. 19.8	59	−25

One observes the contrast between the height of the summer navigation season and the depth of the winter that seals it. On a summer night Montreal seems all leaves and lights, and people out of doors at all hours, with long-drawn steam whistles from the boats in the Lachine Canal soft on the night. But compare a February night, in the cold heart of winter, twenty below zero,

[1] R. O. Campney, special article, Canada Year Book, 1940.

with a blizzard raging over the city in conflict with the great rotary snow plows, electric lights dimmed and blurred by the snow, and nothing moving in the street.

Such is winter in Montreal. Consider then the condition of winter navigation above and below it. The maritime harbors of Canada on the Atlantic do not freeze up, but the Strait of Belle Isle, Cabot Strait, the Gulf of St. Lawrence, and the river below the Island of Orleans are so blocked with moving ice, ice floes, and the solid ice along shore that there is no question of winter navigation beyond the smashing of a ferry passage from Quebec to Levis. When Cartier spoke of six feet of ice around his winter-bound ships in the Ste. Croix (beside Quebec) he spoke what is known to be true. The river freezes solid above Quebec as does Lake St. Peter, and not only freezes solid but tends from the movement of the current below the ice to pile huge ice jams far thicker than the average two feet of ice. Above Montreal the St. Lawrence freezes solid, and with it the connecting water sections all the way to Lake Superior, except where the fiercer current of the rapids breaks a way open to the surface. The Great Lakes do not freeze but their harbors do. Navigation comes to a full stop.

Montreal is thus blocked on both sides.

Nor are the winters getting milder. That ancient myth goes back to the earliest-known Canadian history. They were said to be growing milder in Frontenac's time. Peter Kalm, the Swedish traveler mentioned previously in this book, was told in 1749 by an ancient habitant that the winters when he was young were much more severe. But the thermometer will have nothing of it. It shows no general change over the whole period of definite record, now at least a century. The winters of 1933 and 1934 were, for many parts of eastern Canada, the coldest ever recorded.

So much for the fallacy of milder winters. Now take the fallacy of the conquest of the ice. In some senses, and very important ones, ice engineers have overcome the problem of the ice, more by the achievement of Howard Barnes of McGill University than by that of any other one man. People seldom realize what a triumph of engineering they are witnessing when they drive past a great Canadian power house and power dam thrown across a river a quarter of a mile wide, operating in midwinter at twenty degrees below zero, with two feet of solid ice above and the broken water of the tailrace below, smoking into the frozen air. This was not possible till the engineers learned how to deal with "frazil ice," which means not honest, solid ice two feet in the chunk, but the dirty, mean stuff all half afloat in little broken bits like smashed-up rock candy. This stuff used to clog the flues and the turbines.

If anyone interested wishes to see a queer memento of this let him drive out along the Lower Lachine Road till he reaches, near to Lachine itself, the remains of what was the first attempt to supply electric light to Montreal. A queer old building, squat and low and long, runs straight out into the water to catch hold of a natural strip of rock which rises above the river. With the help of a little damming this enabled them to cut off a little section of the Lachine Rapids—a very little bit was enough—in order to turn it into light. It worked provokingly well in summer in the long daylight. It wouldn't work in winter, and the engineers used to sit in their electric-light building, trying to figure out by lamplight what was the matter with electricity. That day is passed. That problem is solved. We can generate electric power all over the Arctic regions from the great reserve of water power, to send out light and heat to less favored areas, to carry human life and industry to the farthest north. This triumph of engineering probably means more to the future of Canada than any other mechanical invention.

Thus much for power; not so for navigation. There the ice must have its way. Any idea that the Port of Montreal can be kept open all winter is just a dream. It is a fancy that has often been encouraged, especially during the days of rapid advances made with icebreakers and the impressive results of the use of the chemical mixture called "thermit." Thermit is a mixture of aluminum in fine grains with an oxide of a chemically weaker metal, usually iron. On being heated by a priming, as of magnesium powder, the aluminum combines violently with the oxygen of the oxide, generating great heat and setting the other metal free in the molten state. It does not explode but splatters the molten metal while burning. To the innocent eye it seems to be burning up the ice. Hence hope improved on success and rumor outstripped achievement. Newspapers at times report inventions, or suggestions, for keeping open the river channel all winter by installing warm electric wires along the ice. Another good way would be to pour hot tea on it.

It is evident then that, generally speaking, the ice conditions in the Gulf and in the Cabot Strait govern the length of the season at Montreal. On this point Mr. J. G. Macphail, the Director of Transport, writes: "It is to be observed that in 47 of the 55 years of the table (of annual first arrivals of ships at Montreal) the first arrival from sea was generally much later than the date of channel-opening from Quebec to Montreal. In only eight of these years did the first arrival from sea come within two days of the date of open channel.

"Last departures for sea are governed by conditions in the river itself and in the Gulf. This is due to the desire of ship owners to profit by every possible day and is made possible by the use of the Department's icebreakers both in the river and, in some cases, in the Gulf."

One may perhaps quote further, since the point is one of illimitable importance to Montreal and of direct bearing on the seaway problem, the dictum given by Sir Alexander Gibb in his National Ports Survey, a report of 1931–32:

"In dealing with the Ship Canal, it is opportune to refer to the question of winter navigation, which from time to time receives a certain amount of publicity. The introduction of icebreakers has extended the season of Montreal by sixteen days; it previously averaged 7 months and is now 7½ months. Theoretically, the earliest and latest dates yet recorded are respectively March 29 in 1921 and, until the present 1931–32 abnormal conditions, January 6 in 1929. For all practical purposes, however, the season may be said to open in the third week in April and to close in the first week in December. This is as much as can be certainly secured by the present methods; the expense is considerable but the results have been very valuable. To go beyond this would require a revolutionary change in method and even if the object could be secured, which is exceedingly doubtful, there would be no justification for the expenditure necessary to maintain navigation through the whole winter.

"Apart, however, from the technical and financial considerations that would face the Government, the excessive cost to shipping of hull and cargo insurance, the difficulties of navigation and the risk of serious delays would be insuperable obstacles to the commercial use of the St. Lawrence in the winter. Unless and until entirely new methods are devised, it is, I think, idle to bring the idea of winter navigation into calculations regarding the St. Lawrence route; and I think the reputation of the route is only likely to be tarnished by efforts to extend unnaturally the season of navigation."

Icebreakers indeed can do wonders. They originated from the Arctic whaling ships specially strengthened at the bow to be able to charge against the ice. The first recognized icebreaker, designed for that purpose only, was put on by Russia (1870) to keep open the Port of Cronstadt. After that they were much used in the Russian and Swedish ports. The earlier icebreakers such as the *Lady Grey* and the *Montcalm*, which were put on the St. Lawrence early in this century, were built spoon-shaped in the bow, and relied chiefly on lifting themselves on the ice, like a seal, and breaking it with their weight. More recent types resort also to cutting a passage through the ice with a propeller at the bow as well as at the stern. The great Russian icebreaker the *Baikal* works on keeping open a channel across Lake Baikal, a body of water over four hundred miles long, the lower part of which lies right across the path of the Trans-Siberian Railway. The channel kept open is fifty-two miles long through ice extending all the way and three feet thick.

It would be possible to keep the St. Lawrence channel open if we had icebreakers enough, working hard enough. But the cost of operation would be out of all proportion to any benefit received by the Port of Montreal; especially as the benefit derived from the earlier spring opening of the river, as far as ocean steamers are concerned, would be nothing at all, not one red cent, red or frozen. The point is that the Gulf of St. Lawrence and the Cabot Strait leading out of it could not be kept open. The Gulf does not freeze over as a solid mass, but the winter makes it an area of drifting ice floes with all shore lines and straits blocked with heavy ice. Commercial navigation is impossible. It is the opening of the Gulf which regulates now the opening of navigation up to Montreal. In old days the river was open for only a little over five months. The Gulf opened first and closed last. Ships waited for the river. Hence the prospects of early navigation in the season of today depend on the reports constantly sent in from the Gulf by aviation and telegraphed upriver to the Department of Transport at Ottawa from an Atlantic station, which is not to be named in wartime, but which is a city of over 60,000 inhabitants with a university in it and called after the head of the Board of Trade under George the Second.

Such reports, carrying the same old charm of the sea in its newest form, run in such a tone and tune as this:

FLIGHT NUMBER TWO STOP 1658 HOURS STOP PROCEEDED DIRECT TO NORTH PT P.E.I. THENCE TO GASPÉ TO HEATH PT ANTICOSTI TO CAPE GEORGE NFLD TO CAPE RAY TO 46.00 N 59.00 W TO SCATARI ISLAND AND ALONG COAST TO HALIFAX LANDED 1552 HOURS STOP ICE SIGHTED EN ROUTE STOP NORTHUMBERLAND STRAIT FROM CAPE TORMENTINE EASTWARD TO HILLSBOROUGH BAY OPEN WATER THEN CLOSE PACKED ICE AS FAR AS CAN BE SEEN STOP FROM CAPE TORMENTINE WESTWARD THROUGH STRAIT TO WEST PT P.E.I. CLOSE PACKED ON SOUTH SIDE AND EXTENDING NORTHWARD TO A LINE FROM MIRAMICHI BAY TO NORTH PT P.E.I. STOP WESTWARD OF A LINE FROM NORTH PT P.E.I. TO SOUTH PT ANTICOSTI OPEN WATER WITH EXCEPTION SMALL STRING TEN MILES EAST OF BIRTH PT STOP NORTH SIDE BAY CHALEUR OPEN WATER AS FAR AS CAN BE SEEN

Mr. Alexander Ferguson, the Port Manager of the Harbour of Montreal, makes the following interesting analysis of the situation from 1871 to 1940:

It is found that during the past seventy years the period of time the harbour is open to ocean navigation has definitely increased. This fact is clearly shown by the following averages:

70–year average—1871	to 1940,	inclusive—218 days.
60 " " —1881	to 1940,	inclusive—222 days.
50 " " —1891	to 1940,	inclusive—223 days.
40 " " —1901	to 1940,	inclusive—226 days.
30 " " —1911	to 1940,	inclusive—228 days.
20 " " —1921	to 1940,	inclusive—231 days.
10 " " —1931	to 1940,	inclusive—234 days.

Analyzing the earlier years still further, we find that during the ten years from 1871 to 1880, the harbour was open an average of only 207 days. Comparing this with the average of 234 days for the last ten years indicates that we can now reasonably expect some twenty-seven more days' navigation than we could sixty-five to seventy years ago.

We have spoken of the typical Montreal citizen who sits and reads the summer sailing list of the port as people in Kentucky read about horse races. A marvelous sailing list indeed it is. The effect is created not so much by the impressive schedule of sailing dates of the great passenger liners, extending for weeks ahead, as by the announced voyages of steamers that seem to be striking out for ports all over the seven seas. Here are ships from Montreal to Amsterdam, Rotterdam, and as many dams as there are in Holland; ships from Montreal to the Baltic; ships direct from Montreal to South Africa, and of late years Montreal to West Africa; ships from Montreal to the Mediterranean and to Greece; and in the contrary direction ships of the New Zealand Shipping Company from Montreal to New Zealand via Cape Horn. Strangest of all are the sailings, not regular but intermittent, and presaging all kinds of things for the future are the sailings and the announced arrivals of ships between Vancouver and Montreal via the Panama Canal, or ships in port at Montreal on a voyage from Toronto and even Fort William to Vancouver. The strangest-seeming cargo route, for those who take an interest in such things, used to be that of the Booth Line out of Liverpool for Iquitos, Peru, not via the Pacific Ocean but up the Amazon, clear through Brazil and out again, to a seaport that ought to be, by school geography, on the top of the Andes. But the voyage from Fort William to Vancouver, in apparent defiance of the Rocky Mountains, is at least a close second.

Most of these boats are merely cargo boats, not tramps, but vessels running on a schedule. A few like the New Zealand boats carry passengers. Indeed, there has always been from the Port of Montreal a sort of specialty of steamers taking a few passengers only—up to a dozen—boats not in a hurry, not precise as to their day of sailing, boats without music or hired amusement, but for those who know enough to secure a passage in them, offering a type of old-time comfort, of undisturbed quiet, lost in the crowded tumult of a fashionable liner. The "economics" of such passenger boats is interesting. After all, a vessel must float. It can't be all full of dead-weight cargo; you must have some air in it or it will sink. So you may as well put some passengers in the air, as you have to have it anyway; not too many or they'll need too much air. In any case, after you pass such and such a number, maritime law on the St. Lawrence, as elsewhere, runs into a new set of regulations, necessary for a crowded ship's company, negligible for a tableful, questions of carrying a doctor, nurses, children's playrooms, sale of liquor, and such. The ships we speak of avoid this higher scale of cost. The passengers, apart from a little bit of table and bedroom service, partly covered by tips, carried thus to fill up the air, are "velvet" to the ship and the voyage velvet to the passenger.

There is no doubt that the psychology of ocean travel, before the catastrophe of the depression, had got hopelessly mixed up with luxury, hurry, and ostentation. The revolt against it takes various forms. One is the revolt of the wholesome-minded young people, students and such, caring nothing for social forms and too sensible to waste money when they can use it better, who deliberately "go third," and in going it have lifted up third till it threatens "first." The other is the revolt, or the reversion, of older people to the ship of the past, sailing its leisurely way with the old-time uncertainty of the sea. Added to both the revolts is the supertravel of the air, out-luxifying luxury, and making the twenty-five knots of the ocean liner look like twenty-five cents. If luxury travels by air, if love travels third, and peace travels slow—how then will float the floating palace? As between such tendencies there might be reason to suppose that the luxury liner may not be the "success" type of ship in a restored world. The Port of Montreal might reflect on this awhile.

But to appreciate in the concrete the varied character of the ocean shipping entering the Port of Montreal, one should turn to the pages of Mr. Lawrence Tombs's masterly technical study of the port. Mr. Tombs presents a very vivid picture of the varied cargo trade out of Montreal by giving some "specimen export cargoes" of outgoing ships of the period just following the Great War (season 1925). Here is the steamship *Grey County*, May 8, Montreal to the Havre, carrying *54,000 bushels of wheat; 455 pieces of timber; 2 cases of cotton goods; 1 case sundries; 3 bales woolens; 2 cases silks; 21 packages; 1800 bundles hides; 192 rolls paper; 4968 packages implements; 1289 billets copper; 268 cakes copper; 12 cases dry goods; 50 cases catsup; 14 barrels of graphite; 14 boxes engines; 600 bags of asbestos; 1220 bales wood pulp; 1 case canoes; 37 boxes mica; 1118 bags w. shanks; 2 boxes of books*—a cargo which looks like something for everybody in the Havre, with even canoes and books to read.

Yet here on the same morning is the *Bretta* outward bound for Cardiff and Bristol, with *59,600 bags of sugar*—just that. Going down the river the same day is the *Canadian Victor*, also bound for Cardiff but carrying *175,000 bushels of wheat; 28,000 bushels of oats; and a list of items as long as that of the Grey County* with not a single one, except "wheat," the same.

With these ships goes the steamship *New Aster*, off for Limerick; *178,000 bushels of wheat*—nothing else.

Next day there follows the *Manchester Regiment* bound for

Manchester. She is carrying as the main item of her cargo 727 *head of cattle*. This means to those who know the St. Lawrence that the cattle trade has been opened again after its long cessation. In the old days of steam and sail discussed in an earlier chapter the cattle trade out of Montreal was one of the outstanding features of the port. Canadian cattle were taken over thin— "store cattle," they called them—and fattened up for the British butcher after their arrival. Even some of the passenger steamers, the old *Laurentian* and such, carried cattle, and the cattle boat played a peculiar part in offering a free ocean trip to young men willing to help look after the animals. The British apprehension of "foot and mouth disease" being brought over by Canadian cattle—a very acute apprehension since there was none of the disease in Canada—led to the prohibition after 1893 of this trade in store cattle. This kept the British market for the British stock farmer. The cattle boats disappeared from the river. When the embargo was lifted in 1923 it was necessary to secure new boats of a suitable type. A ship of eight thousand tons with permanent fittings for the cattle pens will carry at least five hundred cattle, needing the care of about twenty cattlemen. But tariff changes and other causes have rendered the cattle trade of later days varying and uncertain.

But the cattle on the *Manchester Regiment* are only the main item of a manifest that carries thirty-eight others. Apart from 646 bags of cattle feed, the 2309 bales of hay, and the 101 bales of straw which constitute the cattle's own board and lodging, the ship carries *1250 sacks of flour, 16,977 pieces of pine, 1941 boxes of cheese, 776 barrels of apples, 60,600 maple blocks*, and so on, endlessly. Some of the items, like the wheat, the flour, the cheese, the apples, the 9350 boxes of lard, are agricultural products of the farm and grist mill, others represent agriculture plus the factory—*346 boxes of canned beef, 2000 cases of evaporated milk*, etc., others purely manufactures, as *67 boxes of auto tires and 21 reels of cable, 40 boxes of steel nails*, etc.; others were things purely of the mind and imagination as the four cases of advertising matter.

This *Manchester Regiment,* by the way, is a typical ocean cargo boat of large size as contrasted with the typical large-size lake carrier. With a total length of 471 feet, 6 inches she has a beam of 57 feet, 9 inches with a speed of 14½ knots. If loaded with wheat only she could carry 397,787 bushels on a draft of 30 feet, 2 inches. A Canadian lake freighter of the largest class carries 500,000 bushels with a draft of only 18 feet, 6 inches. But her superficial measurement would show a length of 633 feet and a beam of 70 feet.

On the next day the *Doonholm* sails for New Zealand and Australia with a manifest list that covers half a page of print and makes the others look simple. It is notable that the items are all manufactured goods. The largest single item is that of 4685 packages of agricultural implements. On the other hand the *Aldermin* sails next day for Rotterdam carrying nothing but wheat, rye, and oats. The "opposite number" of the *Aldermin,* the import vessel in the other direction, would be one of the famous "gin ships," carrying gin to Montreal from Holland (and nothing else). The green and red cases of DeKuyper breathed, or seemed to breathe, a soft atmosphere over the port. Their arrival was always specially announced in the Montreal press, half jocosely, half joyously.

Among this unending variety of exports and imports one can, however, form a good idea of what are the principal items of the ocean trade of Montreal and of their relative importance from the tables published each year by the Dominion Department of Marine and Fisheries. They are for calendar years, not fiscal, and therefore the year 1938 is the last one that is undisturbed by war conditions.

The statistics here presented must be taken with a word of caution, or a grain of salt, or with any of the things that statistics are usually taken with. It is evident that some of the commodities in question are loaded off, and then loaded on, to vessels in port and hence counted twice, or twice less the amount of the commodity consumed in Montreal. Others come by rail, or are made in Montreal, and thus count only once. Note the cases of cement, sugar, etc.

PORT OF MONTREAL

Principal Commodities in Water-borne Cargoes Landed from
and Loaded to Vessels of Montreal, 1938

Commodity	Total, 1938, Tons
Grain	5,002,755
Coal, bituminous	2,114,141
Petroleum, crude	2,624,206
Coal, anthracite	1,681,826
Petroleum products (except gasoline)	673,564
Gasoline	1,018,593
Sugar	355,588
Flour	234,120
Wood pulp	378,520
Base bullion, matte, pig and ingot (nonferrous metals)	209,767
Cement	107,692
Canned goods (except meats)	103,130
Lumber, timber, box, crate, and cooperage material	134,248
Iron and steel (bar, sheet, structural, pipe)	96,939
Automobiles, auto trucks, and auto parts	82,005
Molasses	52,138
Dressed meats	74,485
Ores and concentrates (except iron)	31,855
Sulphur	35,173
Newsprint	49,056
Mill products (except flour)	121,514
Totals (21 Commodities)	15,181,315
Grand Totals, All Commodities	16,193,805

Montreal stands in most intimate relation to the export of
grain (mainly wheat) and its equivalent, flour, and hence to the
production of western wheat, and hence to the economic life
of the Northwest. Wheat is no longer the main product nor the
mainstay of Canada. Gold alone runs it close, and in the gross
value of the product it is rivaled by pulp and paper, by the pack-
ing industries, and far exceeded by textiles as a total class. In
many recent years the tourist trade has run ahead of it in dollars
and cents. Indeed the whole product of agriculture only repre-

sents about a quarter of Canadian production today. But agriculture builds a nation. Tourist trade sells it. Tourist trade is indeed the worst of national economies, mere economic serfdom that tends to turn a nation into hotelkeepers selling scenery with waiters serving supper to people on vacation, whose work is to make iron and steel and such things in real industries.

Wheat and its equivalent, flour, is the chief grain export as the crop of rye, oats, and barley is largely used for animal feed and for distilling. Canada consumes about twenty per cent of its wheat at home; its people eat about four bushels each; the rest is fed to poultry, etc. A hen will eat (gladly) a bushel a year.

Since the opening of the Panama Canal Montreal loses all the wheat export that goes out by Vancouver and the Panama Canal, an unexpected commercial phenomenon. This meant 38,000,000 bushels in the total export crop of 146,000,000 bushels in 1938–39. Only a small part, what is called diplomatically a "token," goes out by the Hudson Bay Route, 916,913 bushels in 1938. The season is not only short but even shorter than it looks, opening before export is ready. In any case the Churchill route is handicapped by the fact that there is no market for shipping. Everything must be done by previous charter. Moreover, delay means imprisonment for winter, perhaps on a rising market. Montreal has nothing to fear from Churchill, but much from Vancouver-Panama. Nor does the West any longer worry over Churchill. The route is now unimportant politically. The railway was built as the prairie farmer's safety valve. Panama supplies a better: it takes all the British Columbia wheat, practically all the Alberta export, and a fringe of the Saskatchewan.

The bulk of the export wheat moves to Fort William, thence by water down the lakes to the Lake Huron ports and Port Colborne on Lake Erie, the head of the Welland Canal. But at Lake Erie the moving stream is tapped by exports via Buffalo to American ports, chiefly New York, where the advantage of a continual and competitive market for shipping offers a great advantage. Cut rates at New York at times have turned wheat into ship's ballast at Montreal. In 1938–39 (July 31–July 31),

30,000,000 bushels of Canadian export wheat went out by that route.

Navigation ends at Montreal only to begin again. The river and lake navigation extends, in its first stretch, 369 miles to reach Lake Erie at Port Colborne, the head of the Welland Canal; 237 miles more to the head of Lake Erie at Toledo; 389 miles more, past Detroit and up Lake Huron to Sault Ste. Marie, and from there 273 miles to Fort William, a total transit to the Canadian head of Lake Superior of 1168 miles. The full distance to the head of the lake at Duluth is 1245 miles. The distance from Montreal to the tail of Lake Michigan at Chicago is 1200 miles. In this vast area of inland navigation there moved in 1938 through Canadian canals about 20,000,000 tons of shipping.

More than that. From Chicago navigation connects, not yet in great volume, with the whole inland water system of the Mississippi, the Missouri, and the Ohio, reaching thus to the Gulf of Mexico. This system once held all the national importance of a main system of communication, all the peculiar splendor and romance that went with the Mississippi passenger steamboats of the days of Mark Twain. The railroad humbled all its pride, into lifeless levees, with grass among the cobblestones, a few dingy scows, and a few dilapidated excursion steamers, calling "Ho! for Barnes's Point," to people who could drive there in fifteen minutes in their motorcars.

All this has changed. Water-borne traffic is coming back to its own. The world of today moves dead-weight cargoes, heavy as lead, heedless of time, careless of wind and weather, and influenced only by the inconceivable cheapness of transit by water. The new bride of the waters is the cement barge, moving as majestically as the water funeral in Tennyson's poem.

It was this development of water-borne inland traffic which led to the wide popular demand for the creation of a seaway from the St. Lawrence to the Great Lakes, by which is meant a deepening of existing canals so as to allow the passage of ocean vessels. By this the shipping on the inland waters and the shipping on the ocean routes would be amalgamated into one great system of water transport, and the sea would, as it were, wash the shores of Toronto Bay and the Lake Front at Chicago. The great inland cities, from Chicago, Duluth, and Fort William all the way down to Kingston and Oswego, would become ocean ports enjoying that outlook on the seven seas now possessed by Montreal and Quebec alone. The project has in it all the appeal that goes with those vast achievements of man over nature which revolutionize the globe we live on—the digging of the Suez Canal, the far greater achievement of Panama, the vast schemes of irrigation dams that turn a desert to a garden, Assuam and Boulder and Grand Coulee, and the projects still unrealized for flooding the low-level part of the Sahara Desert to bring rain to the rest of it and turn it again to what it was thousands of years ago.

None of these projects has a more generous appeal, a nobler outlook than the project of the St. Lawrence Seaway. Agitated and discussed for years, the plan was at last definitely accepted and the Seaway Pact signed by the President of the United States and the Dominion Government in 1941, accompanied by a parallel pact as between Ontario and Ottawa. It calls for the completion of the seaway by 1948. Delayed by the opening of war, it appears probable that construction may be undertaken as a work contributing itself to victory.

Many of us cannot help but endorse the plan of the seaway for the sake of this very grandeur of outline. On general principles it seems as if opening up a water connection from the heart of North America out to the open sea must be of benefit to mankind at large. Nor would it seem to involve any greater cost in human labor, the ultimate cost of all production, than to set to work the idle millions fed free in bad times by the rest of us. But these generous and general speculations must not blind us to the serious aspects to be considered in regard to the seaway as a "business proposition."

One point of discussion, however, hitherto in the front line of argument, has unexpectedly vanished, and may now be mentioned first, only to be dismissed. A serious objection to the ship canal was its creation of needless power to the detriment of existing power enterprises. This objection was hitherto very generally regarded as sound, though not of necessity final as other advantages might offset it. The conclusion of the Brookings Institution in its admirable study of the project in 1929 ran: "Our analysis indicates that, although the development of the St. Lawrence hydroelectric energy will in the course of time doubtless be economically profitable, its exploitation at present would be premature." The hand of war has wiped the objection away as easily as a child's writing off a slate. It appears now in this hour of stress that we have not too much power but too little. We must develop more. When peace comes we shall need it even more for it is already seen that the only way to prevent peace from precipitating disaster by dislocation of employment is to turn war industry into peace industry at the same tempo with work for all as easy and as lucrative as now. For us in Canada this means work spent in the development and settlement of our still empty country. For that we can harness all the power in the Great Lakes watershed and find it still insufficient.

All opponents of the seaway project stress the evidence that is given by experts as to the essential difference between lake vessels and ocean vessels. This, of course, leaves out of count the vessels of war, a negligible quantity on the lakes in peacetime, prohibited by treaty and existing only in indirect form. It leaves out of count all the sailing yachts, sailing dinghies and "motor-boats" (not motor-driven cargo boats) of all sizes and forms, the whole apparatus of sport on the water; fun is fun anywhere but fun fourteen feet deep is deep enough anyway. The reference, of course, is to the vessels of commerce, not those of war and sport.

In the case of passenger vessels the distinction between an ocean liner and a river steamer would be obvious even to the eye of an Idaho miner—without coming up to look. The river steamer has developed lines of artistic beauty far more attractive to the untrained eye of the land than are the mixed superstructures, the humps, gaps, and derricks of most ocean steamers. The ocean boat never recaptures its lines till it reaches the superior tonnage of a duchess. But to the nautical eye the river steamer is all wrong; it carries its center of buoyancy too far up in its chest. It is liable to "turn turtle," as did even the ocean ships in the period when the designers first struggled with the problem of carrying heavy guns on the upper decks of iron ships; as witness the loss of H.M.S. *Captain* in 1870; or when designers went too far in carrying weight of superstructure—the probable cause of the mysterious loss of the *Waratah* in 1909—vanished with all hands. But the river steamer in the ocean would not only be liable to upset but certain to, in upsetting weather. It could only cross the ocean if the ocean stayed quiet enough. But for its own line of work, it can carry more passengers in less space for less cost than is possible for an ocean vessel.

Discussion centers around the cargo boats. "The lake freighters," writes the naval architect, Herbert C. Sadler, "are the last word in a type of vessel especially developed to do the business of carrying bulk commodities, such as iron ore, coal, etc., in the most economical way between the lake ports. Their business is on the lakes, not on the ocean. To alter the design to allow them to go to sea would be suicidal."

Ocean boats are essentially stronger and deeper. Stress is laid on stability in navigation, but for the lake boat on rapidity and mechanical cheapness in loading and unloading. An average of ten modern Upper Lake freighters shows a length of 535 feet to a beam of 58 feet and a draft of 27½, along with 303 horsepower. The corresponding ocean freighter has a length of 427 feet to a beam of 55 and a draft of 32 with a horsepower of 533. The lake freighter's hatches are in a continuous series on 24-foot centers, the ocean boat quite diversified. The lake boat is loaded and unloaded by gear on the dock, the ocean boat by gear on the deck.

The highly specialized appearance of the lake freighter in its extreme form leaps, as the French say, to the eye. Here is the great wheat carrier *Gleneagles,* 582 feet long but throughout nearly its whole length presenting nothing but a flat deck, all battened down, not even a chair to sit on; the only superstructures are the tiers of little deck houses four stories high, away up in the bow, and a group of others rising behind the funnel away at the stern. The boat has a beam of sixty feet, a molded depth of thirty-two feet, and a draft of twenty-one. But thus fashioned for one purpose the *Gleneagles* can carry 445,000 bushels of wheat.

Yet a part of this argument is not so sound as the other part. Granted the difference in gear and hatches, it may be that these differences are a consequence, not a cause. They may exist because the Welland Canal has a depth of twenty-five feet and not of thirty-six; and other boats may owe something of their shape to the limitations of the fourteen feet of Lachine and the canal system of the St. Lawrence above it.

One limit, however, is permanent. It is not possible to deepen the ship canal below Montreal to a depth to accommodate the world's great ships. Digging a canal is one thing; digging and blasting rock for two hundred miles is another. Some of the world's ships never will, never can, come up the seaway. How many are shut out? Here we may take the evidence presented in the Brookings Institution Report of 1929, very generally regarded as perhaps the best and most unbiased summary of the economic side of the case. It has to be admitted that the report makes out a bad case. We must remember that a twenty-seven-foot channel doesn't float a twenty-seven-foot draft ship. It can't scrape the bottom. You must give it, in salt water which floats it best, two and a half feet under the bottom, and in fresh water, three feet.

The tables cited in the report endeavor to show what proportion of existing ocean shipping could enter a seaway according to the depth of channel offered. Thus a twenty-five-foot St. Lawrence Great Lakes channel would only permit the passage of ships with an ocean draft of twenty-two feet, six inches. But if you take the cargo ships in the U.S. foreign trade as illustrating the traffic that the seaway would be supposed to bring up the river, you find that 88½ per cent of them are of deeper draft than twenty-two feet, six inches. These figures are those of 1926, but as ships tend to grow bigger rather than smaller they apply as well, or better, today. Hence it is argued that a twenty-five-foot canal "would exclude all important ocean shipping." A twenty-seven-foot channel as favored by the Canadian section of the Joint Board of Engineers (1926) would admit ships with an ocean draft of twenty-four feet, six inches. Even this, the report argues, would greatly restrict the availability of the seaway. Of the passenger cargo ships now in the U.S. foreign trade, this would admit only 37 of the total 277. Of cargo ships it would admit only 1504 out of a total 3103. Even of the tonnage operating (at the time of the report) on a regular schedule out of Montreal and Quebec, in all 82 steamers of which 59 were British, only 13 per cent could go on up the seaway with a twenty-seven-foot channel. Similarly a twenty-seven-foot channel would exclude 60 per cent of the tramp grain ships that come to Montreal from using the seaway above and 81 per cent of the cargo vessels and the tankers engaged in the intercoastal trade. The report argues that a channel depth of thirty-three feet is the minimum that could serve the supposed purpose of the seaway. Even that would exclude—a quite obvious fact—the great luxury liners.

The opinion of what are called Montreal "interests" are strongly against the seaway. By "interests" we mean people affected in dollars and cents by the project, either directly as shipping men or indirectly as shareholders. Naturally, since "interests" are as human as the rest of us, they cannot help seeing the project from their own point of view—through the bottom of an empty pocket. The Port of Montreal, they say, and indirectly much of the city, lives on the transshipment of cargo, ocean to lakes, lakes to ocean. The seaway, if successful and in proportion to its success, would substitute passage-through for transshipment. It would do to Montreal what Montreal did to Quebec. Hence the bigger the success made in Toronto and Duluth, the less in Montreal. If, on the other hand, the seaway failed, it would leave a vast burden of taxes for no tangible benefit.

Thus having been as thoroughly damned as the rapids themselves, as badly scraggled as the Jackdaw of Rheims, it is pleasant to know that the seaway plan is to go right ahead. As agreed in the Pacts of 1941 it calls for a twenty-seven-foot channel through the St. Lawrence and the lakes and the connecting waters. The heaviest work to be done will be in the international section of the St. Lawrence between Lake St. Francis and Lake Ontario. Here the proposal involves great physical changes; the heavy dam needed to get the twenty-seven feet of depth will flood out many islands and half islands in the river all the way from Cornwall to Cardinal (about 40 miles), drown out a long stretch of the existing highway, and even of the track of the Canadian National Railway.

A unique part of the plan, a queer example of the romance of engineering, will be the arresting of some of the rivers that now flow north to James Bay and recalling them to the St. Lawrence watershed, to guarantee a sufficient head of water. This indeed is already being done by the diversion of Long Lac, which hitherto drained into the Albany River, into Lake Superior and the diversion of the Ogoki, a tributary of the Albany into Lake Nipigon and thus to the St. Lawrence watershed. The estimate of cost made by the Joint Board of Engineers (1926) was $427,-000,000. In the light of the war finance of the hour this seems a mere bubble.

The truth is that arguments against the seaway never reached home, as compared with the vast and obvious general truth of the physical utility of water connection halfway across the continent. It has been seen that the power objection has vanished into mist. The rest will go also. We must look at the long run, not the short. The life of a ship is little more than a generation. In forty years a new set of ships will sail the seas anyway. The existence of the seaway will alter all conditions. It may place such a premium on ships of a twenty-two-foot draft as to alter the world's shipbuilding. It may be that even with transshipment at Montreal a new era would open for larger vessels out of the great inland cities with other and more varied cargoes than grain and ore and such single dead weight. Even the passenger trade will have its surprises. Large liners may move on lazily past Montreal all the way to Chicago, with a new set of passengers taking a lake cruise with the music and luxury of the supership.

Compare the cruises "New York to Montreal" via ocean liner which no one foresaw. And finally the construction and extension of the seaway may afford exactly the kind of postwar activity needed for the out-of-work millions of veterans and ex-munition makers.

CHAPTER XIII

French and English

How French Is Montreal? First and Second Impressions. Statistics of Racial Origin. The French Language in Montreal. As Good French as the English Is Good English—Old French and New. Extent of Bilingualism. Separation of the Races. Division of Education, Family, and Social Life. The Two Universities. French and English Street Names.

AN APOLOGY, or at least an explanation, is needed for the use of "English" at the head of this chapter. This generalized use of "English" and "England" has become a matter of great sensitiveness. Time was when world-famous books could be written under such titles as *The Expansion of England, The English Constitution, England in Egypt,* and the *Government of England,* with no outcry from Wales or protest from the Isle of Man. A poet could write that the "*sands of the desert are sodden red . . . and England far and honour a name,*" without being asked the distance from Glasgow or Dublin. The words "England" and "America" are both used in senses quite wrong, and exactly right.

The trouble was that the United States never had an adjective; hence "American" and therefore "America." The mother country didn't have a single name; all the various terms meant too much or too little. "Great Britain" left out Ireland. "Britain" left out the "British Empire." The British Empire took in India, and the "United Kingdom" is a law term. "Britain" was, till very recently, a poetic term. Forty years ago a person would no more think of taking a trip to Britain than he would to Caledonia or Erin. Only poets went there. Nor has "Britain" any fully competent adjective, since "British" won't translate and is especially unsuitable for Montreal as the French cannot say "les Britanniques" and must say "les Anglais."

The usage in Montreal has always been for English people to say "the French and the English." French people used also to say "les Canadiens" to mean themselves, but seldom now, and the English never. "British" is used only for the special distinction of British race as opposed to English speech.

Montreal is overwhelmingly a French city by racial origin as compared with British and by a heavy majority even when we include among the "English" (English speaking), the Europeans, other than French, the Jews, the four or five thousand Asiatics and the handful—if one thousand makes a handful—of Negroes. The latest classified census returns show the city as 64 per cent French, 22 per cent British, 5 per cent Jewish, and 9 per cent something else.

This great predominance of the French is entirely contrary to the first general impression of casual visitors and tourists. These visitors see only certain parts and certain aspects of Montreal—the railway stations, the steamship docks, the big hotels, the main shopping district, and, perhaps, McGill University. They can form no idea of how French the city really is. It seems an English-speaking city, except that a lot of the people speak a rather queer but not unattractive English. The true racial aspect of the population is concealed from casual visitors partly because they do not go into the specially French parts of the town, and also because the section of the population that is neither French nor British, which includes the large element brought by the European migration of this century, learns to speak English rather than French. To this is added the fact that the great bulk of the French are bilingual to a certain extent and use English in the current intercourse of shops and streets. The last classified census returns show that of the total French population of the province of Quebec, 71 per cent of the French speak French only; and even on the Island of Montreal 38 per cent of the French people speak French only. But this is partly because the island includes a large semirural area, and all French children under five are classified as not speaking any other language, which is just like statistics. These "children under five" represent one tenth of the whole population, or the equal of one third of the class in question. Count them out altogether and the 38 per cent changes to about 25.

On the other hand, many British people live and die in Montreal and make no attempt to learn to talk French, getting no further with it than the bilingual call of the streetcar conductor giving them a choice of *Guy!* and *Ghee! Prinsse Arthur* and *Prinsse Arthúr.*

We have also to realize that, as far as present vision can go, the French language in Montreal, as in French Canada, is there to stay. The mass of the people speak it as their mother tongue; it has behind it all that goes with a system of public education, covering eleven years of school, the four years of college, the law school, the graduate school, the medical clinic, and the laboratory of science, with French as the medium of instruction throughout. Add to this the French metropolitan press of Montreal with daily and weekly editions comparable to those of any great American city. To this is added the unending outpour of French that comes from the private radio stations speaking French and the government (C.B.C.—"Radio-Canada"), which is compelled to be bilingual at the peril of its life. By these combined good offices the Montreal taxi driver may hear as he drives the appealing accents of a *chanson d'amour*. This bilingualism, we say, is at the peril of the political life of Radio-Canada, because the French are intensely jealous of their language, insist on its use in street signs, traffic directions, and other wastes of paint. People in Montreal keep off the grass in two languages and are directed on their way by such signs, imbecile at first sight, as "Pont Victoria Bridge," "Parc LaFontaine Park," "School Zone École," and so on. Insistence goes further and puts French needlessly on our paper dollars with a "CINQ" that looks like "One"—and acts like it; insists on it for railway stations and timetables where much of it is an amalgam of English and wears a suspicious look. A train in Montreal is marked up as *due* in English and *dû* in French, a thing unknown in France. But this distorted language is mostly forced by the exigencies of translation, not, as will be shown later, by the "badness" of French in Montreal.

But the main factor in the retention of French in Montreal is its rootage in the history of the country and its embodiment in the sacred offices of the church. "When a people lose their liberty," says Alphonse Daudet, "as long as they keep their language it is as if they held the key to their prison." For the French in Canada the doors of what was once their prison have long since been thrown wide open. But they keep the key.

A rough-and-ready, very rough and not quite ready, division of the area of Montreal shows the French on what is called the east side—east of St. Lawrence Main Street—and the English on the west side. The division came about as follows. As the old French town was more and more taken over by shops, business houses, and public institutions, the families moved out into the suburbs. The richer ones began building houses even beyond these original "faubourgs," up the slope toward the mountain— the old Torrance House, Simon McTavish's famous house (afterward haunted), and similar suburban manors. The English (in this case many of them Scottish), growing rich and controlling capital, bought up the beautiful farms that stretched away from the crown of Beaver Hall Hill to the very foot of the mountain—the McGill farm, the McTavish farm, and others, some once French, as seen in the City Map of 1836. The central and best part of this became the English residential district of the richer class already described. From this district English settlement spread west, taking the second best when the first was gone. The French, moving from the old town, of necessity, went further east, along Sherbrooke and up the beautiful road that became St. Denis, and so, eastward and northward, out over Logan's Farm and down the river endlessly.

Yet this general division was broken by many exceptions. The French area was the first to extend to encircle the mountain so that, on its rearward side, Outremont and the Côte des Neiges village are French. Yet when settlement was further extended by the tunnel, Mount Royal was occupied by the English. The French also originally spread in St. Ann's suburb beside what had been the river, St. Pierre, but the influx of Irish into Griffintown made an "enclave," or whatever is Irish for it, among the French. Verdun and the factory area, as already seen, became mainly English-speaking but with many French intermixed. On the French side, the east side, the factory districts that grew up and the Canadian Pacific (Angus) Railway shops drove a wedge of English-speaking workers into what had been an entirely French area.

These general tendencies are illustrated statistically by the map of the municipal wards of Montreal and the areas of municipalities surrounded by Montreal, viz., the cities of Verdun, Westmount, Outremont, and the town of Mount Royal.

The question naturally arises as to what extent this large predominance of French people implies the use of the French language. There is very much misunderstanding in regard to the French spoken in Montreal. It happens once in every while that some English visitor, meaning no harm, refers to it as a "patois." The effect is like throwing a brick into a beehive. There is no point of their nationality on which the French Canadians are so touchy as on their language. Proud and confident of their quite imperfect English, they are sensitive to a degree about their practically perfect French.[1] All the more so as many people, both in Great Britain and the United States, suppose that what is spoken in Montreal is not really French.

The point is one that will stand some explanation. The written French of the books and of the journalism of Montreal, and of

[1] L. de Montigny, *La Langue Française au Canada*, 1916.

the speech of educated French Canadians in Montreal, is just as much French, just as much and just as little, as the speech of the English people is English. We are speaking here, of course, not of Frenchmen who have come out from France, or English people just out from England, but of people born and raised in this country or brought to it in such early childhood as fully to take on its accent. On these terms English Canadians, however well educated, going over to England are never mistaken for English, nor are Irish from Dublin, nor Australians from under the Equator. Which speech is best and which worst, and which worse still, there is no need to discuss. Certainly the English of darkest Ontario sinks low; "current" is pronounced "curnt," and an orange becomes an "ornge." On the other hand, there are circles in England where a railway becomes a "wailway," from which the 4.04 train leaves at "faw faw."

Such superiority in general as the English language of the "old country"—England, Scotland, and Ireland all three—has over the English spoken in Canada comes from the greater attention paid to voice and its cultivation in the schools. Reading aloud is almost disregarded in public education in Canada, a result of the curse of standardizing matriculation, which omits it because it "doesn't count." The result is well-known to anybody who ever asks a McGill student to read aloud from a book to his fellow students in the class and then lets him sit down and allows a public-school boy from England to do it. The poor old school tie has been at least good for the throat.

But this is mere rivalry of language. For the unlucky French Canadian there is no rivalry, nothing but (linguistically) master and servant. He is measured against Paris and there is no appeal. He has had to tolerate as best he could that peculiar arrogance of the old world toward the culture of the new, which, until yesterday, the new world had to bear. Such values are all shifting now and are sliding the same way—Spanish courtesy, German culture, Italian honor, and French generalship—in the wreckage that was Europe. Presently the French Canadian would perhaps rather not be mistaken for a Frenchman.

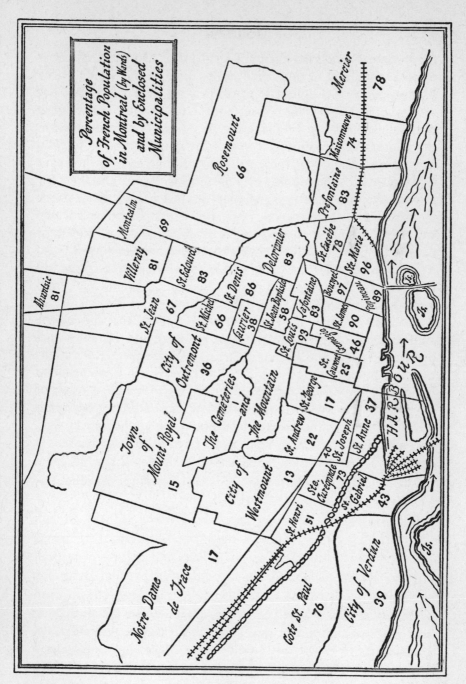

Percentage
of French Population (by Wards)
in Montreal and by Enclosed
Municipalities

Rosemount 66

Mercier 78

Maisonneuve 74

Prefontaine 83

St. Eusebe 78

Ste. Marie 96

Montcalm 69

Villeray 81

St. Edouard 83

St. Denis 86

Delorimier 83

Bourget 97

St. James 90

Papineau 89

Ahuntsic 81

St. Jean 67

St. Michel 66

Laurier 38

St. Jean Baptiste 58

Lafontaine 83

St. Louis 93

Duvernay 46

City of Outremont 36

The Cemeteries and The Mountain

St. Laurent 25

HARBOUR

Town of Mount Royal 15

St. Andrew 22

St. George 17

St. Anne 37

St. Joseph 40

City of Westmount 13

Ste. Cunegonde 73

St. Gabriel 43

St. Henri 51

Notre Dame de Grace 17

Cote St. Paul 76

City of Verdun 39

273

The speech of the French-Canadian habitant and the speech of the Montreal French working class is a different matter. It is not intelligible to English people who have learned French elsewhere and not mixed with French-Canadian working people. French people from France understand it easily enough, just as any of us understand the English of Somerset and very nearly understand the English of Yorkshire.

So much for comprehension. As to the words used, there are in both the spoken and printed French of Montreal, innumerable English words, some taken over without change and some with shifts of spelling or oddities of pronunciation. But so there are, though not so many, in the French spoken in Paris. Most English people know very little of the French language, little more than lies within the circle of an Ollendorff, or other "grammar," and a few trips across the Channel. Yet they have an easy and arrogant assumption that they know French. When such people come to Montreal and see in the newspapers and hear in speech this peculiar vocabulary of English words they think how different it is from the purity of Paris. They find themselves invited to *lunch* (*longsh*), even to *luncher*, to take a *biftek* in a *bar* with a *songwidge*, to attend a *mitting* where they meet *un gentleman* or *une flirt*, *un jocky* or *un dandy*, and so on endlessly—not realizing that all these terms are Parisian French. So, too, a long list of words dealing with railways and transportation, where England led France—*railway*, *express*, *tramway*—and so on, just as the English language bows to the *cuisine* of France and talks of a *soufflé à pâté*, a *filet mignon*, etc. The list of these words is not only endless but includes many words hidden under a new spelling such as *boulingrin* and *rosbif*. Others have a shift of pronunciation, very droll to English ears, such as the sporting term *outsider*, pronounced in French with the accent changed and turned into *oot-see-dáre*. Naturally in Montreal, and in all French Canada, there appears also a long list of locally accepted English words, names of companies, localities, organizations, etc. Not one could be bothered talking of the Y.M.C.A. to call it anything else; or to translate "*le McGill Cricket Club*," or to call the C.P.R. *le Say-Pay-Air*. There are a lot of words that arise from the workingmen of both races being under one boss: *boss* itself, and *job*, and *foreman*, *freight*, and *switch*, *shed*, *winch*, and so on. Some combinations are very odd, "*saut morisette*," the French-Canadian spelling for "*somersault*," the two spellings both missing the mark, like bracketed shots of gunfire. Compare *Sainte-Folle* for *Stanfold*, and wind up with *Saint-Abroussepoil*, which means *Sandy Brook Point*.

But when allowance is made for all these peculiar factors of the situation the written French of the metropolitan journals of Montreal is just as good French as the English of the English newspapers is good English.

Some French Canadians would go further and say "better." They like the idea that their language in Canada has retained the original purity of the seventeenth century, the age of Louis XIV, of Racine and Molière, lost in France under later innovation. They like to recall that Father Charlevoix, in his visit to Quebec and Montreal in 1721, said that nowhere was the language spoken with greater purity (*plus purement*).

It is hard to sustain or refute this claim without getting lost in philology. Charlevoix probably meant by "purity" freedom from alien elements. But the original French of Canada was mixed as between Île de France (Paris), Brittany, Poitou, and so on. Moreover, old French is not necessarily good French any more than English must be good if it can be proved to be old. Compare in the Ontario English of the farmer and laborer the phrase, "*You hadn't ought to go*," this, especially when pronounced, as they do pronounce it, "*You hedden't ought to go*," is enough to bring tears of joy to the failing eyes of a philologian. It is a beautiful old Anglo-Saxon pluperfect subjunctive preserved in the people's speech a thousand years, like a fly in amber, a toad in a stone, or any other such ecstasy. Except on such ground as this we cannot rejoice over Montreal workingmen still saying *icitte* for *ici*.

Similarly the French-Canadian habitants of the countryside using bygone forms of bygone French dialects when they make a number of nouns feminine which at Paris are masculine: *une incendie, une honneur, une orage, une (e)squelette,* and so on.[2] These only reflect the confusion of the old Latin genders (masculine, feminine, and neuter) breaking down into two, like waters in a Canadian rapid divided by a rock. There seems to be no sense in retaining such divergences. Nor the antique dropping of vowels which changed *sud* to *su* and *œuf* to *oe;* nor the mixed-up use of what grammarians call *liaison* and *hiatus,* as when a French-Canadian habitant turns the Parisian *cent hommes* into *cenz' hommes, avant hier* into *avanz hier,* changes *donne-m'en* into *donne-moi-z-en,* or rather not changes, but retains an old form. Compare, on either side of the Atlantic, *"Malbrough s'en va-t-en guerre. Il reviendra-z-à Paques,"* etc.

Such vagaries are for the peasant to use, the philologian to put on a card index, and the *Société du Parler Français* of Montreal to exterminate at sight. They have no more place in the cultivated speech of Montreal society than *"them there"* has in a London drawing room.

If one turns from the French spoken in Montreal to the English spoken by the French the case is quite different. Almost all the French people understand English and speak it well enough for the business of the day in shops or factories; understand it to the full satisfaction at movies and at public meetings. All young French Canadians, even below the college class, can read English books if light enough but sink easily among hard sentences and long words. Anyone in Montreal unable to speak English and asking his way in French is probably newly arrived from a locality where French is used. In this "bilingualism," as far as it goes, the French are immeasurably in advance of the English. Most English people in Montreal cannot follow a French movie or a French speech or buy and sell in French. They don't need to. The French, conversely, have to.

But one must not exaggerate, as the Montreal French themselves do, the extent of their bilingual grip on English. Real bilingualism is very rare, in Montreal or anywhere. It can only exist where necessity and opportunity combine, and where a

[2]A. Rivard, *Bibliographie du Parler Français au Canada,* 1906.

native taste and aptitude give a further aid to circumstance. Many Montreal French people speak French with their children at home and send them to the English schools and colleges. Such children, if they continue to mix in both circles, become bilingual to a great extent.

Yet where the French fall short is when they try to write in English, not casual writing but books intended as literature. Here something is wanting, and the something wanting means, in a sense, everything. The English written is all right, the words all right, grammar and sentences, punctuation and paragraphs all right. Everything is correct—but that is all. There is a dead flatness, a dull uniformity of style, nothing of that turn and touch of language that illuminates and attracts. What they succeed in doing would be, of course, utterly beyond the English to do in reverse direction. Yet of the dull biographies and such, written in English by French Canadians, the best one can say is that they convey the truth, the whole truth, and nothing but the truth.

There is here intended nothing derogatory, no fault implied. People who can write at their very best in each of two languages must have a very low best to write at.

Most of the French in Montreal mispronounce English to a certain extent, offering no injury to an English ear. It is our English habit to throw a heavy accent on the first syllable of all combination words like *crow-bar*, *sheep-skin*, etc. The list is legion. A French Canadian, talking English, is detected as such at once by saying *crow-bar* (both alike), *sheep-skin*, and so on.

The almost complete social separation of the French and English in Montreal is as extraordinary as it is unfortunate. It seems to have begun very soon after the conquest. A certain number of newcomers, as notably and typically James McGill, mingled with the French and married among them. But most of the British traders who first came up to Montreal from the provinces were, as seen above, very unpopular. Other British people, coming out from home, kept themselves to themselves as soon as there were enough of themselves to keep to. This separation persisted. It was an object of frequent remark a hundred years ago.

The separation no doubt arises from the historical relation of the two races, from the difference of religion (as apart from the later influx of Irish), from the separation of the children at school, and from the fact that British people have an insular difficulty in learning a foreign language. Each race sees too well the faults, too dimly the merits, of the other. The English think that many of the French are priest-ridden; the French think that many of the English are badly in need of a priest. The English think that those of the French who are crooked are crooked in a selfish, petty way, using favoritism for little jobs. The French think that the English, when crooked, are crooked in a big, unselfish way, stealing a million at a time out of a franchise and giving silver cups to golf clubs. Merit, we say, passes unrecognized. All the English admit that, but for the French, Montreal would have had prohibition. But they differ in their degree of gratitude.

Nor does intermarriage help. There is very little of it; it is discouraged, generally speaking, on both sides, yet not discouraged enough to make it romantic and attractive. There is no civil marriage in Montreal (law of Quebec Province); marriage is only by the clergy, and for mixed marriages the Roman Catholic Church refuses to recognize the status of Protestant ministers. An example of this relative rarity of intermarriage is seen in a family history book recently printed (for personal circulation only) by one of the best-known families of Montreal, too well known to mention. The book traces the descent of all the family and its intermarriages since its ancestor arrived in Montreal soon after the conquest. The index of the names of the family includes in all five hundred names, of which one hundred names are those of the family itself, while the other four hundred represent intermarriage and collaterals. Of all these less than a dozen can be definitely distinguished as French.

A certain small number of French families are exceptions to what has been said. French boys are sometimes sent to English boarding schools, for the sake of their traditional form of education—full of open air, exercise, and independence, with study doggedly accepted under threat of punishment. Some French people admire this type of education; most don't. Most of all, French boys have always been sent from Montreal to the Royal Military College at Kingston, a grand old institution, with a sound outlook in all directions, military glory for the French cadets, hard work for the Scots, and Rugby football for the English. The heads of some French families, also, have been business associates with the English in a large way, and have grown too rich to live anywhere else than among the English.

Out of these exceptions is made a considerable group of French who spend most of their time with the English—a group that looks large in a small circle but almost like nothing in the whole ambit of the city. Even at that, these praiseworthy exceptions are often called "*anglifiés*" by their fellow French. In the French language to be "*anglifié*" means something about as rotten as "*Frenchified*" does in English . . .

A visible sign of the separation is seen in the peculiar duality of all social and charitable organizations. The *St. James's Club* of Montreal, its oldest and largest, situated on the English side, has as its opposite number, a mile east, the *Club St. Denis*. The *University Club*, situated, as has been seen, on the site of Hochelaga, corresponds to the *Cercle Universitaire*, a mile and a half away, dispossessed by the everlasting English of what should in fairness be its own bones and pipes and tomahawks. Even the softer bond of innocence and union of the *Junior League* could not encircle the *Ligue de la Jeunesse Féminine*. The *Boy Scouts* must face, or scoot away from, the *Scouts Catholiques*. The *Board of Trade* is not the *Chambre de Commerce*, and money given to the *Federated Charities* is distinct from any contribution to the *Fédération des Œuvres de Charité*. The *Deaf and Dumb* hear nothing of the *Sounds-Muets*. The blind grope their separate ways. There are two ways of being "incurable" in Montreal, two forms of "isolation" and of "insanity," and at least three methods of "maternity"—in French, in English, and in Hebrew.

Certain things, of course, are overwhelmingly French or English (British) by national habit and inclination. Nearly all the golf clubs are British, since the Royal Montreal Golf Club was one of the first founded by the Scots in America (1873). But *Laval sur le Lac* is French. The curling clubs, as far as can be seen through the mist at their Saturday luncheons, are either Scotch or full of Scotch. The great luncheon clubs and service clubs downtown which carry on the Indian tradition of oratory are, of necessity, English-speaking, owing to the rarity in North America of guest speakers to talk in French.

A real exception is the *Alliance Française*, half French, half English, made up of people who can understand French and people who wish they could. Another exception is the Montreal Stock Exchange, knowing only English, and snappy at that, on its "floor," but whose transactions are all translated into terms of French exchange in the Montreal French press.

A happy exception, productive of much good, is seen in the case of the Bar of Montreal. This has to be bilingual—judges, juries, lawyers, jailers, and all. Both criminals and litigants are far too open-minded to confine their activities to their own people. A Roman Catholic would just as soon murder a Protestant as a Roman Catholic, indeed sooner. Real estate has no religion and property no proper speech. Witnesses see with two eyes but testify with one tongue. Hence the English judges and lawyers (at the bar) in Montreal must and do talk French, from which results, as between English and French lawyers in Montreal, a more complete good will (as far as lawyers dare entertain such) than between any other two classes.

Education, the most vital function, we are told, of civilized society, the only hope, it is often thought, for a united people with a common patriotism, is separated in Montreal as completely as with the crosscut of a sword. People are so used to this in Montreal that they do not commonly realize its full significance. Elsewhere it would seem appalling, like Turks and Christians, Moslems and Hindus. "Education in the province of Quebec," writes Dr. Percival, the Protestant Director, "is unlike that in any part of the world."[3] The Roman Catholics have one set of schools, the Protestants another, a Protestant Committee and a Roman Catholic Committee as the head authorities (at

[3]W. P. Percival, *Education in Quebec*, 1941.

Quebec), and everything divided below, school boards, curriculums, matriculation, degrees, etc. There is a Protestant Board of School Commissioners for Montreal, as distinct from the Roman Catholic, other boards for other municipalities on the island, a Central School Board with a (slight) supervision over all Protestant boards, and all utterly distinct from the Roman Catholics. All schools are nominally clerical; a Turk is a Protestant; so is a Jew. There are so few Protestant French that, apart from the Irish, "Protestant" means English-speaking and "Roman Catholic" means French.

There are in Montreal 227 Roman Catholic public schools with 118,000 pupils; for Protestants, 47 schools with 29,000 pupils. For all French pupils the language of instruction is French, that is, they learn arithmetic in French, a thing either done in infancy or never completely done. English children learn in English. Each language is also taught in the schools of the other, and very well taught, as a school subject. Montreal schools use the direct method of teaching, not the wretched grammar and translation of Ontario, New York, and such backward localities, but the natural way of teaching, naming things, not translating names, calling a spade *une pelle*.

Like the lower schools, the high schools are entirely separated on lines of religion and language; so, too, the classical colleges and the universities at the top. The special Irish schools (the Callaghan, O'Connell, and Catholic High) divide off in their own fashion. Slight exceptions are seen in the technical schools of the province which teach both races together, yet at Montreal even the technical school has an English and a French division.

The most peculiar case of all, the *reductio ad absurdum*, is that of the almost complete mutual isolation of the University of Montreal and McGill University. Their present buildings are situated about a mile apart and down the street, with an excellent sidewalk and streetcars all the way. In each college are a continuous series of things "open to the public." There are about six hundred instructors on the staff of McGill. Most of them, it may be said with assurance, are never inside the University of Montreal for years at a time. Many live and die without entering it. The writer of this book can recall personally the case of a McGill professor, on the staff for thirty-six years, a man of some distinction, who entered the University of Montreal (Laval in those days) only once—in his first week at McGill. The students keep entirely apart, except now and again, once in a great while, they meet in hostile clashes as in the time of the South African War. It used to be the custom for Laval students to march over to the McGill grounds in procession once a winter, a custom now fallen out. There is no interlocking of studies or lectures. A student of medicine at McGill does not attend or see or hear anything connected with the lectures or clinics of the University of Montreal. He may, once or twice in his course, hear a distinguished local French doctor lecture on a special topic to the McGill medical public but only as he might, and does, hear doctors from New York or Toronto.

The two universities know each other, of course, officially. They interchange seats of the mighty at convocations. They help install one another's new principals. McGill from time to time confers a degree on a distinguished representative of the University of Montreal, on which occasion the principal of McGill speaks, or, rather, *reads*, a flattering tribute in excellent French—too good to be true, all except the pronunciation. The Montreal newspapers comment, as they have for a hundred years, on the principal of McGill's perfect command of French. But in reality his command is what the restaurants call a "short order."

The question of clashes between the races in Montreal has been mentioned above. This, of course, is the abiding danger in the life of the city. The soil under the feet of its people covers ashes never extinct. Its real volcano still smolders. Every now and then such clashes have occurred, on a minor scale, and occur as election riots. At times in the past they have occurred in a form to create the gravest alarm.

A case in point is the Gavazzi Riot of 1853 to which a reference was made in a previous chapter. Here the danger was heightened by the further intrusion of Irish animosity. The Irish being mainly Roman Catholics, but speaking English, would naturally seem a sort of connecting link, an element of union between the two races. Unfortunately this is not so. Indeed, the case is the other way or at least was the other way during most of the history of the city. The Irish being against England for Ireland's sake, many of them, refugees and outcasts from a land depopulated under British rule, were more anti-British than the French themselves. Whenever all these elements coincide and combine the results have always been terrible to contemplate.

Father Alessandro Gavazzi was an Italian ex-Roman Catholic priest who had given up being that kind of father. He was, or said he was, an Italian patriot, a thing that sounded better then than it does now. For these were the days of the sorrows of Italy under Austrian rule, of England's sympathy, and presently of the hero worship of Garibaldi's red shirt—the shirt now turned to black.

Gavazzi came to the United States, lecturing, on Italian Liberty and Romish Tyranny. He could do a turn on either. He came to Quebec, lectured on the Inquisition, and narrowly escaped from the row that followed. Then he came to Montreal to speak in the Zion Church that stood on what was still called the Haymarket (Victoria Square). The audience, scenting danger, or a good time, came well armed. The garrison contributed a detachment of Cameron Highlanders concealed near the church. The Mayor was there, all ready to read the Riot Act. There was angry controversy afterward as to whether the scene was all set for the riot or the riot set the scene. At any rate, a body of Irishmen tried to break into the church where Gavazzi was lecturing. Firing broke out. The audience left the church. A confused crowd was apparently, as we now say, "milling round" on Beaver Hall Hill, some fighting, some trying to get away. The Mayor, Charles Wilson, read the Riot Act . . . without avail . . . the fight went on; the soldiers fired. Forty people were shot down, others trampled down as the mob broke and ran. Gavazzi got out with his life and was smuggled across the river. The town seemed appalled. There was no inquiry, no arrests—just horror. They had raised the devil.

An interesting light is thrown on the French-and-English aspect of Montreal and of its history by a study of the names of the city streets.

The street names of any great American city offer an interesting study reflecting its historic growth. They are like the concentric rings that indicate, on the sawed-off stump of a tree, the years and the rate of its expansion. Now it shrinks to the narrow lines that mark unfavorable seasons, now enlarges to the broad bands that recall the generous growth of prosperous years. More than that. Street names also tell us much of the culture and the dominant thought of the times, as when the loneliness of exile prompts early settlers to name their forest stream the Thames, their log cabins London, and the bush about them Middlesex. An opposite tendency leads settlers to accept and take pride in the aboriginal names which they find in use among the savages, a pride which gives New Brunswick its proud Mettawomkeag, its Passamoquoddy, and its Skidawabskasis. An equally natural impulse is to name things in a new land in honor of sovereigns and of great men, as evinced by the Kingstowns, Queenstowns, Princetowns, the Delawares, the Jerseys, and the Wellingtons. Equally natural is it, as local history grows, to honor the names of people on the spot, native allies such as Pontiac or an Oshkosh, or patriot leaders, a Washington, a Jefferson, a Dorchester. As time goes on and earlier affections dim, as the demand for business convenience outweighs the romance of history, there appear First Avenue and all that follows, crossing First Street as a system as endless as infinite space and about as interesting. This atrocious system sacrifices all that goes with words—memory, affection, association, and individuality—for the mere convenience of number. It sacrifices history to help an expressman deliver a parcel. We might as well call London No. 1 and Liverpool No. 2 and the Right Reverend William Temple, Archbishop of Canterbury, by his census number at birth, 36,051,328. It is shorter and more exact than his present long and clumsy designation. There would be no mistaking him.

The system, discovered in America, has run across the United States and invaded the Canadian North West, a community always determined to be at one and the same time as up to date as the United States and as out of date as Great Britain. But most Canadian cities still keep thinking out names till weary fancy, in their outer rings, fades out into the names of last year's aldermen.

Oddly enough the latest Montreal maps of the latest area of streets laid out, partly inside, partly outside the city's limits, show a list of avenues running from *"première avenue"* up to 39ème avenue, and a list of streets running up to "trente-quatrième rue." But in French "trente-quatrième rue" doesn't mean Thirty-fourth Street, as a title. It just means that this is the thirty-fourth street. They will think out a name later on, perhaps Jacques Cartier.

The Montreal street names are of peculiar interest, for here we find the contrast of saints and sinners, of French and English, of "bygone history" and present endeavor, of the passing hour and of things eternal. From Athlone Avenue of Outer Montreal we may pass to Laurier Avenue, to Peel Street; we descend to Victoria Square, to McGill, and then by a procession of saints to the street of Notre Dame de Bonsecours.

In Montreal the concentric rings of growth are not to be distinguished until we first separate out the old town, all laid out in one period, all French and nearly all sacred. St. James Street is of course only a translation of Rue St. Jacques.

Where the old French town ends we find the name McGill Street, but it was no part of early Montreal, being only created when the fortification walls were knocked down long after the conquest (1803) and the new fathers of the city—there was a James McGill and a Peter and an Andrew—were gratefully remembered, in the names of its street, or took care to remember themselves. McGill was not named by James, who was dead (1813) before it was made.

But before the walls were demolished new streets were being named or old roads renamed in the suburbs outside the original town. Close by, and all three together, appear the men of the conquest—*Wolfe, Montcalm,* and *Amherst*—all side by side. Amherst afterward rose, or sank, to be a streetcar as well. So also did the Duke of *Wellington*, whose name was given to the long street running out through the old St. Ann suburb. But even before him the early governors, Lord Dorchester and St. James Craig, were commemorated in the new streets outside the old town and running, as we now call it, east and west. Dorchester, as was right, received the fairest portion, the beautiful road along the hill. Craig got the marsh, long a blot on Montreal, filled, even when a street, with the refuse thrown into it, flooded in springtime even within present memory, yet waiting for a glorious resurrection under the new city planning in which in Montreal as in other cities the last shall be first and the slum become sublime.

The Rebellion Days of 1837 and 1838 left their grim writing on the streets with the Place des Patriotes, where their scaffold stood, and the streets *Delorimier, Sanguinet, Robert, Hamelin,* named after the men executed. A higher honor is evidenced in the long *Papineau Avenue* traversing the city in that quarter. More grudging is *Colborne Street,* short and narrow, near *McGill Street,* in what had been at the other end of the town. Durham failed to qualify. The *Durham Avenue* of today, away out near the Rivière des Prairies, is just an act of forgiveness, a gesture toward the past.

The Victorian Age breaks out vigorously in the new advance of the city over ground still largely empty when the Queen began to reign, which climbed Beaver Hall Hill and moved south and west. Here is *Victoria Square* (though not so named till 1860) and *Windsor Street* and *Peel,* just where they should be. The war scare of 1845 gave *Cathcart,* the Crimean War, *Sebastopol.* On the French side the outward-moving rings are less clearly marked, the names of the men of the hour standing in competition with the eternal glory of the saints and with the pride of history never tired of recalling *Cartier* and *Maisonneuve.* Jacques Cartier is a parliamentary riding, a street, a square, a pier, and was a whole town, "Cartierville," as was Maisonneuve, till the city absorbed them both. Cartier reappears in the new bridge.

But the English names keep climbing steadily on. Anyone who knows our history since Confederation could guess exactly where to find *Gladstone Avenue, Lansdowne Avenue*, and *Aberdeen*, how far to go to look for Lord Grey. The Duke of Connaught had long since qualified in his youthful, soldierly days in the Montreal Garrison and gave us the *Prinsse Arthur—Prinsse Arthúr* of the Park Avenue streetcar call. He reappeared triumphantly in an avenue, in Montreal West, as the wartime Governor General with his daughter on *Patricia Avenue* beside him. Joffre and Pau got honorable mention at the same epoch but at the very opposite end of the city. Foch, as who should say, "made" Verdun; Pétain, luckily nothing. But before this, between Prince Arthur's time and that of the Duke of Wellington's, the belt of the Macdonalds and the Tuppers, the Strathconas and the Lauriers carry out our history till the end with all honor in the outer ring of Athlone in the town of Mount Royal.

A few streets, not many, recall in Montreal the great names of English and French literature, but with no great honor. Shakespeare is an empty road, Milton a dingy side street, Dickens and Thackeray are outside the limits, near the streets still waiting for names, Burns not even there. Along with Dickens and Thackeray are Taine and Racine and Ruskin in a new district that has presumably just heard of them. The addition of Hugo, Dryden, and Milton makes this municipality of St. Michel de Laval look like the Poets' Corner in Westminster Abbey. All honor to it for its rescue of authorship. Chateaubriand, champion of the church, has a real avenue nearly three miles long, Molière a street one block in length, and Jules Verne one with three blocks. Most of the literary names seem an afterthought; Montreal was too busy and had so much history of its own, and, after all, other cities are just as bad.

Thus lies Montreal, in two languages, from the Victoria Bridge to the Pont Jacques Cartier repeating its civic official motto, *Concordia Salus*, Our Salvation is in Concord.

CHAPTER XIV

McGill University

Under the Ginkgo Tree. He's Our Father, Oh Yes, Rather. McGill, Its Campus and Its Corpus. Foundation and Stagnation. Sir William Dawson and His Work. Marvelous Growth and Progress of McGill. World Fame of Its Medicine and Applied Science. Scope of Its Work. Men Not Mortar. The University of Montreal. Its Fine Classical Training. Music, Arts, and Letters on Montreal.

NO APOLOGY IS NEEDED for devoting the larger part of a chapter of this book to the discussion of McGill University. Its great success in the past and the reputation which it enjoys throughout the whole world, especially as a school of medicine and engineering, would make it natural that readers would wish to know something of it. One who looks back gratefully to thirty-six years spent in its service and six years of leaning upon it in old age, without having ever contributed to its medical and engineering reputation, may perhaps be a fitting person to bear witness.

The grounds of McGill University are beautifully situated in

what is, in a sense, the center of Montreal, the slope at the base
of the mountain running straight down toward the river. Unlike
many colleges buried in commercial cities, it has the great advantage that it can be seen all at once; not really all of it, but
enough to give the finished picture of a college and a campus,
the oldest building, of the greatest dignity, recognizable at once
as such at the top of the slope. The newer buildings, magnificent
in size, frame the sides of the campus. All the central open space
is a playground dotted with great trees, pierced with a central
avenue of tall elms and maples, running up through the beautiful
Roddick Gates from Sherbrooke Street below. The trees verge
already on a hundred years of age. The photographs of past days
show them as slender little saplings when all Montreal made
merry at the visit of the gay young Prince of Wales in 1860. The
old building at the top is the Arts Building, battered, renewed,
built over, pinned under, having lost everything but its beauty.
Again and again common sense whispered, "Knock it down;
build it like Pittsburgh, fifty stories high . . . stick elevators
into it to make it like Columbia. This thing begins to look like
those old places in Oxford." But no one ever dared to. It was the
old dilemma, the old problem as between affection and change,
continuity or a new start. So there it stays.

Before the Arts Building, at the front steps, is James McGill's
grave, with a strange tree, a ginkgo tree, weeping over it, if such
a tree as a ginkgo can indeed weep. This grave seemed so in-
congruous, years ago, that they let the bushes grow around the
foot of the ginkgo, and James McGill slept like the beauty in
the fairy tale, hidden behind the leaves, his gravestone moldered
and illegible. It was forgotten that he was there; the records
said that he was buried in 1813 in the Dorchester Street Burying
Ground. Then an energetic dean—from the States, and hence
careless of antiquity—had an opening cut in the bushes and the
gravestone scraped and the letters rebuilt, and there it was, the
original epitaph of eulogy of James McGill's *loyalty to his
Sovereign and ability, integrity, industry and zeal as a magistrate.*
To this was added, *This Monument and the remains which it
covers were removed from the Old Protestant Cemetery, Dor-*

*chester Street, and placed here in grateful remembrance of the
Founder of this University, 23rd June, 1875.*

So now the students on their evenings of merriment sing,—

> *James McGill,*
> *James McGill,*
> *Peacefully he slumbers there,*
> *Though he knows we're on the tear,*
> *He's our father*
> *Oh yes, rather,*
> *James McGill ! ! ! ! !*

Yet they do say he's not there at all; that he was meant to be there
but was never moved. Some day another American dean may
come and exhume him. Till then we cannot know. It is probable
that this legend of McGill not occupying his own grave arose
from the fact—if one may be pardoned for referring to such
grim details of the record—that James McGill is not all there and
never was. Only the "skull and a few of the greater bones and
the bottom of the coffin" were left to remove in 1875.

The Arts Building is all filled with classrooms, even the left-
hand end of it that was once the Assembly Hall and Library
given by William Molson at the time of the same royal visit. But
the right-hand end, as you face it, is the Administration, renovated from what was once pantries, kitchens, cellars, attempts at
chemistry, as inconvenient, crooked, and impossible as anything
in London. Above it is housed the Law Faculty, crookeder still,
fit to compare with any Inns of Court. Scattered through the
building are all sorts of little odd offices for things left out of
the main buildings, such as the principal of McGill and the
registrar and offices that in American colleges would cover an
acre.

Round the campus, as said, are beautiful and spacious science
buildings, the stately sisters, Engineering, Chemistry, and Physics
—the last one now growing to a legend as the place where Lord
Rutherford, the great physicist, conquered the atom; like St.
George and the dragon in English colleges. The Engineering
Building and the Engineering Faculty (1931) have so christened

themselves in despair. Taunted that they were not "pure," they threw aside the earlier title of "applied science" and admitted straight out what they were: working-class people, not ashamed of it.

On the other side of the campus is the Redpath Library, a marvelous repository of books, a hive of working students, busy as bees and (exactly) as quiet. Beside it, in real silence, is the College Museum. Years ago it carried a sign, "Admission 10 cents." Nobody went in. Professors lived and died (it is literally true) and never went in; the admission, I say, was ten cents. They moved the sign; admission is now free, but people still hesitate. They say that inside are Hochelaga skulls, the oyster shells found on the mountainside by Sir William Dawson (proving the existence of the Champlain Sea), and much else—more than ten cents' worth.

Just outside the college, just technically off the campus, but as close to it as they can sneak, are the affiliated Theological Colleges, not part of McGill but feeding on the bounty of its learning. The Presbyterian College alone is practically on the campus, with the Museum blocking it a little, thus representing the early claim of Scotland on the heart of Montreal.

But in reality the largest buildings of McGill and the widest area of its ground is not on the campus at all but in the background. The chief of these is the (new) Medical Building, the gift of Lord Strathcona, an edifice of great beauty if there were anywhere to see it from. It took the place of the old "new Medical Building" that stood hard by the Arts Building on the campus, before yet Science was. This went up in flames one memorable night of 1907 in a sudden and unaccountable fire, strangely lurid and uncanny from the holocaust of the dissecting room and all that it contained. Wonder and inquiry were still rife when the great glow in the sky and the crash of the fire bells in the heart of the night called Montreal to the second great McGill fire that gutted the Engineering Building. No known cause was ever found. The flames had scorched the doors of Arts. In superstitious fear the professors of Arts moved away the miscellaneous junk they called their "notes." No cause for the fire was found. There was at the time no night supervision of buildings. An estimate was published by the Department of Economics to show that the sum lost in the burning of the Engineering Building alone would have paid for the services of two night watchmen every night from the Norman Conquest until 1907. The department might as well have said "since the Creation," for it is only a matter of annual interest. But "Norman Conquest" sounded better. The governors were convinced. The night watchmen were engaged. Since then each night at stated hours their silent feet perambulate the buildings to call "All well," like the night watch with the blue sticks in the Montreal of 1818, or at least to punch "All well, nothing burning," on a time clock.

So the new Medical Building was built higher up, and the site of the old building and much adjacent ground used for the home —rectangular but all there—of biochemistry and such. Past the new Medical Building, McGill met its medical ally, the Royal Victoria Hospital, and had to move off sideways to build the Pathological Building and the new Montreal Neurological Institute, McGill's latest gift to the world, the latest jewel in the crown of its reputation. Beyond that sideways and a little higher, for the slope of the mountain has begun in earnest, McGill begins all over again with the part of it best known to Montreal at large, the vast playground and amphitheater, the stadium that commemorates the name and is the legacy to his *Alma Mater* of Captain Percival Molson, killed in action on July 3, 1917.

Even at that, the largest part of McGill is still far away, the great Macdonald College at St. Anne de Bellevue at the upward end of Montreal Island, the place of the massacre and the "evening chime" of the church at the meeting of the waters of the wilderness. This, one of the gifts of Sir William Macdonald (1907), contains the Faculty of Agriculture, which includes the School of Household Science, with classes, experimental gardens, and experimental cattle and poultry, the whole of it somehow intertwined with the training of teachers under the Protestant Committee of the Council of Public Instruction. The registrar of McGill is understood to understand the connection.

Such is the outer government of McGill. Now turn to its inward life and mind.

The origin of McGill University has already been indicated. James McGill (1744–1813)[1] was one of the earliest of the British settlers in Montreal and spent there an active, prosperous, and patriotic life. As the British population increased he realized more and more that Lower Canada offered no education suitable and acceptable for the young men of British families. He determined to make a bequest to aid the foundation of a college. He took counsel, as already said, with the young and Reverend John Strachan, the later Bishop. On his advice he left his Burnside Estate and £10,000 to the Royal Institution for the Advancement of Learning, to found a university whose first college should bear his name. Soon after this McGill departed in peace (1813). It was left to his executors (Strachan was one) to carry out the bequest.

This proved a matter of unusual difficulty; indeed it was not until McGill had been dead thirty years that his college began its actual teaching as apart from its legal existence. If early adversity makes for courage and character McGill was blessed indeed.

The difficulties that followed are complicated almost to the verge of absurdity. The French community was bitterly opposed to the creation of the Royal Institution. The British government authorities wanted, above all, peace and harmony. This is often obtained, as it was in the Turkey of the Sultans, by doing nothing. Hence the Royal Institution of 1801 existed as an idea but not as a fact. No trustees had been appointed, so there was no one to receive McGill's bequest. When they did at last appoint trustees (1818) Roman Catholics refused to serve. McGill's heirs-at-law, meaning his wife's former husband's family, refused to surrender the property and refused to hand over the money.

The McGill farm, Burnside Manor, was indeed a beautiful estate. It began at the base of the mountain (roughly the present Pine Avenue) and it came down to the road—it was no more —called St. Catherine Street and a little beyond. On one side it

[1] C. Macmillan, *McGill and Its Story, 1821–1921*, 1921.

reached, as now, McTavish Street; on the other it was a little wider than the present grounds. Through it flowed the pleasant little "burn" that gave it its name, a stream that had meandered down a couple of miles from the northwest (we call it northeast) where now LaFontaine Park is. It was met just before it reached the McGill farm by another little brook that had gathered up the streams off the mountainside. The united rivulet moved in a pleasant curve round the bottom end of the McGill farm. A surviving relic of its course is the sunken tennis court at the foot of the McGill grounds that marks its bed. It was inside this sheltering arm that stood the fort, or camp, of Hochelaga four hundred years ago.

The McGill property had been cleared into fields and gardens and orchards. In it then stood a stone house of two stories and an attic, a barn, and outsheds—buildings all gone long ago. The heirs held it all; they refused to let it go; they claimed that as there was no college there was no bequest. Lawsuits followed, beginning October 20, 1820, and lasting seventeen years. Under the terms of the will the bequest would lapse if not carried out in ten years. To hold the bequest the Board of the Royal Institution obtained a charter for "McGill College" from the Crown, October 21, 1821. They claimed that this brought McGill College into existence. The heirs said it didn't. They said that there was no college, there being no staff, no students, no premises, and no teaching. It was this date, 1821, that was selected for the reckoning of the Centenary of 1921. But there was reason for that. Wise governors saw already the storm cloud of depression on the horizon and wanted to tackle the graduates before they got too wet. Since the real date of the first teaching is 1843, the happy end of the war might give McGill another chance to rejuvenate itself back again to one hundred years, blushing at its first century.

To make the college more real the Board of the Royal Institution appointed an imaginary staff, Dean Mountain as principal and four imaginary professors. The heirs still laughed at them. At last the Privy Council, in 1829, after nearly ten years of legal fights, awarded the estate, not yet the money, to the board. They held a formal opening June 24, 1829, with speeches in the farm-house from the Bishop of Quebec and from Dean Mountain and the reading of a biblical quotation, selected, so the Montreal *Gazette* said, "as suitable to the occasion." It contains the verse, "The lines are fallen to me in pleasant places; yea, I have a goodly heritage." Heritage, but no money, the heirs refusing to sign any surrender of the funds. Failing other use, the board rented McGill "on halves" to a farmer, to work the university half and half. The farmer bought, on credit, £3 worth of garden seeds. McGill was sued for it. That was its first financial breath —a deficit.

The college being now officially open, "governors" were ap-pointed, so that henceforth the parties concerned were the heirs, the executors, the Board of the Royal Institution for the Ad-vancement of Learning, and the governors of McGill College, the shadow staff, and the farmer in occupation. There was still no money except any sum that the board could get as apart from the bequest. The heirs remained obdurate. Yet the Board of the Royal Institution conferred a degree, May 1833, on Mr. Wil-liam Logie on behalf of the Montreal Medical Institution already mentioned and since 1824 at work and teaching students. The secretary used the words "the Medical Faculty" in recording the degree. This was in accordance with the fact that at the time of the "Opening" of the college, as described, in 1829 a resolu-tion was passed at the first meeting of the governors "that the members of the Montreal Medical Institution be engrafted on the College as its Medical Faculty." The Montreal Medical In-stitution had begun teaching classes in 1824, occupying a wooden house, No. 20 St. James Street, on the site of the present Bank of Montreal on the Place d'Armes. They moved their classes in, or possibly before, 1833 to the tall, narrow building of three stories, described by the present registrar of McGill, who has followed out the peregrinations, as "a strategic site for a medical faculty"—being just over the fence from the cemetery. This, too obvious abode, was exchanged in 1841 for premises on St. George's Street just above Craig. They did not teach on the campus till after Arts lectures began. Even at that they moved off again. They entirely controlled their own funds, their own property, and their own activities. It is hard to say when they became an organic part of McGill. "Engrafted" is a slow process, yet in many an orchard the graft presently is the best of the tree.

Principal Mountain, weary of office, retired. His post was offered to the Rev. Mr. Wood, rector of Three Rivers; he refused; to the Rev. Thomas Littlehales of Oxford; he refused. Three professorships, also vacant by disuse, were offered and refused at Dublin, Aberdeen, and Edinburgh. The Board then offered the Principalship pro tempore to the Rev. John Bethune, rector of Christ Church, Montreal. Bethune was an upright, forcible man who spoke his mind. The only question was what was in it; certainly not a college education. Bethune's father was a Scottish minister, an army chaplain in the American Revolution, who settled among the Glengarry Highlanders. John Bethune was a soldier in the War of 1812. After it was over he entered the Anglican ministry, the gate swinging easily then. He was rector of Christ Church for fifty years (1818–68), dying in 1872 at the end of a long and honorable career. He was, along with this, acting principal of McGill from 1835 until 1846. He accepted it pro tempore, stipulating that he would not get out pro tempore—that is, in favor of any pro tempore substitute.

With that began the four- or five-cornered quarrel at McGill that lasted for years. The money was at last wrested from the heirs (December 1837) but the governors fought the board as to who controlled it now. Bethune moved into the farmhouse and ran up a bill for fuel.

At last, however, McGill College, using the meager interest on its money, decided to open in earnest. As the principal refused to hand over the house, the governors got the board to ask the government for money to build. Not getting enough money they sold off some of the Burnside property, a dangerous expedient, like sawing off a branch while sitting on it. They were thus enabled to erect, not yet to complete properly, buildings that were at least fit to use. They represent a part of the present renovated Arts Building. College teaching began September 3, 1843, with a staff of Principal Bethune; the Rev. F. J. Lundy, an Oxford graduate in classics, who was made also vice-principal and touched up with an LL.D. degree; a professor of mathematics on £300 and fuel; a professor of divinity at £250 a year "as soon as funds admit it"; a bursar-secretary-registrar at £100 a year and fees; a beadle at £30 a year and board. There were twenty students, of whom seventeen were classical and three mathematical. The fees were £5 a year. The Medical Institute, going strong, was still outside of all this.[2]

On this frail raft McGill pushed out from shore. Nor was the opening voyage easy. Governors and board disputed constantly over authority, the Board of the Royal Institution accusing the governors of McGill College and Dr. Bethune of "wasteful and extravagant expenditure." At this time the available income was £500. Bethune was spending £750. The distinguished historian of McGill, the Hon. Cyrus Macmillan, M.P., Dean of the Faculty of Arts, says that the college was "suffering for lack of funds." The inference seems a fair one.

The quarrel went from bad to worse. There was finally nothing to do—there never is anything to do—but to get rid of the principal. Here came in, most opportunely, the ancient and useful British fiction, connected with all public institutions, of the "Visitor." American visitors to McGill, studying its calendar and its "literature," feel perplexed, and perhaps pleased, to see that the Governor General of Canada is the "Visitor." This means that he is, or represents, in the last resort for those in distress, King George, who by prerogative can set right anything outside of the Statutes. In this case the Bishop of Montreal wrote to Lord Metcalfe, who wrote to the Right Hon. W. E. Gladstone (Colonial Secretary), through whose mouth spoke the Queen. Each said straight out, in three pages, that Dr. Bethune was only principal pro tempore, never confirmed, and that he had never been to college. That was all the Queen needed. Dr. Bethune must go.

After which the governors, unofficially, and the staff, informally, sent warm expressions of appreciation to Dr. Bethune.

In this uncertain and impoverished fashion McGill dragged on

[2]M. Abbott, *History of Medicine in the Province of Quebec*, 1931.

as best it could for another ten years (1846–55). It was probably only saved from extinction by the existence of the Medical Faculty, always strong in capacity and endeavor, even when as feeble financially as the college itself.

Then came salvation with the advent in 1855 of William Dawson, as principal of the college, the second founder and the real maker of McGill. Dawson was a great man, one of the great men of the nineteenth century. More than that of any one man or group of men, McGill is his work. Dawson was born in Nova Scotia, trained in Edinburgh, a student of geology and natural history, a man of religious conviction and moral purpose. He found McGill a sort of bats' nest. Its incomplete buildings, half dilapidated before they were finished, were occupied by professors and students. Classes were held in the old high school, in any outside buildings available—none on the campus. Medicine had lectured there awhile (1845–46) and abandoned the premises as hopeless. They were now teaching in a house on Cote Street, the doctors paying expenses as best they could.

Dawson drove at this system as with the sword of the Lord in Gideon. In less than no time, it seems, he had the professors and students out and the classes in. He brought medicine back. He found money as he could, begging, borrowing, and even selling more of the campus. He went at the city, lectured to it on Natural Science and at it on natural duty. People rallied to his call. The stream of benefaction flowed from the stricken rock of Montreal. Money was found for a building for medicine (1872), not *the* Medical Building, a building. The Molson Hall (1861), with the Library on its upper story, turned, with a little other improvement, the Arts Building (1855) into a thing of beauty, a real college. Students came. There were 105 students in 1860 outside of those in Medicine. Law had become a separate faculty in 1853. A new Faculty of Applied Science was created out of Arts in 1878, an Adam from the ribs of Eve. The Theological Colleges came as lambs to the new fold, the Congregational, 1865, the Presbyterian, 1873, the Methodist, 1876. The Anglican Church, tempted to follow the precedent by which, led by Bishop Strachan, it had repudiated the "Godless univer-

sity" of Toronto, surrendered and came in in 1880. In 1872 Mc-
Gill built a real and equipped Medical Building and from it
graduated that year, its first and most famous product, Dr. (Sir)
William Osler; all the world was later to be his classroom.

The generosity that gave the Molson Hall was followed by
that embodied in the Redpath Museum (1882), the Redpath
Library (1893), and the Workman Engineering Building. Then
came Donald Smith (Lord Strathcona) with large donations of
funds (1882–1901) to help organize classes for women (first
taught at McGill in 1884) and then with the building and endowment of the Royal Victoria College, McGill's resident
women's college. When William Dawson, crowned with honors and a knighthood, laid down his task in 1893, McGill was
made.

Yet, in a sense, the greatest remained to come. In sheer volume
the flood of benefaction was only beginning. Even before Dawson resigned, the magnificent gifts of William Macdonald had
begun. These took shape in the Science Buildings (1893), which
led the world at the time of their first erection. Soon after came
the gift of eight hundred acres and the huge endowment that
made St. Anne's Macdonald College, an Agricultural Faculty
and School of Education. With that went substantial money en-
dowments for professional chairs which set the professors up,
as tight and comfortable as children round a supper table. The
great fires of 1907 only kindled a warmer generosity. Strathcona's answer was the new Medical Building. He and George
Stephen (Lord Montstephen) had already provided the Medical
Faculty with the priceless facilities of the Royal Victoria, later
increased by the gift of the Ross Pavilion, the gift of J. K. L.
Ross in memory of his parents. Of a different kind, but enlisting
equal gratitude, was the gift of Sir William Macdonald of a great
stretch of the near-by wooded slope at the foot of the mountain,
preserved there for the future of McGill. A part of this was to
become the stadium already named. All through the period
(1893–1939) the achievement of McGill in the academic world
had kept apace with the rising glory of its physical surroundings.
It is fitting to mention only those gone; but in addition to Osler

such names as those of Sir William Peterson, Sir James Grant, Sir William Hingston, Sir Thomas Roddick, of Rutherford, Soddy, Macphail, McCallum, form a roll and scroll of honor unsurpassed. As the years of peace closed in, they record the name of the soldier principal, Sir Arthur Currie, than whom no institution ever had a more beloved or more inspiring commander.

Such is McGill. A wonderful heritage. Now, as careful as children with a gold watch, let us open the works and look in.

The present organization, scope, and size of McGill may be summarized on paper thus. McGill is a trust, administered under a Royal (British) Charter of 1821, amended and amendable by the Legislature of the Province of Quebec. Its property and money are controlled by a body of governors, acting for the still-existing, imaginary Royal Institution for the Advancement of Learning. These governors were, until 1935, a self-perpetuating body, now only partly so since no governor holds for a longer term than five years at a time, and in addition to governors named by the governors themselves, representative governors are elected for terms of three years by the graduates.

For the organization of faculties, schools, courses, and the curriculum, the academic authority (but without control of money) is the senate. The presiding head of the governors and of the senate is the chancellor. Some chancellors accept their office as purely one of honor. Others undertake to give administrative and academic help. Next in dignity is the principal (who is also by title vice-chancellor), standing at the head of all faculties. This was not true of the Medical Faculty until 1905. Until then it retained its own budget, its own control, and was not under the headship of the principal. The idea was that doctors were supposed to be the only people who understood medicine and medical studies. In the day-to-day life of the college the principal is monarch of all he surveys unless he doesn't care to survey it and leaves to others things of which he knows nothing. Some principals have known everything. Next to the principal there is for each faculty a dean, managing the internal faculty affairs. His boundaries with the principal and with the professors of the departments allow for a good deal of what is called "latitude" or "friction" according to the individuals concerned. But until very recently there was the tradition of each department (meaning what ordinary people call a subject, Classics, History, Physics, etc.) as a kind of little island fortress by itself with the head of the department as a sort of independent native prince.

The existing faculties in order of historic priority are those of Arts (Arts and Science since 1931), Medicine, Law, Engineering, Agriculture, Dentistry, Music, Graduate Studies, and Research.

REGISTRATION OF McGILL STUDENTS, 1941–42

	Men	Women	Total
Faculty of Arts and Science	791	495	1286
of these:			
In Arts	245	382	627
In Science	381	98	479
In Commerce	165	15	180
Faculty of Engineering	478	6	484
Faculty of Medicine	359	28	387
Faculty of Dentistry	54	2	56
Faculty of Law	54	0	54
Faculty of Graduate Studies and Research	184	54	238
School of Household Science	0	81	81
Faculty of Agriculture	89	2	91
Faculty of Music	5	2	7
Totals (Degree Students)	2015	684	2699

These figures, to those acquainted with the staggering totals of institutions like Columbia, seem very small. But there is an explanation. A state university has to teach everybody. McGill doesn't have to teach anybody. In medicine, McGill, from the richness of its soil, restricts its crop as they restrict coffee in Brazil and hogs in Missouri. The enrollment is only a fraction of those applying. Particularly notable is the way in which the Medical Faculty attracts students from beyond Montreal and indeed from beyond Canada. In the enrollment above, of its 387 students, only 115 came from Montreal; 32 came from Quebec Province outside of Montreal; 140 from other Canadian provinces, and the rest from the United States. The Law Faculty is small because it represents study for the Bar of Quebec, a theater of French customary law, isolated, along with Louisiana, in a whole continent of English Common Law. McGill, moreover, in its registration only counts students actually attending degree courses, not casual people taking evening classes or afternoon extension lectures.

Among the things long lacking at McGill was a residence for the male students, a need now partly met by the endowment of Douglas Hall. Among those still lacking is a university press with all that goes with it to stimulate the literary impulse—the weak limb of a strong body. McGill, to its shame, has nothing to compare in a literary way with the *University of Toronto Quarterly*, the *Queen's Quarterly*, and the *Dalhousie Review*.

In its relation to the churches, McGill is a nonsectarian college, chiefly attended by Protestant students but with a large number of Jews, especially in the Faculty of Arts, and a certain number of Roman Catholics. It draws no color line, there being, in Montreal climate, no color line to draw. But it has a certain aspect of Protestantism in that all the chief Protestant sects have Theological Colleges affiliated with McGill and the Jews and Roman Catholics have none. Under its charter and statutes it is entitled to hold College Chapel, and used to do so, praying daily in its days of poverty, but easing off as there was less and less to pray for. McGill has no classes in religion, a contrast with the practice in the University of Toronto where "religious knowledge" is a curriculum study of the first year, with as much "credit" as mathematics. The proposal made at various times to give "lectures on the Bible" as a general subject in the Faculty of Arts, which gives lectures on almost everything else, was never carried. It proved impossible to decide whether the lectures were to be on the Bible as God's Word or as King James's English. The Department of English, however, maintains a course —optional and biennial—on the English Bible.

McGill, though in no sense a provincial university, is fortu-

nate enough to receive a considerable financial support, without
any academic control, from the provincial government. This
arises from the peculiar situation of education in Quebec. It is
impossible to find sufficient common ground as between English-
speaking Protestants and French-speaking Roman Catholics to
allow for a unified department. Education is left on the clerical
basis and the so-called Council of Public Instruction operates
through two separate branches, the Protestant Committee and
the Roman Catholic Committee. Education under the Catholic
Committee is clerical both in name and in fact, inseparably connected with the Roman Catholic religion and its clergy. Under
the Protestant Committee, education is much the same as secular
education under any state or provincial government. The pro-
ceeds of local school taxes are divided according to the declared
religious faith of the taxpayers. These, however, fall hopelessly
short of maintaining education in all its branches. Hence the
provincial treasury, in default of any other method, makes large,
direct grants to a long list of schools, colleges, organizations, and
objects not administratively controlled by the provincial government. The allocation is made on a rough-and-ready basis of population classified according to declared religious belief. About
$8,000,000 a year is the present total of all these sums. McGill
University gets a general grant and special grants for such things
as its Neurological Institute, Teachers Training, etc. The University of Montreal receives more than three times as much with
special capital grants for construction. Bishop's College, at Len-
noxville, the Classical Colleges of the province, and a lot of institutions gather round to get their share. There seems no particular system. It is what is called, in other than clerical circles, a
"pork barrel."

It seems to work reasonably well. To outside eyes the only
amazing feature is that there is in Quebec no compulsory education. It won't fit into this dual control.

In the matters of terms and sessions McGill follows what is
called the Scottish model. This was commended to James McGill
in the Rev. John Strachan's first letter of advice. It remains still
as the basis of McGill's studies, though much broken into of late

years and almost shattered in wartime. The Scottish system was especially suited, in Scotland and in Canada, for a population strong in industry and effort, but little blessed with inherited family wealth. The young men were to work on the land in summer and study in the winter. Hence the single short session, which as late as 1900 had lectures only from September 22 to March 22, with exams all over in mid-April. It was hardly broken by holidays, a continuous unflagging effort, the "vacation" being in its own way harder still. Thus did generations of Canadians pitch wheat in July and pitch medicine in January. What sort of men the system produced it is not for those of us left over from it to say. The present session, with lectures from October 1 to May 1 and examinations in May, is extended more or less all summer by special schools. But it is broken with many holidays, breaks, gaps, and stops, and is throughout so punctuated with "student activities" that it is hard to say where activity ends and study begins.

The Faculty of Arts of McGill shares with those of all other great colleges the perplexities of the expanding curriculum. The distressed Alma Mater is like the Old Woman in the Shoe. The children clamor round her, asking for all sorts of new things, commerce and social science, music and housekeeping, and some of the little ones crying for salesmanship and beekeeping. She does what she can, gives out Greek for little clergymen, English to make boys gentlemen, Economics for those who don't want to be, and compulsory Latin in a medicine spoon, marked B.A., "a spoonful before and after matriculation." Commerce students don't take this spoonful.

Old-fashioned professors think that more than half of the present Arts Course is just tinsel and frills and fun. Old-fashioned men in colleges think that Commerce can only be learned in a counting house. But if old-fashioned men in counting houses endow a course in Commerce in a college, what are you to do? "Commerce" disrupts modern arts courses like a bombshell. Students flock to it, by preference, not for what they learn, but for what they don't. At McGill Latin is compulsory for entrance to Arts, not for Commerce. Many professors, old- or new-fashioned, think Latin a great training, even for business purposes. Businessmen don't. Businessmen want their sons to learn business English. There isn't any, except bad English. Businessmen want their sons to learn business psychology; there is none, or none inside the law. Businessmen want their sons to learn accountancy because they never learned it themselves. . . .

But all of this is common ground to McGill and all similar places. McGill has here no particular success or solution to offer for study.

The case is different with endowment. The experience of McGill, as a great endowed university, may be of a certain interest at the present time. A controversy, and indeed something like a national problem, has arisen in both England and America over the question of endowed versus state institutions. In England the question concerns the so-called "public schools" (that is, endowed secondary schools such as Eton and Rugby), as against schools conducted by the government. In America the problem turns on the rival merits of state universities and endowed universities. The controversy gathers urgency in proportion as the increasing scope and cost of education and the decreasing funds available from endowment begin to threaten the future of endowed universities.

The latter, however, have found voices raised in their defense. One of the most prominent among the presidents of endowed universities argues that without their competition the curriculum of the state university would deteriorate. Legislatures elected by the people would clamor for a sort of free-for-all, pleasant and easy higher education, with degrees for everybody. At present they are held back from this by the stern example of the private, endowed colleges, still teaching Greek and trigonometry.

At first sight the outstanding success of McGill would seem a strong case in point. But it is not so simple. McGill owes much, not only to its peculiar basis as endowed, but to the peculiar atmosphere in which it grew up, the traditions brought from Scotland, the scholarship from England, the class of people from whose sons it drew its students, and the attitude toward learning current in their homes. McGill did not make these things. It found them. We realize this when we remember that McGill is not the only great Canadian college. One other, the University of Toronto, rivals it and in many things exceeds it. Yet Toronto is a provincial university, born by act of Parliament, cradled in legislation, and suckled and fed on taxes.

Toronto is dependent on the provincial legislature. McGill is not, except in the inapplicable sense of constitutional law whereby a province is supreme in education, so that the legislature at Quebec could legally abolish McGill tomorrow. It could also, if it liked, make it legally a Roman Catholic institution open only to Negroes. Such things have no bearing on the case. Indeed, it has been argued, no doubt incorrectly, that McGill, having been created by Royal Charter before Confederation, is not fully amenable to the province.

But the point is that the legislature controls Toronto, at one remove, through a board of governors and the legislature does not control McGill. But is this good or bad? It all depends on how the legislature acts, as compared with how the self-perpetuating Board of Governors acts. Either body may be wise or foolish, sagacious or inept.

At the same time colleges of both types, private or state, seem to meet the same troubles and fall into the same sins. State institutions run the obvious danger of political favoritism; private institutions to danger of control by money. Endowment, after all, is just the sister of capitalism. Both kinds of colleges suffer from the intrusion of business ideas belonging to another sphere; suffer from the peculiar dry rot of "efficiency," the attempt to make all educational values provable, measurable, divisible into credits and units, to make professors work on time, "produce" by the cubic yard, and be "hired and fired" according as to whether they "show results."

In any case, the days of endowment are measured. No such funds will again exist under arbitrary personal control. We cannot, of course, see far into the veiled future of the hour. But the sweeping tax power called forth in war will carry forward for the aims of peace. A myriad voices call for it. Failing hands are lifted up for it. Never again; never again the rich and poor as they were. Never again will any individual, however philanthropic, have the chance to give $80,000,000, even to education.

In the main McGill was made, not by its system, but by its circumstances, by the models from which it drew, the generous and unconditioned help of those who paid its cost, and above all by the men who served it. Men, not mortar, make a college. Trustees and governors at times get a glimpse of this in their sleep and then wake up and buy more mortar. . . . And not only the great and outstanding men—the Dawsons and the Oslers —but all the men, all who are given the peculiar and proper tenure of a university chair, as abiding as marriage, no hire and fire, no time clock, room for individuality to shape and grow, for scholarship to walk its own queer path, as odd as Isaac Newton, as freakish as Edward Gibbon.

A university is hard to recast. We should watch that we do not break the mold.

It is important to notice that benefactions given to McGill in its great formative period from 1860 to 1914 were given from pure public spirit, without self-interest, and carried with them no conditions, no "strings," no intrusion on the conduct of the university. On these terms alone is a benefaction worth accepting. Anything else is just a handful of poisoned thorns hidden in a bouquet of flowers. After all, the benefactor gets much, gets in the long run the best of the bargain. That tablet of Latin, high on the corner of a McGill building, *To Commemorate the Notable Bounty of* —— —— ——, what a legacy to leave to one's descendants. The "Macdonald" Physics Building, known to the world as the cradle of modern atomic physics, rocked by Ernest Rutherford, how much better than if the name had ended with the "Macdonald's ten-cent plug."

So there were no strings. Sir William Macdonald of the "plug" had made his vast fortune out of tobacco. But he never insisted that professors must smoke or even chew. The Chair of Economics was endowed by members of a family whose name was associated with their proprietary interest in a great brewery. But they made no conditions that the occupant of the chair must drink beer. If any strings there were, they arose by general consent out of the ideas of the moment as apart from the personal interest or advantage of the donor. Thus Sir Donald Smith (Lord Strathcona), in his foundation, some fifty years ago, of the Royal Victoria College (the more feminine part of McGill), laid down certain restrictions. Sharing the fear of women common to his time, he insisted that the college girls must not come near the men for two years. The Royal Victoria opened thus, as safe-guarded and secluded as an Indian purdah, a harem in Hydera-bad. Its very doors and its curtained windows looked mystery. Its entertainments were open only to professors over sixty and governors over seventy. Old graduates of McGill, quite old now, will remember the glorious incident when two college boys, dressed up all in flounces and fans and feathers, entered a Royal Victoria entertainment with bogus cards of admission and were shown into their seats by an eager and competitive group of elderly governors and professors.

The restriction proved a nuisance, especially as applied to what were then the best classrooms and the best assembly room at McGill. A legal fiction was eagerly found. The men students came over to the "R.V.C." not as men but as students, members of a class. The governors thought of this idea, submitted it to themselves, asking what they thought of it, and approved it. This illustrates the ease of operation without a legislature. At present, of course, women enter all buildings and attend all lectures, and in the Faculty of Arts outnumber the men 382 to 245.

If no apology was needed for saying much of McGill perhaps some apology, or at least explanation, is due for saying little of the French University of Montreal. In point of fact this univer-sity, if taken in connection with the parent institutions of Laval University of Quebec (1852) and the antecedent "Séminaire de Quebec," can boast a far higher antiquity than McGill. In the number of its registered students of all faculties and departments it exceeds McGill, according to the last available figures, by approximately eight thousand to three thousand. A beautiful and extensive site was given for its new buildings, beyond the moun-tain, on the elevated mountain slope itself, looking out toward the setting sun of summertime over a landscape that seems boundless in extent, the stretch of river and river land, rising slopes and distant mountain, the *"vaste et belle contrée"* of the departing Governor Vaudreuil. This incomparable site exceeded in opportunity anything that McGill ever had; it is doubtful if many colleges in the world ever had as good. Whether the architectural opportunity has been rightly used, whether the buildings even face the right way, and whether they are pleasant to look at are matters for individual judgment. The University of Montreal has been unfortunate in the devastating effect on it of the great depression which prevented, and still prevents, the full completion and equipment of the premises and, until 1942, the installation of the classes. The university is not, like McGill, an endowed institution. It is financed by the province of Quebec, though controlled by the Roman Catholic Church. As a result it felt the full strain that went with the crippled budget of the province.

But apart from these considerations the interest felt in the University of Montreal by the world at large cannot be compared with that long felt for McGill. Its admirable courses (while still Laval) in theology, classics, rhetoric, etc., were offset by a relative disregard of the technique of modern science, a study obviously lower from a certain point of view. Its work being entirely in French, it could not easily, even as a medical school, invite students from the outside. Of necessity its scope and utility are domestic to its own surroundings and belongs especially in the orbit of its church. Yet those who know its work both in its main courses and in such branches as its commercial *École des Hautes Études* realize how thorough it is and how well it maintains, perhaps even better than its English counterpart, the tradition of hard work, of real study, the thoroughness that went with the Jesuit schools and became a tradition of classical education.

We really touch here, but touch only to abandon, one of the greatest problems that face the French Canadians. To what extent must their education be directed toward learning English, toward acquiring the scientific and practical knowledge that means a career and success for English youth, without which the world offers few openings beyond the range of the learned professions? The whole world of business success is shut. Hence some French Canadians, especially in the dual area of Montreal, advocate compulsory English, more science and more practical training. Yet the discussion no sooner enters the door of the legislature than apprehension beats against the windowpane. This looks to many minds, even legislative ones, like the danger of losing the distinctive French nationality, of gaining the whole world to lose one's own soul—a bargain long since repudiated.

It is not possible in such limited compass to say much of Montreal as the home of arts and letters. Nor is there much to say. No one can deny the charm of Montreal's history or the splendor of the commercial development of which it has been the center. But having brought forth a great university it does not appear to have been capable of a wider motherhood of letters and science. It has always been notoriously what is called in the Broadway offices a "poor theater town," equally a "poor lecture town." Montreal is notoriously not a publishing town, the whole Canadian publishing business centering in Toronto with the lion's share of the magazine and editing business.

Music seems to be something of an exception to Montreal's general place in the world of culture. Just as Montreal is a "bad" theater town, so it is notoriously a "good" musical one. It is possible to gather larger and more frequent musical audiences in Montreal, even in proportion to its size, than in any other Canadian city. This is a matter not so much of outstanding musical talent in execution as the widespread appreciation of good music; and this again is due in great measure to the presence of the French Canadians. The British, at any rate the English, in Montreal resemble those in England in showing what is called in electrical science a strong "resistance" to music. They are able to go without it as uncomplaining as a camel in the desert. Hence in Montreal at a performance of either one of its two admirable symphony orchestras, many of the English present represent social rather than musical behavior, admiring what it is the thing to admire, rapt in their attention, no doubt, but not really difficult to unwrap. With the French, genuine appreciation reaches the saturation point.

Montreal is decidedly not a (English) literary center; still less is there a Montreal school of English literature. It is, of course, the center of the Metropolitan French Press and of the publication of French books, extremely numerous and of high merit, considering the limited area at command. Such literary life as there has been in English-speaking Montreal has centered round various little organizations past and present, of which the Pen and Pencil Club is without doubt both the most venerable and the most notable. This organization, meeting every fortnight in the half-light of a studio, falling asleep over essays read to it, and waking up to look at pictures or drink scotch and soda, developed a life and character all its own. Its records hold the names of Sir Andrew Macphail and of John McCrae, author of the immortal *Flanders Fields*. But as a matter of fact it lived rather on brush than on ink. The pencil was mightier than the pen.

For painting is perhaps something of an exception to what was said above. If there is no distinctive Canadian literature, that is, no Canadian way of writing, there is a certain distinctive Canadian art, a Canadian way of painting. What foreign painter ever put on canvas the melting snow and the black open water of the Canadian spring, the tremble of the birches, and the glory of the autumn all tawny and red and gold? Perhaps the painters of Montreal, the young men of forty years ago, Maurice Cullen and such, gone now, represented a real and unique contribution to the history of art.

No doubt this work was helped by the existence in Montreal of the notable private picture galleries. They were the outcome, it is true, of private taste. But they helped to give opportunity to rising artists privileged to see them. They helped also to stimulate the foundation and aid the future of the Montreal Art Association. Its beautiful building on Sherbrooke Street, its annual spring exhibitions, and its constant special displays of individual and particular exhibits render it a factor in the cultural life of the city. Yet here again a complete discussion would be beyond the scope of the present volume.

CHAPTER XV

Come Up on the Mountain

The Ascent of the Mountain. The High Altitude Cab. The Extinct Volcano. A View of Sixty Miles. And a Vision of the Future.

COME ON UP to the top of the mountain. For no tour of Montreal, no book on the city is complete without such a visit. And this lovely afternoon of the closing month of May shows the mountain at its very best, unsullied as yet in its billows of luxuriant green.

The mountain, it is true, seems to have dropped out of this volume since its earliest chapters. It always does in the pages of Canadian history. Jacques Cartier goes to the top of it; Maisonneuve erects a cross upon its summit, and then, apparently, no one goes up it for three hundred years. It does not appear in history again until in 1920 when a pious and energetic provincial secretary re-erects Maisonneuve's mountain cross. There with its vast frame of steel at the loftiest corner of Mount Royal, it stands visible in daylight from the city below and with its myriad lights visible at night over river and country for fifty miles. The Cross of Christ, in this case frequently spoken of as Athanase David's Cross, still guards the city.

The writer of this book—by which I mean myself, for I wrote it—can well act as guide, having walked the mountain now for

Montreal Today, the Farthest Inland Seaport of Any Importance in the World

forty-two years. But let us on such a pleasant excursion dismiss the formal dignity as between writer and reader and talk as between ourselves.

You note at once how relatively insignificant the mountain appears at a first view from the city. This is like the disappointment so generally felt, at first sight, at the small size of Niagara Falls. But just as Niagara gains in majesty from day to day, so does the mountain gain a loftier attitude. This is partly an effect of the weather and the atmosphere. At times, as on a clear winter day, it shrinks till it seems little more than a rim of frost above the city sky line. But at times of gathering thunder it rises high like a shield of rock towering to protect its city.

But the diminution of the mountain arises also partly from the fact that the city has climbed halfway up it. What Cartier and Champlain saw from the riverbank was vastly different from what is seen now. The St. Lawrence River at Montreal in mid-summer has an altitude of thirty feet above the level of the sea. The harbor wharves lie twenty feet above that. The Windsor Station is one hundred and ten feet above sea level. As you go uptown you come to the tunnel that plunges under the mountain just beside the great Roman Catholic Cathedral. The tunnel must be on a level almost the same as Windsor Station, and McGill University when the tunnel dives under it is eighty feet above the tunnel, and the city reservoir is, at a guess, almost one hundred feet above McGill, and eighty feet, say eighty feet, above the reservoir level again, there runs Pine Avenue belted round the waist of the mountain. These altitudes, except the sea level itself, may not be absolutely correct, but they are good enough for your trip up the mountain. They only mean that you are nearly halfway up, over 350 feet of its total 763, before the mountain gets a chance to begin. Indeed, private land, built on or ready to be built on, climbs so high and so eagerly all around the slopes of Mount Royal that it is too late to save it now as what it should have been. It would have been so easy at the start. It is everywhere. Ask anybody from Philadelphia what might have been done with Philadelphia, or ask anybody from San Francisco why they did to it whatever it is that they have done to it, and the answer is always the same. As to New York, it was ruined before it began, and London has never recovered from the Saxons. But if there is ever again a new city, let it learn to beat down private property as you beat down house dogs from the breakfast table.

So let us go up. You ask how do we go? Well, that's just the trouble; there isn't any real way to go. In fact, the great majority of the 1,476,737[1] of Greater Montreal have never been to the top of the mountain. There are no statistics on this question, and I admit that if you took one of the popular polls that now obviate and obliterate popular thought, you would find that 99 per cent of the Montreal people have been up on top of the mountain. But that is because the kind of people who go up to the top of a mountain are the kind of people who send an answer to a popular poll; and the kind of people who live beside a mountain and never go up it are the kind of people who never answer popular polls. But if you take the common experience of those who walk Mount Royal you will find it always comparatively empty. Often, even at nine in the morning, on a fine day, you may walk around a half-mile circuit on its open summit and see not a living soul: you may walk easily a quarter of a mile, and perhaps half a mile, down the winding road and still look in vain for that same soul. It is true that for three hours on a fine Sunday morning the mountain becomes a promenade, but this is a special crowd like the flock of young skiers that tears its frozen snows on a winter day, telemarking among the trees.

As we say, there is no easy way up. Years ago there was an inclined railway, but it was so wheezy and uncertain, its beams trembled so much at its own temerity, that they *disinclined* it. While it was there it started from the streetcar level in an attractive open car, all fresh air and wickerwork, up a slope as pleasant as that of sin itself; it ran to the most precipitous face of the mountain, then shifted into a caged-in car, all set on a slant so as to come straight on a track that was crooked, and then, with a clanking of cables and a wheezing of machinery, up it went above the treetops, its passengers turning green at the ascent.

[1]Lovell's *Montreal Guide.*

Women didn't mind it so much, since women always trust machinery as they do men; but men who distrust machinery as they distrust women were glad to get out of it. So it was disjointed and never rebuilt.

Nor can you ride up in your motorcar, since motorcars are excluded from the mountain. Excluded also is the streetcar company. It is true that the streetcars have found a cunning way round, by the back of the mountain where the slope is gentler, a route as strategic as Napoleon's plan of invading Europe by going to Egypt. It winds its hidden way behind a screen of trees and conceals itself cleverly under the hillside of a cemetery, and so crosses the entire mountain, reaching quite an altitude, then runs down a concealed ditch and out again, without anyone suspecting it. All cities have these engineering triumphs.

No, we have to drive with a horse. Since it is too far to walk all the way up and around the top and down again, we must take one of those special Montreal mountain cabs for which the route is reserved. These open cabs, carriages if you will, or *calèches* if you like, or victorias if you must, are the last survivors of a past age like the sailing whaling ship and the sedan chair. The horse ended in Montreal as elsewhere in a cloud of gasoline. Time was when it was not so. The city of forty years ago lent itself to the glory of the private carriage. Along the firm winter snow of its wide upper streets swept the open supersleighs that bore the superrich, buried deep under astrakhan fur, in front of them two flunkies in tall bearskins and fur capes, one to drive and one not to drive. Between the beautiful horses that seemed to dance before the equipage rang tall silver bells on a prong like a Russian troika. In summer beneath the leaves a lesser glory displayed an even greater luxury, silk hats for bearskins and livery replacing fur.

All that is gone. The mournful hackman sits his box, waiting for us to embark. We see as soon as ever he begins the ascent that he is one of two kinds, of only two. He may sit sunk in dejection, his head bowed like Rodin's Thinker while his tattered horse hauls us its gradual, laborious way; or he may commence at once, gesticulating with his whip, that flow of information that in some hackmen is not to be quenched, not even by alcohol.

But it is better to pay little heed to his murmurings. His mountain is not yours. You will get no history out of *him*. Don't ask him about Cartier and Maisonneuve. Especially not about Cartier; for if you do he'll wave his whip sideways and tell you that right over there you can see the top of Cartier's monument, the tall stone pillar with a bronze angel on top. He says it is just close to where they used to build the Ice Palace. Having said this and started a thrill of historic interest, he will then spoil it all by adding that his father always voted for Cartier. After which you have to sleep that off among the leaves as best you can.

You see, he lives here. He is only interested in what happened yesterday. He will show you where they held the horse show last year and where the Mayor of Montreal shook hands with the Mayor of Westmount; if you let him he will drive a little out of the way to show you where one of the city aldermen lives. Even as it is, he begins as soon as you reach the first slopes of the mountain road to point down to the houses below and say where people live. There is the house where Sir Edward so and so lives, and there is the one that used to be Sir Henry so and so's. Sir Henry, it appears, was a very fine man, very fond of driving up the mountain with him, our hackman, just as we are doing. Sir Henry was a generous man; it seems he always paid a dollar extra over the regular fare. He used to say, "Take that for the horse"; yes sir, always that extra dollar for the horse. The last time they drove it was a day just like this one. What's this? —the thirtieth of May. Well, that's odd, because the last time the hackman drove Sir Henry up here it was on a thirtieth of May. That's queer, isn't it? Sir Henry, it seems, is a great loss. We need men like that. . . .

So it is well, perhaps, not to talk with the driver. Let us think of his figure as there in front of us, like what the mathematicians call a constant in a function. If you pay no attention he will cancel out. . . .

We wind up a road that has been cut as a spiral of gradual

ascent, never too steep for the horse to walk, just too steep for the horse to run. All the mountain has a thin cover of trees through which one sees more and more of the widening prospect below—the city, the river, and the country beyond. Then as we turn the last wind of the winding road round a corner of rock we lose sight of the city, and there we are on the open "top" of the mountain—not the highest point but what is evidently the top. It is a great hollow space, mostly open grass dotted with bushes, sunk like a shallow bowl with banks of trees rising all round it. Sometimes we can see no further than these trees, but here and there we can see, through gaps in them, ever so far away, a glimpse to the north of a "vast and beautiful country"— the woods of Vaudreuil—reaching to the Laurentian Mountains.

Sunk in the bottom of the bowl is a beautiful artificial pond, almost a little lake, with flagstoned banks and beds of flowers all in a row—a bit of art against nature. This, we are told, was long ago a beaver pond.

The mountaintop suggests, you say, the crater of a volcano. Why, that's exactly what it is, not exactly what the geologist would call a crater, but the stump of a volcano that has blown its top off, crater and all. This that is left is what geology calls the "plutonic core," once just a shapeless bulk of bare rock. Time's hand has long since covered it to make it nature's garden.

That was long, long ago, long even to a geologist, although they have their own way of reckoning time. One of the most distinguished of our Canadian geologists wrote, as a part of his legacy to us, a marvelous book on the formation of this part of North America. He called it *The Last Million Years*.[2] He didn't mean to be funny; he only meant that he was not dealing with antiquity. But even he would admit that it must be a long time since the Mount Royal volcano was active. Dr. Frank Adams, the distinguished professor emeritus of McGill, the leading authority on the subject, reckons it from thirty to forty million years. Yet even that, from Dr. Adams' point of view, was not the geological beginning of Montreal. Deep down under the mountain itself is the bed of old Laurentian rock; overlying that

[2] A. P. Coleman, *The Last Million Years*, 1941.

is what is called familiarly (by geologists) the Ordovician, a bed of rocks mostly limestone in which are found marine fossils from the ancient sea and through which the mountain broke upward. The volcanic action shot a great shaft of steam and ashes and uptorn rock toward the sky. As the column fell it tore away the core of the volcano itself, leaving only this core. Later came the glacial age, burying all under ice, to leave behind the "moraine," boulder clay. Over this came the present upper surface of post-glacial deposit, clay and sand.

This means, then, that there was a time when these pleasant hollows, this wide sunken cup that marks the empowered summit of Mount Royal, showed the place where the volcano, long ages ago, blew off its top. Time must have been when the glow of the angry fires lit up the sky and reflected on the waters of the inland sea that then lay at the foot of the mountain, must have carried far across to the north to be reflected from the fireless stones that are the Laurentian Hills.

The fires died. The rock cooled into a solid mass, riven here and there with faults and channels, to be filled later with other molten rock, their traces visible today. Over the surface the wind and sun and rain, the bursting ice and the melting snow, broke and wore down the rock to form the thin soil that now covers Mount Royal and clings to its abrupt sides. Down from its sides the streams and rivulets carried the soil to the mountain foot to spread it wide at the base. This flat layer of uneasy sand and clay could bear the trifling weight of Cartier's Hochelaga, even as magnified into Ramusio's fanciful drawing. But it was to become the despair of the modern architect and builders, whose houses leaned crookedly sideways, leering with premature old age, till they learned to pierce down and search for a foundation on the moraine, or lower still on the plutonic core, or lower still on the Ordovician rock. The bedrock of Laurentian they cannot reach. As the mountain cooled and crumbled the great inland sea beside it shrank and drained away from the upheaving earth, to leave nothing but the three streams of the St. Lawrence, the Ottawa, and the Richelieu hurrying along the hollows of its lower bed. Seen thus, what Cartier saw, the waving trees, the grassy slopes, is but a thing of yesterday. Nature with a twist of the hand (or of the equinoxes) could turn it all back again to the fierce, lifeless panorama of fire and rock from which it began.

Cartier dreamed of empire and of the Kingdom of Faith. . . . Champlain, of inland waterways and a metropolis. The geologist, of these vanished fires and this forgotten sea. Which dream is the dreamiest?

But that's enough geology. As we drive along the high side of the bowl the city is hidden still but one sees, off in the other direction, and rising clear above the trees, the great dome of the basilica of the Shrine of St. Joseph, so vast that it seems to dwarf even nature itself. Indeed the nature lover, if unaware of its meaning and sacred character, might well think it a blot on the landscape. Yet this shrine has acquired within the last forty years a reputation almost equal to that of the famous Ste. Anne de Beaupré beside Quebec. Here was built at the close of the nineties by the Corporation of Our Lady of the Sacred Heart, whose college stands near by, a chapel to contain a statue of St. Joseph. Here began the ministrations of Brother André, presently called the Miracle Man of Mount Royal. The wonderful cures effected and the spiritual relief afforded to thousands of the sick and the lame led to the building, behind this shrine, of the great basilica. It stands on the rising slope at the foot of the Little Mountain. It can accommodate five thousand people. It rises two hundred feet high. Up the one hundred stone steps that lead to its doors the supplicants climb on their knees, in the two great public supplications for divine intercession held every year on May 10 and on Labor Day.

But our winding through the trees on the mountaintop has now brought us from the bowl back again to the face overlooking the city and we are now at the point of the mountain called Observation Point, or commonly the Look Out. It is by no means the highest point on the mountain but it commands the widest prospect. A natural projecting ledge of the rocky mountainside here falls away sharply so that a wide-open view, a panorama, is afforded, both far to the right and far to the left, over the trees and the city and up and down the river and across the river. This ledge has been converted to a wide, semicircular pavement, some two hundred feet across, with a cement balustrade over which, on such a lovely day as this, lean little groups of people, looking at the view.

Suppose we let the cabman go; we don't need him—we can walk down. What about giving him . . . You remember what he said about Sir Henry? Good, I will.

As we look out over the balustrade it is the sense of distance that first strikes us, just as it did Jacques Cartier: miles and miles of it, clear away to a dim, flat horizon with mountains on it here and there, each little block of them dimmer than the last. We are looking right out over the city, over the trees just below us —we can almost touch the tops—and beyond it over the St. Lawrence coming down from our right, as far away as we can see, passing below us in the foreground, and then moving on to the left to be lost again where the shoulder of the mountain blocks our sight.

But for the moment the distance holds us. Those nearest mountains—they are over twenty miles away—are over beside the Richelieu. The tallest one, reaching to a high point from which there must be a wonderful view all round the compass at once, is Beloeil—or "good eye"—which is the French for what they call Bellevue in the States. It overlooks the Richelieu. Our little guidebook tells all about Fort Sorel and Fort Chambly and the Indian Wars and the Patriots of 1837, but we don't need that. We had that in Chapter Four. Our cabman, if we had kept him, would have told us about the horse show at Sorel last fall and say we ought to come back for it this fall, but he's off, trundling down the winding slopes at a pleasant jog trot, half asleep under the leaves, as happy as the horse. So we can pick the mountains out for ourselves—Rougemont, and that one like a sugar cone must be Johnson. How far away is it? Let me look it up—a hundred and twenty-four miles! Just imagine that! A hundred and twenty-four miles!—oh, wait, I beg your pardon—twenty-four miles!—imagine that instead! Further still to the southeast is the dim outline of the Green Mountains in Vermont, seventy-eight miles away, and almost straight south, the top end of the Adirondacks, sixty miles away. Looking at them, our eye catches the river again, far away to the right; the Lachine Rapids—we can just see them or just not see them—they are half hidden by islands. To see them you must take a flying carpet and fly to them from the mountain, and make it not the end of May but the end of March, with the river breaking open and all one wild roar of rushing water and breaking ice that you hear half a mile away. Stand at the turn of the old Lachine Road, lonely still, and you can hear the sound come from across the river and from down the stream, the "hiss" of the smashed ice rushing past your feet and the undertone, the "roar," from a mile away . . . "My hair stood on end," said Champlain at the terror of it.

But come back; get on the carpet and come up; turn it back to the thirtieth of May. And let us look down at the nearer view, the city itself, the towering stone buildings of the Sun Life and the Royal Bank—that beats any rapids, doesn't it?—and the great grain elevators . . . There's so much on the river front that we can't see the ships, not the ones in dock. The harbor lies framed between great bridges, the Jacques Cartier downstream and the Victoria up. The shipping we do not see. But look off to the left, away off; you wouldn't realize that that's an Atlantic liner coming up, but it is.

Then we look nearer—all the business city seems a tumble of houses and all the huddle of the slums smothered over and looking all right at a distance, as poverty always does. As we follow the city up the slope of the town, trees break out in it, and then more trees; that enchanted wood with stone tops sticking out of it is McGill University; the small object moving slowly along a road in front of it is a professor hurrying to his lecture. Beside the university lies the residential district of the rich that were—you remember we talked of it—beautiful indeed, as seen from above, as seen from here, for the trees cover all traces of the demolitions and the placards of houses for sale are too far away to read.

Even above this the houses among the trees climb higher and higher still, unwilling to let go, unwilling to admit the mountain too steep, till they reach the last, their highest thrown, in the beautiful little Redpath Crescent whose slated houses and lovely gardens we can see just below us. Just below? Why, it looks as if we could almost touch them. . . . It can't be more than, what, two hundred feet? Why, look! You can see the people, almost hear them, look at the bright dresses. Why, of course, it must be a wedding party! How charming on this lovely thirtieth of May! Good luck to them, whoever they are, starting life together, high, high up. . . .

As we reach this point in our speculations we hear beside us, as coming up from among a little group of visitors looking over the balustrade, the voice of a statistician (they are not forbidden on the mountain) or, what is worse, the voice of a statistical tourist who only lives to give information, explaining:

The Island of Montreal is thirty miles long and between seven and ten miles wide. The city occupies almost one quarter of it. Montreal itself has a population of a million and Greater Montreal a million and a half. Montreal has 127 parks, playgrounds, and gardens. It has 247 churches. It has 907 miles of streets. It has 19 hospitals, 2600 manufacturing plants and 773 miles of sewers . . .

Come away! It's time to go. And don't admire the man's erudition. He got it all out of the blue pages of the Montreal Telephone Book except the population: he makes that up, himself. But in any case we want to move on so as to get to the top of the mountain in the literal sense, for the high shoulder where the great cross stands is far higher up than the Observation Point. We reach it by the winding road, or, if we like, straight through among the sparse trees of the summit of the mountain. We wish now that we had kept the cabman—it's quite a walk. But it has been worth it, for now we can see all the lovely country beyond the mountain—the islands of Montreal and Jesus and the Laurentian Slope. Let me show you the Sault au Recollet rapids, away off this way, and now, if you want to see the St. Vincent de Paul Penitentiary, look right out toward—— You don't? No, perhaps not. Seems terrible, doesn't it?—those great high walls with guards on top, walls so high that the people in the yards can never see the beauty around them; they can hear the river and not see it. . . .

Look further then. Away off there is St. Eustache, where they killed the rebels—you can't see it, but it's there. And away at the end, most beautiful of all, is the Lake of the Two Mountains, lovely as its own name. The island ends there and where it ends is Ste. Anne's, the village of the "evening chime" that we spoke of (you haven't forgotten Chapter Three?), near it, mentioned three times already? Well, never mind, it's worth it. Close by St. Anne's—you can't see them but you can see where they are—are some of the most beautiful country estates and lake-shore houses in all America. They look out over the lake toward the sunset. Some are historic too. They represent, and here and there part of their buildings actually were standing then, the old French "fiefs" granted and occupied as a sort of first line of defense from Indian raiders coming down the two rivers. Such is Boisbriant, just beside the little village of Senneville. It was a fief granted to Sidrac du Gue (1672), then passed into the hands of the famous Charles le Moyne de Longueuil, then to Jacques le Ber and later to Le Ber de Senneville. A round stone tower was built as a fort and windmill (1686). It underwent fierce attacks by the Iroquois in 1687 and 1691 in the first of which, at any rate, several people were massacred. A real Fort Senneville was built in 1692, its ruins still existing. After that a manor house was built, which itself was enlarged into a fort. It had a long history extending to an attack made by Benedict Arnold in 1776.

All about the present manor house and the beautiful lawn and gardens which surround it are the characteristic memorials of two and a half centuries of history, which lend distinction to these surviving remnants of New France.

When Jacques Cartier looked around this vast circuit he saw a country that seemed empty—north and south and east and west —just as nature made it. All the fifteen hundred miles south to Florida, empty; all the fifteen hundred miles north to Ungava, empty. The visitor of today looks south over the same fifteen hundred miles that is now the greatest area of industrial civilization in the world. He looks north, but beyond the Montreal islands and a little strip of ski-side of the hills all is empty still, empty, largely unknown.

Yet on the north side the available energy of water power and the latent mineral wealth (apart from coal) are incomparably greater than that to the south.

Come, it is time to get down from the mountain. There are things to do.

CHAPTER XVI

L'Envoi: The Problem of a Great City

THE ROMANS had a saying to the effect that from any one thing you could judge all others of the same class. So it is with our great American cities. If you study one, you study all. They have all had something of the same origin in the adventurous days of early settlement, of Indian warfare. All carry the same pride of achievement in the record of their foundation. Boston thinks of the Puritans and the Massachusetts Bay Colony; New York, of Hudson's ship entering the spacious shelter of its waters; New Orleans, of old French days; and Chicago and the cities of the Mississippi Valley recall the stockade forts of the plains and the lonely grandeur of the prairies. Our early American founders stand in stone, Winthrop looking toward Maisonneuve, John Smith searching the horizon for Iberville, and Pontiac sending across the lakes from Detroit a message of good cheer to Oshkosh of Green Bay.

Hence it is that in North America we can all read the story of one another's cities with a peculiar sympathy and understanding which we cannot bring to bear on Europe. Our interest in the origins of Rome and London or in the lost antiquity of Athens may be profound, but it lacks the peculiar appeal of the cities on our own side of the ocean.

Nor is it only the origin of the cities. Their history from stage to stage runs a similar course—the early years of struggle, the beginnings of comfort, the building of real houses, the first meeting of a city council. Later comes transport, highroads that replace the trails through the forest, canals, a very wonder of

the age, with canal boats seeming to the pioneers of the bush
floating palaces of luxury; the railroads all put together in little
bits, then turning, overnight as it seemed, into trunk lines, and
with that the oncoming of the machine age; the millions of immigrants that turned frontier towns to metropolitan cities; the age
of electricity and power that annihilated nature; the vast ac-
cumulations of wealth that made Europe look poor, and the
spread and growth of the new industrial poverty, the reproduc-
tion of the European slum in the New World, a thing so sudden,
a poverty so unexpected, that it made the life of the pioneer in
his log cabin in the forest seem wealth itself.

All of our cities wear these marks of history, traced on their
streets and evidenced in their monuments. Each of us can read
the story of any American city without a guidebook from what
we know of our own. That stone figure in the breastplate and
the plumed hat, with a drawn sword, that is, of course, the
founder of the city. The bronze Indian crouching below the
pedestal—the proper place and proper attitude for him—recalls
the salvation of the city by the founder. Those military figures,
with little three-cornered hats, knee breeches, and stockings,
their hair in pigtails, those are the great American generals who
beat the British and the great British generals who beat the
Americans, and both of whom beat the French.

In another concentric ring of history are solid metal statues
of men in frock coats, wide iron trousers, and wearing semicircular metal beards, their faces absolute calm, more in calcula-
tion than in anger. These are the city patriots who first built
docks or urged for years the construction of a tunnel, or worked
hard till they at last persuaded the city to lay out the great wood-
land cemetery, a very dream of rest, where they now lie.

Nor do we need to be told where we are when we enter the
college area—where the Medical Building alone cost ten million.
In front of such a building is again a statue, this time of a man
in more modern dress, like an office coat, and with an air of
shrewdness not seen in the broad face of the man who made the
cemetery. This man built railroads, an uneducated man but with
the peculiar driving force that was developed in the transcon-

tinental days of the railroad. Beneath his feet is a Latin motto, crisp and terse—the kind of thing he would have said if he had known Latin. He can't read it, least of all now: he doesn't know, never did, whether it means "Labor conquers everything," or "Look out, low bridge." But the motto dates him as a period. Inside the building, done in great canvases in oil, are the portraits of the later donors, indoor men, who never drove anything, never saw the plants and labor other people drove, but just organized things and then reorganized them and when they fell apart organized the pieces of them bigger than ever, and gave what was left over to the college, which now rest in shadowed rooms, dark in oil, looking a little darker perhaps as time wears on.

All that we have in common. It is a wonderful record of human achievement, a wonderful story of energy and progress. And yet can we feel as sure of it all as we had expected to? Are we quite certain of its outlook on the future? This city of yours and mine and of all of us, so beautiful in its leafy residential streets, so inspiring in its college area, so triumphant in its downtown section jostling with wealth and luxury, ostentatious with plate glass—does it not contain, like all its sister cities, those tangled, narrower streets of the part of the city where the poor live, and the long miles of crowded tenements and inglorious apartments, just room to turn around, just room to breathe, except in the hot weather; is all that, even with its lighted streets and its picture shows, is all that so much better than what was there before we conquered nature?

So it comes that in all our cities we are busy in the same way with city planning for the future, with city housing, with the demolition of the slums. To shovel up the slums, to shovel up half the city and throw it away, that is the word of the day in every great North American city. The biggest man is the man who will throw it furthest. Later he will have a statue with a Latin motto on the base to mean, "Knock it all down."

It seems strange, doesn't it, after so much effort, after so much that seemed a continuous triumph, that it has come to this? The city—my city and your city—is all wrong. The thing has got to go. It's built wrong. It's congested. It hasn't got light enough, air enough, space enough. It's full of noise, strident and discordant, not like the noise of the wind and the sea that used to be here. There's no place for the children to play in, no fit apartments for them to live in, and so there are no children to play, or not enough of them. The founder was one of ten, wasn't he?—and even the sheet-iron man with the broad face one of six. But now? Why, a lot of the city fathers are unmarried women.

So we must knock it all down and start over. Everybody must live in a place fit for everybody to live in. The trouble is that the poor are too poor to afford it; so it won't do to have any poor: they must either get rich or get out. So the problem of city planning somehow turns in our hands to the problem of the rich and poor, the problem of poverty, of starvation in the midst of plenty, which all now see and none as yet alleviate.

But we must be at it. If our city means anything, at least it means inspiration. If it all has to be done over again, let's do it over, with the same courage as that of the first settlers. Remember what the founder did—drew his sword and said, "Come on!" Let's do that.

Appendix No. 1

POPULATION OF MONTREAL

		Estimated
1642	First Settlement	50
1642	End of Year	72
1650		196
1660		472
1667		766
1710		3,492
1720		5,314
1730		6,351
1750		8,244
1800		9,000
1809		12,000
1825		22,000
1831		27,000
1839		35,000
1844		44,000
1852		57,719
1861		91,169
1871		115,000
1881		155,238
1891		219,616
1901		328,172
1911		400,504
1921		618,506
1931		818,577
1941		890,234

Appendix No. 2

CHRONOLOGICAL HISTORY OF MONTREAL

1535   Jacques Cartier at Hochelaga.
1603   Champlain at the Grand Sault.
1611   Champlain laid out Palace Royale.
1642   Maisonneuve founded Ville Marie.
1660   Dollard des Ormeaux was killed at Long Sault, May 21.
1665   Maisonneuve dismissed, returns to France, 23 years after founding Ville Marie.
1667   Census of Montreal, 766 souls.
1673   Frontenac arrived in Montreal.
1676   First market place opened.
1682   Frontenac recalled by the King of France, May 10.
1689   Massacre of Lachine, August 5; Return of Frontenac, October 15.
1694   Two watchtowers built as part of the Fort of the Sulpicians and still standing beside the Collège de Montréal.
1700   2100 population of Montreal.
1734   "The Great Fire."
1759   Fall of Quebec.
1760   Montreal capitulated, September 9.
1774   Quebec Act.
1775   Montgomery entered by the Recollet Gate, November 13.
1782   John Molson came to Montreal. Northwest Company formed.
1785   The Beaver Club started.
1791   Canada divided into two parts, Upper and Lower, May 14.
1800   Montreal Waterworks.
1809   The *Accommodation* made her first trip from Montreal to Quebec, November 3.
1811   James McGill made a will, January 8, leaving forty-six acres on Burnside and University streets and £10,000 for a university.
1817   Formation of the Bank of Montreal.
1821   Work commenced on Lachine Canal.
1825   First Lachine Canal completed.

1830   Montreal Harbour Commission.
1832   Visitation of the cholera.
1837   The Rebellion.
1846   Montreal Telegraph Company organized.
1849   Parliament Building burned.
1854   First pier of Victoria Bridge laid.
1857   St. James Club, Dorchester Street, West, established.
1858   Decimal currency.
1860   Victoria Bridge opened by the Prince of Wales.
1861   Montreal Street Railway.
1870   Fenian Raid.
1879   Art Association of Montreal opened.
1882   Electric Light Company.
1886   Nearly one quarter of Montreal flooded.
1892   Montreal Street Railways (electric).
1893   The Royal Victoria Hospital opened.
1899   Royal Victoria College opened.
1902   The Duke and Duchess of Cornwall, King George V and Queen Mary visited Montreal.
1909   The Children's Memorial Hospital opened.
1917   Mount Royal Tunnel finished.
1919   Cornerstone of Sun Life Building laid.
1920   General Sir Arthur Currie made Principal of McGill.
1930   Harbour Bridge opened.

INDEX